"Lindsay Hilsen's *A Step-by-Step ABA Curriculum for Young Learners (Age 3–10)* is a welcome extension of her well-received earlier w[...] *for Early Learners with Autism Spectrum Disorders*. Writing with clear, and instructions, Hilsen provides a useful format that can be applied to additional behaviors and more advanced skills as the child's behavioral repertoire continues to expand. This book is well written and organized, making it easy to locate programs for the assessment and teaching of specific behaviors developmentally appropriate for young learners. It will not only be useful to experienced ABA practitioners, but also should be helpful to practitioners less familiar with ABA and those using a non-ABA approach."

—*Albert Kearney, clinical psychologist and author of*
Understanding Applied Behaviour Analysis

"Lindsay Hilsen's first book, *A Step-by-Step Curriculum for Early Learners with Autism Spectrum Disorders*, truly works. It made a huge difference in my son's life as the transformation of his overall development has gone beyond all expectations. His negative behaviors significantly decreased and his receptive and expressive language skills tremendously improved since the implementation of the curriculum. I wholeheartedly believe in Lindsay Hilsen's curriculums and would recommend them for any child that can benefit from ABA therapy. It is evident from my own son's success that Lindsay Hilsen has a true understanding of children with ASD and her curriculums are definitely one piece of solving my son's ASD puzzle."

—*Michele Irizarry, parent to a son on the autism spectrum*

A Step-by-Step ABA
Curriculum for
**Young Learners
with Autism
Spectrum Disorders
(Age 3–10)**

A Step-by-Step ABA Curriculum for **Young Learners with Autism Spectrum Disorders (Age 3-10)**

Lindsay Hilsen, M.Ed., BCBA

Jessica Kingsley *Publishers*
London and Philadelphia

First published in 2013
by Jessica Kingsley Publishers
116 Pentonville Road
London N1 9JB, UK
and
400 Market Street, Suite 400
Philadelphia, PA 19106, USA

www.jkp.com

Library of Congress Cataloging in Publication Data
A CIP catalog record for this book is available from the Library of Congress

British Library Cataloguing in Publication Data
A CIP catalogue record for this book is available from the British Library

ISBN 978 1 84905 928 2
eISBN 978 0 85700 728 5

Printed and bound in the United States

This book is dedicated to my husband Alex for all his encouragement, my father for all of his support, and my daughters Abigail and Emily. I love you all.

Contents

Part I: Assessment

Classroom and Social Skills

Handwriting

Reading

Math

Language Arts—Receptive Programs

Language Arts—Expressive Programs

Sort and Categorization

Conversation and Social Skills

Self Help and Daily Living Skills

Part II: Curriculum

Classroom and Social Skills

Handwriting

Reading

Math

Language Arts—Receptive Programs

Language Arts—Expressive Programs

Sort and Categorization

Conversation and Social Skills

Self Help and Daily Living Skills

Part III: Mastered Programs

Classroom and Social Skills

Handwriting

Reading

Math

Language Arts—Receptive Programs

Language Arts—Expressive Programs

Sort and Categorization

Conversation and Social Skills

Self Help and Daily Living Skills

Book Overview

This curriculum was designed to be used with preschool and elementary students, aged approximately from three to ten years, depending on the extent of the child's developmental delays. The basic layout, the ease of implementing the programs, and the overall design were developed so that any adult can utilize this curriculum. It is recommended that anyone involved in the student's life should follow this curriculum so that generalization is fluid. Generalization allows us to ensure that the child is able to perform a skill in any setting, with any person, and with different materials. Therefore, our goal should always be to achieve generalization.

When you first start implementing this curriculum, or if it is the beginning of the school year, teachers, parents, or therapists should do a full assessment. The assessment should be conducted again in the spring. Therefore, the assessment should be given twice a year. The purpose of assessing in the fall is to see if skills are being maintained. You assess again in the spring to see the progress that was made and to help devise goals and objectives for the upcoming school year. The curriculum section is basically the student's lesson plan. Once you complete the assessment and calculate the percentages of independence for each program you will be able to determine which programs the student will need to work on. Once you choose which programs to work on, you will then locate those curriculum pages and follow the steps on each curriculum page. When a step or program is mastered from the curriculum section, it then becomes a mastered step or program. The mastered steps/ programs should be run at least once a month to ensure that the mastered skills are retained. More in-depth directions are provided at the beginning of each section.

Applied Behavior Analysis Overview

Applied behavior analysis (ABA) is a methodology that is used to help children and adults diagnosed with autism spectrum disorders and other developmental delays to learn and function within society. Research has shown that the earlier a person receives intervention, the more likely that person is to acquire the skills necessary to do this. Experts in the field of autism have seen the constructive effects ABA has on people with autism.[1] Applied behavior analysis looks at socially significant behaviors (communication, self help, fine motor, gross motor, etc.) and breaks each program down into small steps so that a child will build up an understanding of how to complete the skill. Applied behavior analysis is based on encouraging positive behavior through prompting, reinforcement, shaping behaviors, and generalization.[2]

Applied behavior analysis has had some negative criticism in recent years. The traditional approach of ABA is to place a child and a teacher at a desk, with the teacher instructing the child to perform a certain skill (such as clapping hands), and, subsequently, the child would have to perform this skill ten times in a row. This traditional approach has caused many to think of ABA as robotic, repetitious, and not practical.[3] However, research demonstrates that ABA works and is effective at teaching this population. The best known research study was conducted by Ivar Lovaas in 1987. Lovaas[4] showed that close to half of his students with autism who were receiving an ABA program were able to attain a normal intelligence quotient (IQ) and tested within the normal range on adaptive and social skills.

In ABA practice today there is much more of a focus on working in a natural environment, with one of the main priorities being to achieve generalization. For this ABA curriculum to be successful it is helpful to have the following components: a program book, data collection, graphs, prompting, prompt fading, shaping, reinforcement, and generalization. All of these components are explained below.

---

1   Lovaas, I. (1987) "Behavioral treatment and normal educational and intellectual functioning in young autistic children." *Journal of Consulting and Clinical Psychology 55*, 3–9.

2   Cooper, J. (2007) *Applied Behavior Analysis.* Saddle River, NJ: Pearson Education.

3   Smith, T., Groen, A. and Wynn, J. (2000) "Randomized trial of intensive early intervention for children with pervasive developmental disorder." *American Journal on Mental Retardation 105*, 4, 269–285.

4   Lovaas, I., *op. cit.*

Applied Behavior Analysis Components

Program book

This is the go-to location to find anything pertaining to the child. The book can be a ring-binder file that has several sections/dividers within it:

- assessment

- IEP (Individualized Education Plan) goals/objectives

- curriculum/program pages with the graphs that correspond

- mastered section

- sections for occupational therapy, physical therapy, and speech therapy if applicable

- behavioral data (this can be anecdotal data or actual behavior plan information).

Prompting

Prompting helps to teach children a particular skill by helping them to feel encouraged and giving them guidance to make the goal easier to achieve. We want to provide children with prompts so that they will learn the skill the correct way. If we are teaching a child to clap his hands and we say "clap hands" but the child touches the floor we then just taught the child that "clap hands" means to touch the floor. If we say "clap hands" and then immediately prompt the child to clap his hands by using a physical prompt, for example, we teach him the direct correlation between "clap hands" and him actually performing the action of clapping his hands. We also use prompts to maintain the child's motivation and self-esteem. If we are working on a new skill and we continuously perform it incorrectly, our motivation to perform that skill is going to lessen. In addition, we are going to become very frustrated, which will then lead to possible negative behaviors. All of this can be avoided if we use prompts and know when to fade our prompts in a systematic manner so we do not promote prompt-dependency.

The most *common* prompts are provided below in a most to least intrusive hierarchy.

PROMPT NAME	PROMPT ABBREVIATION	PROMPT DESCRIPTION
Physical Prompt	P	You use hand over hand so there is no room for error.
Faded Physical	FP	You guide the child towards the correct answer by touching either their elbow or shoulder. It is not as intrusive as a physical prompt and allows the child a little more independence.
Gesture	G	You point to the correct answer. You can also use your eyes to "gesture" or look at the correct answer.

The prompts below are used when you are trying to get a child to engage in verbal language. You should not provide a verbal prompt unless you are looking for a verbal response.

PROMPT NAME	PROMPT ABBREVIATION	PROMPT DESCRIPTION
Verbal	V or VP	You provide the child with the exact word/words that you want them to say (e.g. "what is your name— Johnny" and the child then says "Johnny").
Faded Verbal	FV	You provide the child with the start of the word/words that you want them to say (e.g. "what is your name— Joh" and the child then says "Johnny").

There are many different ways to prompt and many different ways to write the abbreviations. For example, some people abbreviate Physical Prompt as PP, whereas I like to abbreviate it as a P. It does not matter which abbreviation you use as long as you have a key indicating the prompts you may use and which you are using as the abbreviations. I have listed some other possible prompts below.

PROMPT NAME	PROMPT ABBREVIATION	PROMPT DESCRIPTION
Shadow	S	This is similar to a faded physical, but you are not touching the person at all. You are shadowing his body or the hand to the correct answer.
Visual	Vis or V depending on what you are using for the verbal prompt abbreviation	You provide an actual visual of the answer (e.g. "how old are you" while holding up the number 5 because the child is five years old).
Textual	T	You provide the child with text to help him get the answer correct. An example is putting the child's name where you want him to stand.
Model	M	You provide the child with an example or you demonstrate first and then ask him to do it.

Prompt fading

A big part of prompting is to make sure you fade the prompts in a systematic manner. Children can become very prompt-dependent very quickly, so if you are using prompts, make sure you have a plan in mind for how and when you are going to fade the prompts. On the one hand, we do not want the child to make a mistake, we want to make sure that the direction that is given to the student (the discriminative stimulus or Sd), e.g. "clap hands," "sit down," "touch red," is causing the child to get the answer correct, but we also want to make sure we are teaching to independence and not to prompt-dependence.

Shaping

Shaping is important because most students will not get something exactly right on the first try. So we need to let them know that what they did was a great try and reinforce it. However, the next time, in order to receive a positive reinforcement, they need to perform at least as well as they did the last time, if not better. If they do it better than the previous time, we provide them with a bigger reinforcement. If the following time they do not at least perform at the same level as the time before, we do not reinforce. The big picture when discussing shaping is providing reinforcement for approximations that come closer and closer towards the ultimate goal.

Reinforcement

- Positive reinforcement.

    ○ A stimulus is presented immediately following a behavior which should encourage the child to repeat the behavior and therefore will cause the behavior to increase.

    ○ Example: your student really likes to play with puzzles. You say to your student "clap hands" and once the student claps his hands you say "great job clapping your hands lets go do a puzzle." The puzzle is the reinforcement for clapping hands.

- Negative reinforcement.

    ○ A stimulus is removed immediately following the behavior, which will in turn increase the likelihood of the behavior occurring.

    ○ Example: a student in the class has a tendency to cry a lot. Your student does not like it when his peer cries. You teach your student to ask for a walk whenever the other student in the class cries. Therefore, by the student asking for a walk (the behavior) you take him out of the room which in turn removes the stimulus (the crying).

- It is important to note that not every student likes the same reinforcers. We need to make sure we are constantly varying the reinforcement. We want to use the stronger reinforcers for novel or harder programs. Make sure students know what they are working for by allowing them to choose their reinforcers before starting to work.

- We need to vary the amount of reinforcement provided depending on the child's response.

- A task that is mastered may not receive as much reinforcement as a novel task that the student is learning.

Data collection

Data can be collected in numerous forms. For the purpose of this book I recommend taking data through either discrete trial or probe data.

Discrete trial is when you take an isolated task and present the child with a cue that indicates to him what he needs to do. If the child engages in the correct behavior, we will provide him with reinforcement. This is considered one trial. If when we present the child with the cue (discriminative stimulus, Sd) he does not respond, we will need to prompt him to ensure errorless learning.

When looking at a discrete trial data sheet, it will typically have ten trials and ten boxes, so that we can collect ten single instances of data pertaining to that one skill. You can use any number of trials; however, ten is the easiest because it is very simple to calculate the percentage of independence at the end.

1. Present the Sd (discriminative stimulus, cue).

2. Wait 3 to 30 seconds (processing time depending on student's needs).

3. *Correct response:* mark a + (for independent).

4. If response is *incorrect:*

• present Sd

• wait time—student begins to respond incorrectly/does not respond

• immediately try to interrupt and prompt to the correct response

• then do a teaching trial—represent Sd and immediately prompt correct response. Remember this is all one trial.

Remember prompt hierarchy and fade prompts as quickly as possible. When using discrete trial data collection, do not move on to the next step until the child has reached the criterion. The criterion suggested in this curriculum is 90 percent or greater for three consecutive sessions. This means the child will need to get a 90 percent or better for the current step for three consecutive sessions. This may not necessarily be three consecutive days. It could mean that a teacher works with the child in the morning, then another teacher works with the child on the same day but in the afternoon. This would count as consecutive sessions.

Adult: Sd: "Touch head."

Child: correct response, child touches head (see the "Receptive Body Id" row, column 1, of the table below).

Adult: "Great job touching your head. Do this" (open mouth).

Child: child opens his mouth (see the "Oral Motor" row, column 1, of the table below).

Adult: "Wow! I love the way you opened your mouth, now give me a high five."

Child: no response.

Adult: physically prompts child to give a high five and then does a teaching trial (immediately represents Sd "give me a high five") and immediately prompts the child to give a high five. This is all one trial (see the "Follows One-step Directions" row, column 1, of the table below).

Since the child did not respond when asked to "give a high five" the adult needed to prompt the child. The adult used a physical prompt (P). Although a teaching trial was used, this still only counts for one trial (which in this case was trial 1). Therefore, a P (abbreviation for physical prompt) was written down in trial box 1 for the program One Step Directions.

Adult: "Johnny, do this" (open mouth).

Child: correct response (see the "Oral Motor" row, column 2, of the table below).

Adult: "You are awesome. Touch head."

Child: goes to touch his feet.

Adult: immediately prompts so that the child touches his head (the adult used a faded physical prompt—FP) while saying "this is touching head." Then the adult and immediately represents Sd "touch head" and immediately prompts so that the child touches his head (see the "Receptive Body Id" row, column 2, of the table below).

Adult: "You are doing a nice job sitting. Give me a high five."

Child: correct response (see the "Follows One-step Directions" row, column 2, of the table below).

Child's Name: Johhny											
PROGRAM NAME	**STEP/ SET**	1	2	3	4	5	6	7	8	9	10	**TOTAL PERCENT**
Receptive Body Id	Head	+	FP									
Oral Motor	"Do this" (open mouth)	+	+									
Follows One-step Directions	"Give me a high five"	P	+									

Probe data is a quick, easy way of seeing where the child is in terms of knowing the skill or not. A lot of therapists can become overwhelmed with data collection, but probe data will give you accurate information quickly and you won't have to spend the entire session collecting data.

Probe data can be collected either daily, weekly, bi-weekly, monthly, etc. From my experience as a behavior analyst, I have learned that the more data collected, the more accurate the results, so I recommend collecting data daily. However, not everyone has the same opinion as mine so there really is no rule as to how often you collect probe data. You should just be careful that you are not missing an opportunity to move the child up to the next step if you are not collecting data daily. For example, if you see a child five times a week but you only collect data every other week, that child could master some of the steps in that time frame but you will not be able to move him up to the next step because you do not have the data to verify it. It should also be noted that just because you are not collecting data throughout the entire session it does not mean that you are not teaching the skill. The same principles hold true; you want to prompt to ensure errorless learning, and you want to fade your prompts so that you do not promote prompt-dependency.

So the question is how do you take probe data? The purpose of probe data is to test to see if the child has the skill the first time the probe is presented that day. So that is exactly when you take the data. At this point you will present the Sd and if the child can do it independently then you will circle Y (yes) or if the child could not do it independently then you will circle N (no). You will then move on to the next program and probe that skill. Once you have finished probing for the day, you can then put your data sheet away and just focus on teaching the skill.

The criterion for mastery is that the child should score three consecutive "Y"s. It is not necessary to transfer your data from the data sheet to a graph with probe data; your data sheet is your graph. An example is provided below. The highlighted letter is the answer. When you fill the form out, just circle the correct answer.

PROGRAM: <u>Gross Motor Imitation</u> . . . . . . CRITERION: <u>three consecutive Ys</u>

Step	4/1/11	4/2/11	4/4/11	4/8/11	4/8/11	4/9/11					
Clap Hands	Y/N	Y/N	Y/N	Y/N	Y/N	Y/N	Y/N	Y/N	Y/N	Y/N	Y/N
	4/10/11	4/11/11	4/12/11	4/14/11							
Stamp Feet	Y/N	Y/N	Y/N	Y/N	Y/N	Y/N	Y/N	Y/N	Y/N	Y/N	Y/N

First trial probe with prompt level

When I use probe data, I really like to see the prompt level that was required in order for the child to be successful so that I can tell if he is making progress. For example, if I am working on a skill for two months and all I see on the probe data sheet is Ns circled, I am going to discontinue that program due to lack of progress. However, if I am taking prompt levels, then I will hopefully see that for the first couple of sessions the child needed a physical prompt, then a couple of sessions after, the child needed a faded physical, then a few sessions after that he only needed a gestural prompt and so on. This way I can see that the child is making progress and therefore, the program would not need to be discontinued.

Take the first trial probe with prompt levels in the same way that you take normal probe data. You first need to decide how often you are going to take the data. Again, I prefer daily but that is up to you. Then on the day(s) you are collecting data, the first time you present the child with the Sd, record the results of that trial. If the child got it correct with no prompting, then you record a + or an I for independent; if they needed a prompt, indicate the prompt that was necessary. As far as criteria go, I again like to use three consecutive sessions of independent scores. An example is provided below.

Program Name	Write in the box below the date and the score (P—physical prompt, FP—faded physical, G—gesture, V—verbal prompt, FV—faded verbal, +—independent)					
Gross Motor Imitation (clap hands)	4/1/11 P	4/2/11 P	4/3/11 FP	4/4/11 +	4/8/11 +	4/9/11 +
Receptive Body Id (head)	4/1/11 +	4/3/11 +	4/4/11 +			

For this particular type of data, it is recommended to use a separate graph. The graph that I like to use is shown under the graphs section.

Graphs

Discrete trial graph

It is important to take your data at the end of each session and transfer it to a graph. You will use a line graph when working with discrete trials. You will take the percentage of what the child got correct (or did independently) for each program. If you think back to the second way of collecting discrete trial, the first three steps are written, so mastery is always with a prompt. Therefore, we are not looking for the child to get it correct independently. We are looking for the child to get it correct at that prompt level. This means that criteria for step 1 is 90 percent correct (correct means with a physical prompt) for two consecutive sessions. Step 3 is 90 percent correct (correct means with a gestural prompt) for two consecutive days. For step 3, we are allowing the child the opportunity to make mistakes, whereas with step 1, the child really has little to no chance of making a mistake.

When you are transferring your data to the graph, each program has its own graph. You are taking the percentage of what the child got correct. For this particular way of taking data, correct means doing it independently.

Y = first probe independent
S/G = shadow or gesture
FP/FV = faded physical or faded verbal
PP/VP = physical prompt or verbal prompt

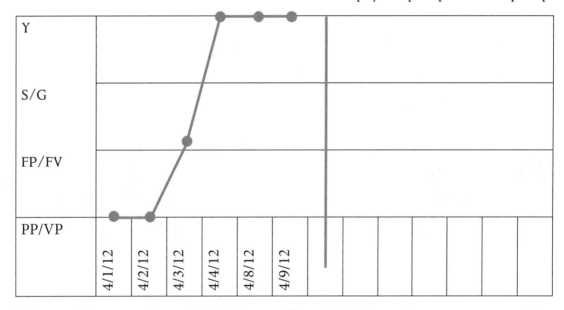

When graphing remember to include the trend line. This indicates that you are now working on a new step.

First trial probe graph

When graphing this type of data, you will take your probe result and place a data point on the correlating line. For example, if the child scored a +/I/Y (indicated by a Y on the graph), then you will place the data point on the Y line; if the child scored a faded physical, you would place the data point on the FP/FV line.

Program Name: Gross Motor Imitation

Criteria: (three consecutive Ys in a row are considered mastery)

Y = first probe independent

S/G = shadow or gesture

FP/FV = faded physical or faded verbal

PP/VP = physical prompt or verbal prompt

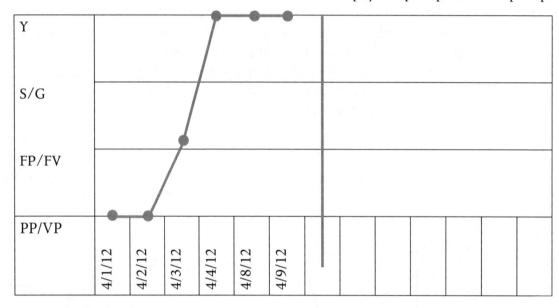

Steps: 1—clap hands

Generalization

Generalization means that the step the child is on should be taught in at least three different settings, with at least three different materials, and with at least three different people. If working on this curriculum within a school system, ask the parents/guardians to see if the child is able to perform the skill at home.

Part I

Assessment

Assessment Directions

Purpose of assessment

The purpose of the assessment section is to provide the teacher or the parent with a baseline to indicate where the child is at the beginning of the school year or when you first start to teach the child. The assessment should be conducted again towards the end of the school year. Goals and objectives for the student's IEP should then be developed based on the results of the assessment.

Directions for assessment

Start with the first column in the assessment section. Write the date of the assessment in the date box. Present the child with the Sd that will be stated on each program page. Then start with step 1. If the child was able to complete step 1 independently, write a + in the box. As soon as you get to a step that the child was not able to complete on his own, write the prompt that was required in order for the child to be successful. At the end of each program page, calculate the percentage of steps the child got correct. To do this you will take the number of steps the child got right and divide it by the total number of steps. The next time you do the assessment you will be filling in the second column. Please note that although a program may only have six steps, it really has 12 because you need to take into account generalization. For programs that build off of each other, as soon as the child gets to a step they cannot complete, the assessment should stop there. If the steps in the program do not directly develop on from each other, the assessment should continue until all steps have been assessed. An example of a program that features steps that do rely on previous steps having been completed is tying shoes. The child is not able to complete the next step without having mastered the previous step. So this would be an example of a program where you do not have to continue with the rest of the assessment as soon as the child gets to a step he cannot complete.

Total percentage sheet

Once you finish the assessment, transfer the total percentages onto the total percentage sheet. Remember to fill in the date in the box that says date, then continue down the column filling in the percentage according to the score on the assessment.

Generalization in the assessment

Generalization is included in the steps during the assessment. It is important that, when we assess, we look at whether the child has mastered the skill in different settings, with different material, and with different people. This means, for example, that you will need to take the child into the kitchen, backyard, or playground; and the child must be able to perform the skills with you, his sibling, and a parent, in addition to being able to perform the skill with different materials, which can include different sizes, fonts, shapes, etc.

Prompts

This curriculum suggests that you use a hierarchy ranging from the least intrusive prompts to the most intrusive. The purpose behind this is so that the child does not become prompt-dependent. However, if a child learns the skills by using a most-to-least intrusive prompt system, then please use that. The least-to-most intrusive prompt hierarchy means that you start with a prompt that is the most hands off. An example would be a gestural prompt. When looking at the prompts below, you will see that a physical prompt is hand over hand. Therefore, this would be the most intrusive prompt. The most important aspect of prompting is to come in with the prompt that will ensure the child will get the answer correct. It is also important to remember to fade prompts as quickly as possible so that the child does not rely on your prompt.

- *Physical Prompt*—hand-over-hand manipulation.

- *Faded Physical Prompt*—the practitioner is guiding the child.

- *Gestural Prompt*—the practitioner points to the correct response.

- *Verbal Prompt*—the answer is provided verbally for the child.

- *Faded Verbal Prompt*—the beginning part of the answer is provided for the child.

A verbal/faded verbal prompt should only be used if you require a verbal response.

Distractors

All programs are designed to be taught in a field of three unless otherwise specified. For example, if you are working on receptive identification of coins, you will put down the coin that you are working on and then an additional two coins. The additional two coins are your distractors.

Assessment Section Example

Child Name: . . . . John Smith . . . .

Playground

Teaching Procedure: When presented with the Sd "go play" while on the playground, the child will engage in three different playground activities for up to 10 minutes.

Prompt Hierarchy: Use the least intrusive prompt required in order for the child to be successful (gesture, faded physical, physical; faded verbal and verbal to be used only with verbal programs).

Materials: Playground equipment (swing, slide, jungle gym).

	STEPS	date: 12/1/12	date: 6/1/13	date: 9/1/13	date:	date:	date:
1	Present the child with the Sd "go on the slide"	P (physical prompt)	I (independent)	I (independent)			
1g	generalization	P (physical prompt)	I (independent)	I (independent)			
2	Present the child with the Sd "go on the jungle gym"	P (physical prompt)	I (independent)	I (independent)			
2g	generalization	P (physical prompt)	I (independent)	I (independent)			
3	Present the child with the Sd "go on the swing."	P (physical prompt)	G (gestural)	I (independent)			
3g	generalization	P (physical prompt)	G (gestural)	I (independent)			
4	Once the child has mastered steps 1–3 tell him to "go play." they will need to start with the slide. Once they are no longer interested in the slide, he will climb on the jungle gym, then they will go on the swings.	P (physical prompt)	I (independent)	I (independent)			
4g	generalization						
PERCENT CORRECT							

Total Percentages Record Sheet

PROGRAM NAME	date:	date:	date:	date:
Classroom and Social Skills				
Playground				
Asks a Peer to Join/Play				
Winning and Losing				
Follows Basic Classroom Instructions				
Sits During Group Time				
Raises Hand				
Weather				
Handwriting				
Writes Lines and Shapes				
Draws Pictures				
Writing Upper Case Letters				
Writing Lower Case Letters				
Writes Numbers				
Reading				
Receptively Identifies the Sound of Letters				
Labels Sounds				
Match Words to Pictures				
Match Word to Word				
Receptive Identification of Simple Words				
Read Simple Words				
Math				
Patterns				
Gives a Specified Amount				
Math Terms				
Receptive Identification of Telling Time				
Expressive Identification of Telling Time				
Receptive Identification of Coins				
Expressive Identification of Coins				

PROGRAM NAME	date:	date:	date:	date:
Receptive Identification of Same and Different				
Expressive Identification of Same and Different				
Language Arts—Receptive Programs				
Receptive Identification of Prepositions				
Receptive Identification of Pronouns				
Receptive Identification of Adjectives				
Receptive Identification of Noun and Adjective				
Receptive Identification of Adverbs				
Receptive Identification of Class				
Receptive Identification of Feature				
Receptive Identification of Function				
Language Arts—Expressive Programs				
Expressive Identification of Prepositions				
Expressive Identification of Pronouns				
Expressive Identification of Adjectives				
Expressive Identification of Noun and Adjective				
Expressive Identification of Adverbs				
Expressive Identification of Class				
Expressive Identification of Feature				
Expressive Identification of Function				
Sort and Categorization				
Receptive Identification of What Goes Together				
Expressive Identification of What Goes Together				
Categorization				
Receptive Identification of What is Not the Item				
Expressive Identification of What is Not the Item				
Sort by Function				

PROGRAM NAME	date:	date:	date:	date:
Sort by Feature				
Sort by Class				
Conversation and Social Skills				
Receptively Identifies Items				
Expressively Answers the Question "Name…"				
Answers Questions About Items				
Answers "What" Questions				
Answers "When" Questions				
Answers "Where" Questions				
Answers "Which" Questions				
Answers "Who" Questions				
Answers "How" Questions				
Answers "Why" Questions				
What Can You Do in the Community?				
"Tell Me About…"				
Recall				
Conversation Starters				
Self Help and Daily Living Skills				
Brushes Teeth				
Washes Face				
Puts Shirt On				
Ties Shoes				
Toileting				

Comments

ASSESSMENT 1 COMMENTS
ASSESSMENT 2 COMMENTS
ASSESSMENT 3 COMMENTS
ASSESSMENT 4 COMMENTS
ASSESSMENT 5 COMMENTS

Classroom and Social Skills

Child Name: . . . .

Playground

Teaching Procedure: When presented with the Sd "go play" while on the playground, the child will engage in three different playground activities for up to 10 minutes.

Prompt Hierarchy: Use the least intrusive prompt required in order for the child to be successful (gesture, faded physical, physical; faded verbal and verbal to be used **only** with verbal programs).

Materials: Playground equiptment (swing, slide, jungle gym).

	STEPS	date:	date:	date:	date:	date:	date:	date:
1	Present the child with the Sd "go on the slide."							
1g	generalization							
2	Present the child with the Sd "go on the jungle gym."							
2g	generalization							
3	Present the child with the Sd "go on the swing."							
3g	generalization							
4	Once the child has mastered steps 1–3 tell him to "go play." He will need to start with the slide. Once he is no longer interested in the slide, he will climb on the jungle gym, then he will go on the swing.							
4g	generalization							
PERCENT CORRECT								

Child Name: . . . .

Asks a Peer to Join/Play

Teaching Procedure: Have two peers engaged in a game or activity that you want your student to play. Make sure the game or activity is motivating to your student. When you are teaching the student to ask a peer to play, have a single peer engaged in an activity by himself.

Prompt Hierarchy: Use the least intrusive prompt required in order for the child to be successful (gesture, faded physical, physical; faded verbal and verbal to be used **only** with verbal programs).

Materials: Activities or games that strongly motivate your student.

	STEPS	date:	date:	date:	date:	date:
1	Ask your student, "do you want to join your friends?" If the student says "yes," prompt him to walk over to the peers and say "can I join you?" Make sure you speak with the other students before contriving this situation so they know they have to say "yes."					
1g	generalization					
2	Say to your student "wow, ___[name] and ___ [name] are playing your favorite game; it looks like fun." Your student will need to go over and ask them to join.					
2g	generalization					
3	Your student should be able to see the peers playing and walk over without any prompt from a teacher.					
3g	generalization					
PERCENT CORRECT						

Child Name: ....

Winning and Losing

Teaching Procedure: Play a game that has a clear winner and loser with your student. Generalization should include peers. Make sure the game you are playing is motivating to the student.

Prompt Hierarchy: Use the least intrusive prompt required in order for the child to be successful (gesture, faded physical, physical; faded verbal and verbal to be used **only** with verbal programs).

Materials: Activities or games that strongly motivate your student and have a clear winner and loser, such as musical chairs and board games.

	STEPS	date:	date:	date:	date:	date:
1	Play a game 1:1 with your student. Make sure your student wins. You say "good game" and teach your student to say "good game."					
1g	generalization					
2	Play a game 1:1 with your student. Make sure your student loses. You say "good game" and teach your student to say "thanks, you played good too."					
2g	generalization					
3	Your student should be able to see the peers playing and walk over without any prompt from a teacher.					
3g	generalization					
4	Once the child has mastered steps 1–3 tell him to "go play." He will need to start with the slide. Once he is no longer interested in the slide, he will climb on the jungle gym, then he will go on the swings.					
PERCENT CORRECT						

Child Name:. . . . .

Follows Basic Classroom Instructions

Teaching Procedure: The child will be presented with the Sd for the step you are working on.

Prompt Hierarchy: Use the least intrusive prompt required in order for the child to be successful (gesture, faded physical, physical; faded verbal and verbal to be used **only** with verbal programs).

Materials: None.

	STEPS	date:	date:	date:	date:	date:
1	Put your backpack in your cubby.					
1g	generalization					
2	Get your backpack.					
2g	generalization					
3	Put your jacket away.					
3g	generalization					
4	Get your jacket.					
4g	generalization					
5	Go line up at the door.					
5g	generalization					
6	Sit in your chair.					
6g	generalization					
7	Get your lunch.					
7g	generalization					
8	Go to the bathroom.					
8g	generalization					
PERCENT CORRECT						

Child Name: . . . .

Sits During Group Time

Teaching Procedure: Present the child with the Sd "let's go sit with the group." Generalization should include using different Sds such as "let's go to circle time."

Prompt Hierarchy: Use the least intrusive prompt required in order for the child to be successful (gesture, faded physical, physical; faded verbal and verbal to be used **only** with verbal programs).

Materials: None.

	STEPS	date:	date:	date:	date:	date:
1	2 minutes					
1g	generalization					
2	4 minutes					
2g	generalization					
3	8 minutes					
3g	generalization					
4	10 minutes					
4g	generalization					
5	15 minutes					
5g	generalization					
6	20 minutes					
6g	generalization					
PERCENT CORRECT						

Child Name:. . . . .

Raises Hand

Teaching Procedure: Teach this program in the natural environment during actual situations in which the child would need to raise his hand. Follow the steps below. If the child talks while teaching this skill, have the teacher non-verbally take his pointer finger and put it up to his own mouth as if he were saying quiet. Do not call on the child if he is talking/calling out while raising his hand.

Prompt Hierarchy: Use the least intrusive prompt required in order for the child to be successful (gesture, faded physical, physical; faded verbal and verbal to be used **only** with verbal programs).

Materials: None.

	STEPS	date:	date:	date:	date:	date:
1	One adult will need to sit behind the child and when the other teacher asks "who wants to answer?" The adult sitting behind the child will physically prompt the child to raise his hand. Make sure that the child knows the answer to the question. Have the teacher leading the group say "I love the way _____ [child's name] raised his hand."					
1g	generalization					
2	One adult will need to sit behind the child and when the other adult, who is leading the group asks "who wants to answer?" The adult sitting behind the child will provide a faded physical prompt to raise his hand. Make sure that the child knows the answer to the question. Have the adult leading the group praise the child for raising his hand.					
2g	generalization					

3	One adult will need to sit behind the child and when the other adult, who is leading the group, asks "who wants to answer?" The adult sitting behind the child will provide a gestural prompt to raise his hand. Make sure that the child knows the answer to the question. Have the adult leading the group praise the child for raising his hand.					
3g	generalization					
4	Have the adult leading the group ask a question to which the child knows the answer. Do not provide any prompt.					
4g	generalization					
PERCENT CORRECT						

Child Name: . . . .

Weather

Teaching Procedure: Ask the child to tell you what the weather is, either using pictures or standing outside, or both.

Prompt Hierarchy: Use the least intrusive prompt required in order for the child to be successful (gesture, faded physical, physical; faded verbal and verbal to be used **only** with verbal programs).

Materials: None.

	STEPS	date:	date:	date:	date:	date:
1	sunny					
1g	generalization					
2	rainy					
2g	generalization					
3	cloudy					
3g	generalization					
4	windy					
4g	generalization					
5	cold					
5g	generalization					
6	warm/hot					
6g	generalization					
7	child will state either warm/hot or cold along with either sunny, rainy, cloudy, windy					
7g	generalization					
PERCENT CORRECT						

Handwriting

Child Name: . . . .

Writes Lines and Shapes

Teaching Procedure: Present the child with the Sd "make a___" (state the items in the step that you are working on).

Prompt Hierarchy: Use the least intrusive prompt required in order for the child to be successful (gesture, faded physical, physical; faded verbal and verbal to be used **only** with verbal programs).

Materials: Paper, crayons, markers, pencil, shaving cream, sand.

	STEPS	date:	date:	date:	date:	date:
1	straight line					
1g	generalization					
2	diagonal line from right to left					
2g	generalization					
3	diagonal line from left to right					
3g	generalization					
4	circle					
4g	generalization					
5	oval					
5g	generalization					
6	square					
6g	generalization					
7	rectangle					
7g	generalization					
8	triangle					
8g	generalization					
PERCENT CORRECT						

Child Name: . . . .

Draws Pictures

Teaching Procedure: Present the child with the Sd "draw a ___" (state the item in the step that you are working on).

Prompt Hierarchy: Use the least intrusive prompt required in order for the child to be successful (gesture, faded physical, physical; faded verbal and verbal to be used **only** with verbal programs).

Materials: None.

	STEPS	date:	date:	date:	date:	date:
1	person					
1g	generalization					
2	house					
2g	generalization					
3	outside (sky, sun, grass, flower)					
3g	generalization					
4	animal					
4g	generalization					
PERCENT CORRECT						

Child Name: . . . .

Writing Upper Case Letters

Teaching Procedure: Present the child with the Sd "write the letter ____" (state the letter in the step you are working on). Make sure you state to the child that you want him to write upper case.

Prompt Hierarchy: Use the least intrusive prompt required in order for the child to be successful (gesture, faded physical, physical; faded verbal and verbal to be used **only** with verbal programs).

Materials: Paper, pencil.

	STEPS	date:	date:	date:	date:	date:
1	F					
1g	generalization					
2	E					
2g	generalization					
3	D					
3g	generalization					
4	P					
4g	generalization					
5	B					
5g	generalization					
6	R					
6g	generalization					
7	N					
7g	generalization					
8	M					
8g	generalization					
9	H					
9g	generalization					
10	K					
10g	generalization					
11	L					
11g	generalization					
12	U					

12g	generalization					
13	V					
13g	generalization					
14	W					
14g	generalization					
15	X					
15g	generalization					
16	Y					
16g	generalization					
17	Z					
17g	generalization					
18	C					
18g	generalization					
19	O					
19g	generalization					
20	Q					
20g	generalization					
21	G					
21g	generalization					
22	S					
22g	generalization					
23	A					
23g	generalization					
24	I					
24g	generalization					
25	T					
25g	generalization					
26	J					
26g	generalization					
PERCENT CORRECT						

Child Name: . . . .

Writing Lower Case Letters

Teaching Procedure: Present the child with the Sd "write the letter ____" (state the letter in the step you are working on). Make sure you state to the child that you want him to write lower case.

Prompt Hierarchy: Use the least intrusive prompt required in order for the child to be successful (gesture, faded physical, physical; faded verbal and verbal to be used **only** with verbal programs).

Materials: Paper, pencil, shaving cream, markers, sand.

	STEPS	date:	date:	date:	date:	date:
1	c					
1g	generalization					
2	o					
2g	generalization					
3	s					
3g	generalization					
4	v					
4g	generalization					
5	w					
5g	generalization					
6	t					
6g	generalization					
7	a					
7g	generalization					
8	d					
8g	generalization					
9	g					
9g	generalization					
10	u					
10g	generalization					
11	i					
11g	generalization					
12	e					

12g	generalization					
13	l					
13g	generalization					
14	k					
14g	generalization					
15	y					
15g	generalization					
16	j					
16g	generalization					
17	p					
17g	generalization					
18	r					
18g	generalization					
19	n					
19g	generalization					
20	m					
20g	generalization					
21	h					
21g	generalization					
22	b					
22g	generalization					
23	f					
23g	generalization					
24	q					
24g	generalization					
25	x					
25g	generalization					
26	z					
26g	generalization					
PERCENT CORRECT						

Child Name:. . . . .

Writes Numbers

Teaching Procedure: Present the child with the Sd "write the number___" (state the step that you are working on).

Prompt Hierarchy: Use the least intrusive prompt required in order for the child to be successful (gesture, faded physical, physical; faded verbal and verbal to be used **only** with verbal programs).

Materials: Paper, pencil, shaving cream, sand.

	STEPS	date:	date:	date:	date:	date:
1	0					
1g	generalization					
2	1					
2g	generalization					
3	2					
3g	generalization					
4	3					
4g	generalization					
5	4					
5g	generalization					
6	5					
6g	generalization					
7	6					
7g	generalization					
8	7					
8g	generalization					
9	8					
9g	generalization					
10	9					
10g	generalization					
11	10					
11g	generalization					
PERCENT CORRECT						

Reading

Child Name:. . . . .

Receptively Identifies the Sound of Letters

Teaching Procedure: In a field of three, lay down different letter cards, one of the cards showing the letter you are currently working on, and present the child with the Sd "touch/point to/show me the letter that makes the _____" (name the sound).

Prompt Hierarchy: Use the least intrusive prompt required in order for the child to be successful (gesture, faded physical, physical; faded verbal and verbal to be used **only** with verbal programs).

Materials: Letter cards.

	STEPS	date:	date:	date:	date:	date:
1	A					
1g	generalization					
2	B					
2g	generalization					
3	C					
3g	generalization					
4	D					
4g	generalization					
5	E					
5g	generalization					
6	F					
6g	generalization					
7	G					
7g	generalization					
8	H					
8g	generalization					
9	I					
9g	generalization					
10	J					
10g	generalization					
11	K					
11g	generalization					

12	L					
12g	generalization					
13	M					
13g	generalization					
14	N					
14g	generalization					
15	O					
15g	generalization					
16	P					
16g	generalization					
17	Q					
17g	generalization					
18	R					
18g	generalization					
19	S					
19g	generalization					
20	T					
20g	generalization					
21	U					
21g	generalization					
22	V					
22g	generalization					
23	W					
23g	generalization					
24	X					
24g	generalization					
25	Y					
25g	generalization					
26	Z					
26g	generalization					
PERCENT CORRECT						

Child Name:. . . . .

Labels Sounds

Teaching Procedure: Present the child with the Sd "tell me what sound ___ [name the letter] makes."

Prompt Hierarchy: Use the least intrusive prompt required in order for the child to be successful (gesture, faded physical, physical; faded verbal and verbal to be used **only** with verbal programs).

Materials: None.

	STEPS	date:	date:	date:	date:	date:
1	A					
1g	generalization					
2	B					
2g	generalization					
3	C					
3g	generalization					
4	D					
4g	generalization					
5	E					
5g	generalization					
6	F					
6g	generalization					
7	G					
7g	generalization					
8	H					
8g	generalization					
9	I					
9g	generalization					
10	J					
10g	generalization					
11	K					
11g	generalization					
12	L					

12g	generalization					
13	M					
13g	generalization					
14	N					
14g	generalization					
15	O					
15g	generalization					
16	P					
16g	generalization					
17	Q					
17g	generalization					
18	R					
18g	generalization					
19	S					
19g	generalization					
20	T					
20g	generalization					
21	U					
21g	generalization					
22	V					
22g	generalization					
23	W					
23g	generalization					
24	X					
24g	generalization					
25	Y					
25g	generalization					
26	Z					
26g	generalization					
PERCENT CORRECT						

Child Name:. . . . .

Match Words to Pictures

Teaching Procedure: Lay down at least three pictures. One of the pictures will be of the object in the step you are working on. Then present the child with the card that has the word written out and ask the child to match.

Prompt Hierarchy: Use the least intrusive prompt required in order for the child to be successful (gesture, faded physical, physical; faded verbal and verbal to be used **only** with verbal programs).

Materials: Cards or pieces of paper that have the words that are in each step below written out, and the related pictures.

	STEPS	date:	date:	date:	date:	date:
1	cat					
1g	generalization					
2	dog					
2g	generalization					
3	hat					
3g	generalization					
4	bat					
4g	generalization					
5	house					
5g	generalization					
6	girl					
6g	generalization					
7	boy					
7g	generalization					
8	train					
8g	generalization					
9	car					
9g	generalization					
10	doll					
10g	generalization					
11	egg					

11g	generalization					
12	phone					
12g	generalization					
13	baby					
13g	generalization					
14	book					
14g	generalization					
15	pencil					
15g	generalization					
16	door					
16g	generalization					
17	bug					
17g	generalization					
18	desk					
18g	generalization					
19	shoe					
19g	generalization					
20	hand					
20g	generalization					
PERCENT CORRECT						

Child Name:. . . . .

Match Word to Word

Teaching Procedure: Lay down at least three words. One of the words will be that in the step you are working on. Then present the child with the card that has the word written out and ask the child to match.

Prompt Hierarchy: Use the least intrusive prompt required in order for the child to be successful (gesture, faded physical, physical; faded verbal and verbal to be used **only** with verbal programs).

Materials: Cards or pieces of paper that have the words in each step below written out, and extra words to be used as distractors.

	STEPS	date:	date:	date:	date:	date:
1	cat					
1g	generalization					
2	dog					
2g	generalization					
3	hat					
3g	generalization					
4	bat					
4g	generalization					
5	house					
5g	generalization					
6	girl					
6g	generalization					
7	boy					
7g	generalization					
8	train					
8g	generalization					
9	car					
9g	generalization					
10	doll					
10g	generalization					
11	egg					

11g	generalization					
12	phone					
12g	generalization					
13	baby					
13g	generalization					
14	book					
14g	generalization					
15	pencil					
15g	generalization					
16	door					
16g	generalization					
17	bug					
17g	generalization					
18	desk					
18g	generalization					
19	shoe					
19g	generalization					
20	hand					
20g	generalization					
PERCENT CORRECT						

Child Name: . . . .

Receptive Identification of Simple Words

Teaching Procedure: Present the child with three cards that have words written on them. One card should represent the word in the step that you are working on. Ask the child to "find/point/show you ___" (name the word in the step).

Prompt Hierarchy: Use the least intrusive prompt required in order for the child to be successful (gesture, faded physical, physical; faded verbal and verbal to be used **only** with verbal programs).

Materials: Different cards that have the words in the steps below written on them. The cards should include different background colors, different fonts, different sizes.

	STEPS	date:	date:	date:	date:	date:
1	in					
1g	generalization					
2	to					
2g	generalization					
3	the					
3g	generalization					
4	we					
4g	generalization					
5	at					
5g	generalization					
6	up					
6g	generalization					
7	go					
7g	generalization					
8	is					
8g	generalization					
9	my					
9g	generalization					
10	me					
10g	generalization					
11	of					

11g	generalization					
12	on					
12g	generalization					
13	it					
13g	generalization					
14	for					
14g	generalization					
15	you					
15g	generalization					
16	can					
16g	generalization					
17	was					
17g	generalization					
18	stop					
18g	generalization					
19	she					
19g	generalization					
20	mom					
20g	generalization					
21	dad					
21g	generalization					
22	that					
22g	generalization					
23	they					
23g	generalization					
24	had					
24g	generalization					
25	but					
25g	generalization					
PERCENT CORRECT						

Child Name:. . . . .

Read Simple Words

Teaching Procedure: Hold up a card that has the word written on it and ask the child "what does it say?"

Prompt Hierarchy: Use the least intrusive prompt required in order for the child to be successful (gesture, faded physical, physical; faded verbal and verbal to be used **only** with verbal programs).

Materials: Different cards that have the words in the steps below written on them. The cards should include different background colors, different fonts, different sizes.

	STEPS	date:	date:	date:	date:	date:
1	in					
1g	generalization					
2	to					
2g	generalization					
3	the					
3g	generalization					
4	we					
4g	generalization					
5	at					
5g	generalization					
6	up					
6g	generalization					
7	go					
7g	generalization					
8	is					
8g	generalization					
9	my					
9g	generalization					
10	me					
10g	generalization					
11	of					
11g	generalization					

12	on					
12g	generalization					
13	it					
13g	generalization					
14	for					
14g	generalization					
15	you					
15g	generalization					
16	can					
16g	generalization					
17	was					
17g	generalization					
18	stop					
18g	generalization					
19	she					
19g	generalization					
20	mom					
20g	generalization					
21	dad					
21g	generalization					
22	that					
22g	generalization					
23	they					
23g	generalization					
24	had					
24g	generalization					
25	but					
25g	generalization					
PERCENT CORRECT						

Math

Child Name: . . . .

Patterns

Teaching Procedure: Start the pattern by completing two full examples and then present the direction "finish the pattern" to the child. The child will need to extend the pattern at least two more times. Example of an AAB pattern: The teacher will start the pattern by doing AAB, AAB and the child will then need to extend the pattern by doing AAB, AAB.

Prompt Hierarchy: Use the least intrusive prompt required in order for the child to be successful (gesture, faded physical, physical; faded verbal and verbal to be used **only** with verbal programs).

Materials: Anything you can make a pattern out of, such as colors, shapes, number, coins, etc.

STEPS		date:	date:	date:	date:	date:
1	can extend an AB pattern using colors					
1g	generalization					
2	can extend an AB pattern using shapes					
2g	generalization					
3	can extend an AB pattern using anything					
3g	generalization					
4	can extend an AAB pattern using colors					
4g	generalization					
5	can extend an AAB pattern using shapes					
5g	generalization					
6	can extend an AAB pattern using anything					
6g	generalization					
7	can extend an ABB pattern using colors					
7g	generalization					
8	can extend an ABB pattern using shapes					
8g	generalization					
9	can extend an ABB pattern using anything					
9g	generalization					
10	can extend an AABB pattern using colors					
10g	generalization					

11	can extend an AABB pattern using shapes					
11g	generalization					
12	can extend an AABB pattern using anything					
12g	generalization					
13	can extend an ABC pattern					
13g	generalization					
PERCENT CORRECT						

Child Name: . . . .

Gives a Specified Amount

Teaching Procedure: When presented with the Sd "give me _____" (a specified number), the child will count out that number while leaving the remaining items where they are.

Prompt Hierarchy: Use the least intrusive prompt required in order for the child to be successful (gesture, faded physical, physical; faded verbal and verbal to be used **only** with verbal programs).

Materials: Objects that can be counted.

	STEPS	date:	date:	date:	date:	date:
1	1					
1g	generalization					
2	2					
2g	generalization					
3	3					
3g	generalization					
4	4					
4g	generalization					
5	5					
5g	generalization					
6	6					
6g	generalization					
7	7					
7g	generalization					
8	8					
8g	generalization					
9	9					
9g	generalization					
10	10					
10g	generalization					
11	11					
11g	generalization					
12	12					

12g	generalization					
13	13					
13g	generalization					
14	14					
14g	generalization					
15	15					
15g	generalization					
16	16					
16g	generalization					
17	17					
17g	generalization					
18	18					
18g	generalization					
19	19					
19g	generalization					
20	20					
20g	generalization					
PERCENT CORRECT						

Child Name: . . . .

Math Terms

Teaching Procedure: Using math manipulatives such as blocks or cubes, set up a situation that would enable the student to be able to receptively identify the step you are on. For example, in step 1 put all of the cubes on the table, then ask the student to "give me all of the cubes."

Prompt Hierarchy: Use the least intrusive prompt required in order for the child to be successful (gesture, faded physical, physical; faded verbal and verbal to be used **only** with verbal programs).

Materials: Manipulatives such as cubes and blocks.

	STEPS	date:	date:	date:	date:	date:
1	all					
1g	generalization					
2	none					
2g	generalization					
3	some					
3g	generalization					
4	more					
4g	generalization					
5	less					
5g	generalization					
6	same					
6g	generalization					
7	different					
7g	generalization					
8	greater					
8g	generalization					
9	add					
9g	generalization					
10	take away (subtract)					
10g	generalization					
PERCENT CORRECT						

Child Name: ....

Receptive Identification of Telling Time

Teaching Procedure: Lay down a minimum of three clocks. Make sure one of the clocks shows the time of the step that you are on. Present the child with the direction "show me/find/point to_____" (name the time for the step you are on). Example of step 1: "show me 01:00."

Prompt Hierarchy: Use the least intrusive prompt required in order for the child to be successful (gesture, faded physical, physical; faded verbal and verbal to be used **only** with verbal programs).

Materials: Clocks that have adjustable minute and hour hands, or pieces of paper that have clocks drawn on them that relate to the steps below.

	STEPS	date:	date:	date:	date:	date:
1	01:00					
1g	generalization					
2	02:00					
2g	generalization					
3	03:00					
3g	generalization					
4	04:00					
4g	generalization					
5	05:00					
5g	generalization					
6	06:00					
6g	generalization					
7	07:00					
7g	generalization					
8	08:00					
8g	generalization					
9	09:00					
9g	generalization					
10	10:00					
10g	generalization					
11	11:00					

11g	generalization					
12	12:00					
12g	generalization					
13	can tell to the half-hour					
13g	generalization					
14	can tell to the quarter-hour					
14g	generalization					
15	can tell to the minute					
15g	generalization					
PERCENT CORRECT						

Child Name: . . . .

Expressive Identification of Telling Time

Teaching Procedure: Hold up a picture of a clock that shows the time of the step that you are on. Present the child with the direction "what time is it?" The child will need to state the correct time.

Prompt Hierarchy: Use the least intrusive prompt required in order for the child to be successful (gesture, faded physical, physical; faded verbal and verbal to be used **only** with verbal programs).

Materials: Clocks that have adjustable minute and hour hands, or pieces of paper that have clocks drawn on them that relate to the steps below.

	STEPS	date:	date:	date:	date:	date:
1	01:00					
1g	generalization					
2	02:00					
2g	generalization					
3	03:00					
3g	generalization					
4	04:00					
4g	generalization					
5	05:00					
5g	generalization					
6	06:00					
6g	generalization					
7	07:00					
7g	generalization					
8	08:00					
8g	generalization					
9	09:00					
9g	generalization					
10	10:00					
10g	generalization					
11	11:00					
11g	generalization					

12	12:00					
12g	generalization					
13	can tell to the half-hour					
13g	generalization					
14	can tell to the quarter-hour					
14g	generalization					
15	can tell to the minute					
15g	generalization					
PERCENT CORRECT						

Child Name:. . . . .

Receptive Identification of Coins

Teaching Procedure: Place the coin you are working on in each step down on a table and provide a minimum of two other coins (the distractor coins need to be different from the coin you are working on) and ask the child to "find _____" (name the coin you are on).

Prompt Hierarchy: Use the least intrusive prompt required in order for the child to be successful (gesture, faded physical, physical; faded verbal and verbal to be used **only** with verbal programs).

Materials: Quarter, dime, nickel, penny.

	STEPS	date:	date:	date:	date:	date:
1	quarter					
1g	generalization					
2	dime					
2g	generalization					
3	nickel					
3g	generalization					
4	penny					
4g	generalization					
PERCENT CORRECT						

Child Name: . . . .

Expressive Identification of Coins

Teaching Procedure: Hold up the coin you are working on in each step and ask the child "what is it?" The child will name the coin.

Prompt Hierarchy: Use the least intrusive prompt required in order for the child to be successful (gesture, faded physical, physical; faded verbal and verbal to be used **only** with verbal programs).

Materials: Quarter, dime, nickel, penny.

	STEPS	date:	date:	date:	date:	date:
1	quarter					
1g	generalization					
2	dime					
2g	generalization					
3	nickel					
3g	generalization					
4	penny					
4g	generalization					
PERCENT CORRECT						

Child Name: . . . .

Receptive Identification of Same and Different

Teaching Procedure: Get at least two things that are either the same or different (depending on the step you are on), or pictures of them, and then at least two more pictures that are not the same and present the child with the Sd "show me which ones are _____" (name the step).

Prompt Hierarchy: Use the least intrusive prompt required in order for the child to be successful (gesture, faded physical, physical; faded verbal and verbal to be used **only** with verbal programs).

Materials: Items that are the same and items that are different.

	STEPS	date:	date:	date:	date:	date:
1	same					
1g	generalization					
2	different					
2g	generalization					
PERCENT CORRECT						

Child Name: . . . .

Expressive Identification of Same and Different

Teaching Procedure: Get at least two things that are either the same or different (depending on the step you are on) or pictures of them, and then at least two more pictures that are not the same and present the child with the Sd "tell me which ones are _____" (name the step).

Prompt Hierarchy: Use the least intrusive prompt required in order for the child to be successful (gesture, faded physical, physical; faded verbal and verbal to be used **only** with verbal programs).

Materials: Items that are the same and items that are different.

	STEPS	date:	date:	date:	date:	date:
1	same					
1g	generalization					
2	different					
2g	generalization					
PERCENT CORRECT						

Language Arts—Receptive Programs

Child Name: . . . .

Receptive Identification of Prepositions

Teaching Procedure: Use cards that show different prepositions and lay down a mimimum of three cards. Present the child with the Sd "show me ___" (name preposition).

Prompt Hierarchy: Use the least intrusive prompt required in order for the child to be successful (gesture, faded physical, physical; faded verbal and verbal to be used **only** with verbal programs).

Materials: Cards that contain different prepositions on them; various objects that can be used to help show the different prepositions.

	STEPS	date:	date:	date:	date:	date:
1	in					
1g	generalization					
2	off					
2g	generalization					
3	on					
3g	generalization					
4	out					
4g	generalization					
5	under					
5g	generalization					
6	over					
6g	generalization					
7	next to					
7g	generalization					
8	behind					
8g	generalization					
9	near					
9g	generalization					
10	far					
10g	generalization					
PERCENT CORRECT						

Child Name:. . . . .

Receptive Identification of Pronouns

Teaching Procedure: Using actual people or pictures, present the child with the Sd "show me ____" (name the step that you are on).

Prompt Hierarchy: Use the least intrusive prompt required in order for the child to be successful (gesture, faded physical, physical; faded verbal and verbal to be used **only** with verbal programs).

Materials: Pictures of pronouns, actual people.

	STEPS	date:	date:	date:	date:	date:
1	he					
1g	generalization					
2	she					
2g	generalization					
3	me					
3g	generalization					
4	we					
4g	generalization					
5	us					
5g	generalization					
6	you					
6g	generalization					
7	they					
7g	generalization					
8	hers					
8g	generalization					
9	his					
9g	generalization					
10	theirs					
10g	generalization					
11	mine					
11g	generalization					

12	I					
12g	generalization					
PERCENT CORRECT						

Child Name: . . . .

Receptive Identification of Adjectives

Teaching Procedure: In a field of three or more, have the student identify the item when you present the direction "show me the____" (name the adjective according to the step you are on). For example, step 1 is colors—you will say "show me the blue one."

Prompt Hierarchy: Use the least intrusive prompt required in order for the child to be successful (gesture, faded physical, physical; faded verbal and verbal to be used **only** with verbal programs).

Materials: Pictures or items of various adjectives.

	STEPS	date:	date:	date:	date:	date:
1	colors (insert various colors)					
1g	generalization					
2	tall					
2g	generalization					
3	short					
3g	generalization					
4	round					
4g	generalization					
5	big					
5g	generalization					
6	little					
6g	generalization					
7	cold					
7g	generalization					
8	hot/warm					
8g	generalization					
9	soft					
9g	generalization					
10	sharp					
10g	generalization					
11	new					
11g	generalization					

12	old					
12g	generalization					
PERCENT CORRECT						

Child Name:. . . . .

Receptive Identification of Noun and Adjective

Teaching Procedure: Present the child with a minimum of two pictures/objects and ask him to "touch/find the _____" (name the object).

Prompt Hierarchy: Use the least intrusive prompt required in order for the child to be successful (gesture, faded physical, physical; faded verbal and verbal to be used **only** with verbal programs).

Materials: A red ball, paper cut into a circle, a big doll, a long pencil, a wet towel, a cold drink.

	STEPS	date:	date:	date:	date:	date:
1	red (ball)					
1g	generalization					
2	circle (paper)					
2g	generalization					
3	big (doll)					
3g	generalization					
4	long (pencil)					
4g	generalization					
5	wet (towel)					
5g	generalization					
6	cold (drink)					
6g	generalization					
PERCENT CORRECT						

Child Name: . . . .

Receptive Identification of Adverbs

Teaching Procedure: You will need to present an Sd that will require the child to demonstrate the adverb in the step.

Prompt Hierarchy: Use the least intrusive prompt required in order for the child to be successful (gesture, faded physical, physical; faded verbal and verbal to be used **only** with verbal programs).

Materials: None.

	STEPS	date:	date:	date:	date:	date:
1	softly					
1g	generalization					
2	quickly					
2g	generalization					
3	nicely					
3g	generalization					
4	quietly					
4g	generalization					
5	happily					
5g	generalization					
PERCENT CORRECT						

Child Name:. . . . .

Receptive Identification of Class

Teaching Procedure: Lay down a minimum of five pictures/objects, where three of them show the step you are working on, and present the child with the Sd "show me which ones are _____" (name the class).

Prompt Hierarchy: Use the least intrusive prompt required in order for the child to be successful (gesture, faded physical, physical; faded verbal and verbal to be used **only** with verbal programs).

Materials: Clothes, animals, food, drink, toys, vehicles, or pictures of them.

	STEPS	date:	date:	date:	date:	date:
1	clothes (shirt, shoes, socks, pants, shorts)					
1g	generalization					
2	animals (cat, dog, horse, pig, cow)					
2g	generalization					
3	food (pizza, cookie, sandwich, burger, soup)					
3g	generalization					
4	drink (water, soda, apple juice, milk, orange juice)					
4g	generalization					
5	toys (bubbles, puzzle, bus, shape sorter, doll)					
5g	generalization					
6	vehicle (car, train, truck)					
6g	generalization					
PERCENT CORRECT						

Child Name: . . . .

Receptive Identification of Feature

Teaching Procedure: Lay down a minimum of three pictures/objects (one of them showing the step you are working on), then present the child with the Sd "give me/show me the one that is _____" (name feature).

Prompt Hierarchy: Use the least intrusive prompt required in order for the child to be successful (gesture, faded physical, physical; faded verbal and verbal to be used **only** with verbal programs).

Materials: Pictures or items that can be identified by color, shape, having a tail, wheels, laces, pages, ears, fur, a point.

	STEPS	date:	date:	date:	date:	date:
1	color (e.g. "give me the one that is red")					
1g	generalization					
2	shape (e.g. "give me the one that is a circle")					
2g	generalization					
3	tail (cat, dog)					
3g	generalization					
4	wheels (car, truck)					
4g	generalization					
5	laces (shoes, boots)					
5g	generalization					
6	pages (book, magazine)					
6g	generalization					
7	ears (bunny, dog)					
7g	generalization					
8	fur (cat, bear)					
8g	generalization					
9	has a point (pencil, scissors)					
9g	generalization					
PERCENT CORRECT						

Child Name: . . . .

Receptive Identification of Function

Teaching Procedure: Lay down a minimum of three pictures/objects (one of them showing the step you are working on), then present the child with the Sd "what do you _____?" (name function).

Prompt Hierarchy: Use the least intrusive prompt required in order for the child to be successful (gesture, faded physical, physical; faded verbal and verbal to be used **only** with verbal programs).

Materials: Pictures or actual knife/scissors, car/truck, pencil/pen, hat/jacket, phone/cell phone, book/magazine, couch/chair, bagel/pasta/food, milk/juice/drink, pot/pan, fork/spoon, brush/comb, pool/ocean, paper/chalkboard, vacuum cleaner/broom, table/desk, cup/mug, bike/scooter, sunglasses/bathing suit, puzzles/trains, bubbles/kisses, blocks/Legos, piano/guitar, crayons/markers, drawer/closet.

	STEPS	date:	date:	date:	date:	date:
1	cut with: knife, scissors					
1g	generalization					
2	drive: car, truck					
2g	generalization					
3	write with: pencil, pen					
3g	generalization					
4	wear when it's cold: hat, jacket					
4g	generalization					
5	talk on: phone, cell phone					
5g	generalization					
6	read: book, magazine					
6g	generalization					
7	sit on: couch, chair					
7g	generalization					
8	eat: bagel, pasta, food					
8g	generalization					
9	drink: milk, juice					
9g	generalization					
10	cook with: pot, pan					
10g	generalization					

11	eat with: fork, spoon					
11g	generalization					
12	brush your hair with: brush, comb					
12g	generalization					
13	swim in: pool, ocean					
13g	generalization					
14	write on: paper, chalkboard					
14g	generalization					
15	clean with: vacuum cleaner, broom					
15g	generalization					
16	work on: table, desk					
16g	generalization					
17	drink from: cup, mug					
17g	generalization					
18	ride: bike, scooter					
18g	generalization					
19	wear when it's hot: sunglasses, bathing suit					
19g	generalization					
20	play: puzzles, trains					
20g	generalization					
21	blow: bubbles, kisses					
21g	generalization					
22	build: blocks, Legos					
22g	generalization					
23	what plays music: piano, guitar					
23g	generalization					
24	color: crayons, markers					
24g	generalization					
25	what you put clothes in: drawer, closet					
25g	generalization					
PERCENT CORRECT						

Language Arts—Expressive Programs

Child Name: . . . .

Expressive Identification of Prepositions

Teaching Procedure: Use items such as a small ball and a cup, put the ball: in, on, and below the cup and present the child with the Sd "tell me where the ball is." The child will name the preposition.

Prompt Hierarchy: Use the least intrusive prompt required in order for the child to be successful (gesture, faded physical, physical; faded verbal and verbal to be used **only** with verbal programs).

Materials: Items such as a small ball and a cup, a piece of paper, and a table.

	STEPS	date:	date:	date:	date:	date:
1	in					
1g	generalization					
2	off					
2g	generalization					
3	on					
3g	generalization					
4	out					
4g	generalization					
5	under					
5g	generalization					
6	over					
6g	generalization					
7	next to					
7g	generalization					
8	behind					
8g	generalization					
9	near					
9g	generalization					
10	far					
10g	generalization					
PERCENT CORRECT						

Child Name:. . . . .

Expressive Identification of Pronouns

Teaching Procedure: Ask the child a question that he would need to answer with the correct pronoun. An example of step 1 would be "tell me what that person is doing." The child would need to answer "he is jumping."

Prompt Hierarchy: Use the least intrusive prompt required in order for the child to be successful (gesture, faded physical, physical; faded verbal and verbal to be used **only** with verbal programs).

Materials: None.

	STEPS	date:	date:	date:	date:	date:
1	he					
1g	generalization					
2	she					
2g	generalization					
3	me					
3g	generalization					
4	we					
4g	generalization					
5	us					
5g	generalization					
6	you					
6g	generalization					
7	they					
7g	generalization					
8	hers					
8g	generalization					
9	his					
9g	generalization					
10	theirs					
10g	generalization					
11	mine					
11g	generalization					

12	I					
12g	generalization					
PERCENT CORRECT						

Child Name: . . . .

Expressive Identification of Adjectives

Teaching Procedure: Hold up a picture or an item and ask the student to tell you about the item. For example, hold up a picture of a red ball and ask the student "tell me about the ball." The student will say that it is red.

Prompt Hierarchy: Use the least intrusive prompt required in order for the child to be successful (gesture, faded physical, physical; faded verbal and verbal to be used **only** with verbal programs).

Materials: Pictures or items illustrating various adjectives.

	STEPS	date:	date:	date:	date:	date:
1	colors (insert various colors)					
1g	generalization					
2	tall					
2g	generalization					
3	short					
3g	generalization					
4	round					
4g	generalization					
5	big					
5g	generalization					
6	little					
6g	generalization					
7	cold					
7g	generalization					
8	hot/warm					
8g	generalization					
9	soft					
9g	generalization					
10	sharp					
10g	generalization					
11	new					
11g	generalization					

12	old					
12g	generalization					
PERCENT CORRECT						

Child Name: . . . .

Expressive Identification of Noun and Adjective

Teaching Procedure: Hold up either a picture or the actual item and present the child with the Sd "tell me about the picture/item."

Prompt Hierarchy: Use the least intrusive prompt required in order for the child to be successful (gesture, faded physical, physical; faded verbal and verbal to be used **only** with verbal programs).

Materials: A red ball, paper cut into a circle, a big doll, a long pencil, a wet towel, a cold drink.

	STEPS	date:	date:	date:	date:	date:
1	red (ball)					
1g	generalization					
2	circle (paper)					
2g	generalization					
3	big (doll)					
3g	generalization					
4	long (pencil)					
4g	generalization					
5	wet (towel)					
5g	generalization					
6	cold (drink)					
6g	generalization					
PERCENT CORRECT						

Child Name: . . . .

Expressive Identification of Adverbs

Teaching Procedure: Using a video, pictures, or by an actual demonstration, ask the child to "tell me how the person is _____" (name the adverb).

Prompt Hierarchy: Use the least intrusive prompt required in order for the child to be successful (gesture, faded physical, physical; faded verbal and verbal to be used **only** with verbal programs).

Materials: None.

	STEPS	date:	date:	date:	date:	date:
1	softly					
1g	generalization					
2	quickly					
2g	generalization					
3	nicely					
3g	generalization					
4	quietly					
4g	generalization					
5	happily					
5g	generalization					
PERCENT CORRECT						

Child Name: . . . .

Expressive Identification of Class

Teaching Procedure: Present the child with the Sd "tell me/name things that are _____" (name the class).

Prompt Hierarchy: Use the least intrusive prompt required in order for the child to be successful (gesture, faded physical, physical; faded verbal and verbal to be used **only** with verbal programs).

Materials: None.

	STEPS	date:	date:	date:	date:	date:
1	a type of clothing (shirt, socks)					
1g	generalization					
2	a type of animal (cat, dog)					
2g	generalization					
3	a food (pizza, cereal)					
3g	generalization					
4	a drink (milk, juice)					
4g	generalization					
5	a toy (puzzle, doll)					
5g	generalization					
6	a vehicle (car, truck)					
6g	generalization					
7	transportation (plane, train)					
7g	generalization					
8	a sport (baseball, basketball)					
8g	generalization					
9	an instrument (piano, drum)					
9g	generalization					
10	a song ("Itsy Bitsy Spider," "Mary Had a Little Lamb")					
10g	generalization					
11	a color (red, blue)					
11g	generalization					

12	a shape (square, circle)					
12g	generalization					
13	a number (1, 2)					
13g	generalization					
14	a letter (A, B)					
14g	generalization					
15	weather (rain, sun)					
15g	generalization					
16	a month (April, May)					
16g	generalization					
17	a day of the week (Monday, Tuesday)					
17g	generalization					
18	a piece of jewelry (ring, necklace)					
18g	generalization					
19	things you take to the beach (shovel, bucket)					
19g	generalization					
20	a room in a house (kitchen, bedroom)					
20g	generalization					
PERCENT CORRECT						

Child Name: . . . .

Expressive Identification of Feature

Teaching Procedure: Present the child with the Sd "tell me about a _____" (name item).

Prompt Hierarchy: Use the least intrusive prompt required in order for the child to be successful (gesture, faded physical, physical; faded verbal and verbal to be used **only** with verbal programs).

Materials: None.

	STEPS	date:	date:	date:	date:	date:
1	dog (tail, eyes)					
1g	generalization					
2	cat (fur, whiskers)					
2g	generalization					
3	car (wheels, horn)					
3g	generalization					
4	house (windows, doors)					
4g	generalization					
5	bunny (tail, nose)					
5g	generalization					
6	book (pages, pictures)					
6g	generalization					
7	phone (buttons)					
7g	generalization					
8	truck (wheels, windows)					
8g	generalization					
9	playground (slide, swing)					
9g	generalization					
10	bed (blanket, pillow)					
10g	generalization					
11	sink (faucet, soap)					
11g	generalization					
12	a classroom has (desks, chairs)					

12g	generalization					
13	a door has (knob, handle)					
13g	generalization					
14	a table has (legs)					
14g	generalization					
15	a library has (books)					
15g	generalization					
16	a desk has (legs)					
16g	generalization					
17	a closet has (clothes, hangers)					
17g	generalization					
18	a family room has (TV, couch)					
18g	generalization					
19	a computer has (monitor, mouse)					
19g	generalization					
20	a sandbox has (shovel, sand)					
20g	generalization					
PERCENT CORRECT						

Child Name:. . . . .

Expressive Identification of Function

Teaching Procedure: Present the child with the Sd "what do you ___" (name function).

Prompt Hierarchy: Use the least intrusive prompt required in order for the child to be successful (gesture, faded physical, physical; faded verbal and verbal to be used **only** with verbal programs).

Materials: None.

	STEPS	date:	date:	date:	date:	date:
1	cut with: knife, scissors					
1g	generalization					
2	drive: car, truck					
2g	generalization					
3	write with: pencil, pen					
3g	generalization					
4	wear when it's cold: hat, jacket					
4g	generalization					
5	talk on: phone, cell phone					
5g	generalization					
6	read: book, magazine					
6g	generalization					
7	sit on: couch, chair					
7g	generalization					
8	eat: bagel, pasta, food					
8g	generalization					
9	drink: milk, juice					
9g	generalization					
10	cook with: pot, pan					
10g	generalization					
11	eat with: fork, spoon					
11g	generalization					
12	brush your hair with: brush, comb					

12g	generalization					
13	swim in: pool, ocean					
13g	generalization					
14	write on: paper, chalkboard					
14g	generalization					
15	clean with: vacuum cleaner, broom					
15g	generalization					
16	work on: table, desk					
16g	generalization					
17	drink from: cup, mug					
17g	generalization					
18	ride: bike, scooter					
18g	generalization					
19	wear when it's hot: sunglasses, bathing suit					
19g	generalization					
20	play: puzzles, trains					
20g	generalization					
21	blow: bubbles, kisses					
21g	generalization					
22	build: blocks, Legos					
22g	generalization					
23	what plays music: piano, guitar					
23g	generalization					
24	color: crayons, markers					
24g	generalization					
25	what you put clothes in: drawer, closet					
25g	generalization					
PERCENT CORRECT						

Sort and Categorization

Child Name: . . . .

Receptive Identification of What Goes Together

Teaching Procedure: Lay down the objects/pictures along with at least two other objects/pictures; present the child with the remaining object/picture and present the Sd "what goes with _____?" (name the object/picture).

Prompt Hierarchy: Use the least intrusive prompt required in order for the child to be successful (gesture, faded physical, physical; faded verbal and verbal to be used **only** with verbal programs).

Materials: Objects themselves or pictures of: sock, shoe, foot, bat, ball, mitt, pillow, bed, blanket, pants, belt, leg, cup, drink, straw, plate, food, fork, toothbrush, toothpaste, teeth, refrigerator, milk, eggs, slide, swing, playground, paper, pencil, crayon.

	STEPS	date:	date:	date:	date:	date:
1	sock, shoe, foot					
1g	generalization					
2	bat, ball, mitt					
2g	generalization					
3	pillow, bed, blanket					
3g	generalization					
4	pants, belt, leg					
4g	generalization					
5	cup, drink, straw					
5g	generalization					
6	plate, food, fork					
6g	generalization					
7	toothbrush, toothpaste, teeth					
7g	generalization					
8	refrigerator, milk, eggs					
8g	generalization					
9	slide, swing, playground					
9g	generalization					
10	paper, pencil, crayon					
10g	generalization					
PERCENT CORRECT						

Child Name: . . . .

Expressive Identification of What Goes Together

Teaching Procedure: Present the child with the Sd "tell me what goes with _____" (name one of the items in the step that you are working on). The child will need to tell you one or two items that go with the item that you named. You can present the Sd as "tell me one thing that go with_____," or you can say, "tell me two things that go with_____."

Prompt Hierarchy: Use the least intrusive prompt required in order for the child to be successful (gesture, faded physical, physical; faded verbal and verbal to be used **only** with verbal programs).

Materials: None.

	STEPS	date:	date:	date:	date:	date:
1	sock, shoe, foot					
1g	generalization					
2	bat, ball, mitt					
2g	generalization					
3	pillow, bed, blanket					
3g	generalization					
4	pants, belt, leg					
4g	generalization					
5	cup, drink, straw					
5g	generalization					
6	plate, food, fork					
6g	generalization					
7	toothbrush, toothpaste, teeth					
7g	generalization					
8	refrigerator, milk, eggs					
8g	generalization					
9	slide, swing, playground					
9g	generalization					
10	paper, pencil, crayon					
10g	generalization					
PERCENT CORRECT						

Child Name: . . . .

Categorization

Teaching Procedure: Present the child with a minimum of eight pictures/objects with at least half of the items illustrating the step the child is working on, and present the Sd "put all the _____" (name step) together.

Prompt Hierarchy: Use the least intrusive prompt required in order for the child to be successful (gesture, faded physical, physical; faded verbal and verbal to be used **only** with verbal programs).

Materials: Items that are the same color, big items, little items, items that are hot, items that are cold, items that are tall, items that are short, items that are wet, items that are dry, items that are rough, items that are soft, items that are broken, items that are sharp, items that are loud.

	STEPS	date:	date:	date:	date:	date:
1	color (all the blue ones)					
1g	generalization					
2	big					
2g	generalization					
3	little					
3g	generalization					
4	hot					
4g	generalization					
5	cold					
5g	generalization					
6	tall					
6g	generalization					
7	short					
7g	generalization					
8	wet					
8g	generalization					
9	dry					
9g	generalization					
10	rough					
10g	generalization					

11	soft					
11g	generalization					
12	broken					
12g	generalization					
13	sharp					
13g	generalization					
14	loud					
14g	generalization					
PERCENT CORRECT						

Child Name: . . . .

Receptive Identification of What is Not the Item

Teaching Procedure: Lay down at least four pictures. At least half of the pictures should be the item in the step you are working on. Present the child with the Sd "show me what is not a ___ [step name]."

Prompt Hierarchy: Use the least intrusive prompt required in order for the child to be successful (gesture, faded physical, physical; faded verbal and verbal to be used **only** with verbal programs).

Materials: Pictures that include cars, foods, shapes, colors, toys, crayons, clothes, buses, drinks.

	STEPS	date:	date:	date:	date:	date:
1	car					
1g	generalization					
2	food					
2g	generalization					
3	shape					
3g	generalization					
4	color					
4g	generalization					
5	toy					
5g	generalization					
6	crayon					
6g	generalization					
7	clothes					
7g	generalization					
8	bus					
8g	generalization					
9	drink					
9g	generalization					
PERCENT CORRECT						

Child Name: . . . .

Expressive Identification of What is Not the Item

Teaching Procedure: Present the child with the Sd "tell me what is not a ___" (name the item in the current step).

Prompt Hierarchy: Use the least intrusive prompt required in order for the child to be successful (gesture, faded physical, physical; faded verbal and verbal to be used **only** with verbal programs).

Materials: None.

	STEPS	date:	date:	date:	date:	date:
1	car					
1g	generalization					
2	food					
2g	generalization					
3	shape					
3g	generalization					
4	color					
4g	generalization					
5	toy					
5g	generalization					
6	crayon					
6g	generalization					
7	clothes					
7g	generalization					
8	bus					
8g	generalization					
9	drink					
9g	generalization					
PERCENT CORRECT						

Child Name: . . . .

Sort by Function

Teaching Procedure: Put down a sample from each category and then hand the child the pictures and present the Sd "sort."

Prompt Hierarchy: Use the least intrusive prompt required in order for the child to be successful (gesture, faded physical, physical; faded verbal and verbal to be used **only** with verbal programs).

Materials: Pictures of things you eat (e.g. banana, cookie, pasta), things you ride in (e.g. car, truck, train), things you wear (e.g. shirt, pants, shoes), things you play with (e.g. puzzle, car, shape sorter), things you sit on (e.g. chair, sofa, bench), things you drink (e.g. juice, milk, water).

	STEPS	date:	date:	date:	date:	date:
1	have child sort things you eat versus things you ride in					
1g	generalization					
2	have the child sort things you wear versus things you play with					
2g	generalization					
3	have the child sort any combination of eat, ride in, wear, play with, in a field of three					
3g	generalization					
4	have the child sort any combination of eat, ride in, wear, play with, sit on, in a field of three or more					
4g	generalization					
5	have the child sort any combination of eat, ride in, wear, play with, sit on, drink, in a field of three or more					
5g	generalization					
PERCENT CORRECT						

Child Name: . . . .

Sort by Feature

Teaching Procedure: Put down a sample from each category and then hand the child the pictures and present the child with the Sd "sort."

Prompt Hierarchy: Use the least intrusive prompt required in order for the child to be successful (gesture, faded physical, physical; faded verbal and verbal to be used **only** with verbal programs).

Materials: Pictures of things with tails (e.g. dog, horse, pig), things with wheels (e.g. bike, car, truck), things that are the same color (e.g. banana, tennis ball, lemon), things that have stripes (e.g. zebra, tiger, striped fish), things that are round (e.g. ball, coin, marble), things that are soft (e.g. rabbit, cotton ball, feather).

	STEPS	date:	date:	date:	date:	date:
1	have the child sort things with tails versus things with wheels					
1g	generalization					
2	have the child sort things with the same color versus things that have stripes					
2g	generalization					
3	have the child sort any combination of things with tails, wheels, same color, and stripes, in a field of three					
3g	generalization					
4	have the child sort any combination of things with tails, wheels, same color, stripes, things that are round, in a field of three or more					
4g	generalization					
5	have the child sort any combination of things with tails, wheels, same color, stripes, round, soft, in a field of three or more					
5g	generalization					
PERCENT CORRECT						

Child Name: ....

Sort by Class

Teaching Procedure: Put down a sample from each category and then hand the child the pictures and present the child with the Sd "sort."

Prompt Hierarchy: Use the least intrusive prompt required in order for the child to be successful (gesture, faded physical, physical; faded verbal and verbal to be used **only** with verbal programs).

Materials: Pictures of colors (e.g. blue, green, purple), food (e.g. pasta, cereal, cookie), clothes (e.g. shirt, pants, socks), animals (e.g. lion, bear, cat), shapes (e.g. triangle, circle, square), furniture (e.g. couch, table, bed), toys (e.g. puzzle, shape sorter, car).

	STEPS	date:	date:	date:	date:	date:
1	have the child sort things that are a color versus food					
1g	generalization					
2	have the child sort things that are clothes versus animals					
2g	generalization					
3	have the child sort any combination of color, food, clothes, animals, in a field of three					
3g	generalization					
4	have the child sort any combination of color, food, clothes, animals, shapes, in a field of three or more					
4g	generalization					
5	have the child sort any combination of color, food, clothes, animals, shapes, furniture, in a field of three or more					
5g	generalization					
6	have the child sort any combination of color, food, clothes, animals, shapes, furniture, toys, in a field of three or more					
6g	generalization					
PERCENT CORRECT						

Conversation and Social Skills

Child Name: . . . .

Receptively Identifies Items

Teaching Procedure: Present the child with a minimum of three pictures/objects and ask the child to "find ___" (name the item in the current step).

Prompt Hierarchy: Use the least intrusive prompt required in order for the child to be successful (gesture, faded physical, physical; faded verbal and verbal to be used **only** with verbal programs).

Materials: Pictures of animals, colors, letters, numbers, shapes, vehicles, things found at a playground (swing, slide, sandbox), things found in a home (couch, TV, kitchen), things found outside (trees, flowers, squirrels), things found in a bedroom (bed, pillow, closet).

	STEPS	date:	date:	date:	date:	date:
1	animals					
1g	generalization					
2	colors					
2g	generalization					
3	letters					
3g	generalization					
4	numbers					
4g	generalization					
5	shapes					
5g	generalization					
6	vehicles					
6g	generalization					
7	things found at a playground					
7g	generalization					
8	things found in the home					
8g	generalization					
9	things found outside					
9g	generalization					
10	things found in the bedroom					
10g	generalization					
PERCENT CORRECT						

Child Name:. . . . .

Expressively Answers the Question "Name..."

Teaching Procedure: Ask the child to "name ___" (present the words in each step).

Prompt Hierarchy: Use the least intrusive prompt required in order for the child to be successful (gesture, faded physical, physical; faded verbal and verbal to be used **only** with verbal programs).

Materials: None.

	STEPS	date:	date:	date:	date:	date:
1	animals					
1g	generalization					
2	colors					
2g	generalization					
3	letters					
3g	generalization					
4	numbers					
4g	generalization					
5	shapes					
5g	generalization					
6	vehicles					
6g	generalization					
7	things found at a playground					
7g	generalization					
8	things found in the home					
8g	generalization					
9	things found outside					
9g	generalization					
10	things found in the bedroom					
10g	generalization					
PERCENT CORRECT						

Child Name: . . . .

Answers Questions About Items

Teaching Procedure: Present the child with the Sd, which are the words not in parentheses in each step.

Prompt Hierarchy: Use the least intrusive prompt required in order for the child to be successful (gesture, faded physical, physical; faded verbal and verbal to be used **only** with verbal programs).

Materials: None.

	STEPS	date:	date:	date:	date:	date:
1	you ride in a ___ (car)					
1g	generalization					
2	you write with a __ (pencil/pen)					
2g	generalization					
3	you wear a ___ (shirt, pants, shoes, etc.)					
3g	generalization					
4	you eat in a ___ (restaurant)					
4g	generalization					
5	you eat with a __ (fork)					
5g	generalization					
6	you sleep in a __ (bed)					
6g	generalization					
7	you wash your hands with __ (soap)					
7g	generalization					
8	you smell with your __ (nose)					
8g	generalization					
9	you blow __ (bubbles)					
9g	generalization					
10	you live in a __ (house)					
10g	generalization					
11	you read a__ (book)					
11g	generalization					
12	you sit on a __ (chair)					

12g	generalization					
13	you drink from a __ (cup)					
13g	generalization					
14	you see with your __ (eyes)					
14g	generalization					
15	you hear with your __ (ears)					
15g	generalization					
16	you cut with __ (scissors)					
16g	generalization					
17	you watch __ (TV)					
17g	generalization					
18	you throw a __ (ball)					
18g	generalization					
19	you listen to __ (music)					
19g	generalization					
20	you play with __ (toys)					
20g	generalization					
PERCENT CORRECT						

Child Name: . . . .

Answers "What" Questions

Teaching Procedure: Present the child with the "what" question in each step.

Prompt Hierarchy: Use the least intrusive prompt required in order for the child to be successful (gesture, faded physical, physical; faded verbal and verbal to be used **only** with verbal programs).

Materials: None.

	STEPS	date:	date:	date:	date:	date:
1	What do you see in the park?					
1g	generalization					
2	What do you see at the library?					
2g	generalization					
3	What do you see at the restaurant?					
3g	generalization					
4	What do you see at the bank?					
4g	generalization					
5	What do you see at the fire station?					
5g	generalization					
6	What do you do at the farm?					
6g	generalization					
7	What do you see at a the ice-cream store?					
7g	generalization					
8	What do you get at a restaurant?					
8g	generalization					
9	What do you see in a supermarket?					
9g	generalization					
10	What do you see at the gym?					
10g	generalization					
11	What do you see at the zoo?					
11g	generalization					
12	What do you see at the mall?					

12g	generalization					
13	What do you see in the cafeteria?					
13g	generalization					
14	What do you see at the bowling ally?					
14g	generalization					
15	What do you see at the movie theater?					
15g	generalization					
16	What do you see at the post office?					
16g	generalization					
17	What do you see at the police station?					
17g	generalization					
18	What do you see at the hair salon?					
18g	generalization					
19	What do you see at an airport?					
19g	generalization					
20	What do you see at a train station?					
20g	generalization					
PERCENT CORRECT						

Child Name: . . . .

Answers "When" Questions

Teaching Procedure: Present the child with the "when" question in each step.

Prompt Hierarchy: Use the least intrusive prompt required in order for the child to be successful (gesture, faded physical, physical; faded verbal and verbal to be used **only** with verbal programs).

Materials: None.

	STEPS	date:	date:	date:	date:	date:
1	When do you sleep?					
1g	generalization					
2	When do you eat breakfast?					
2g	generalization					
3	When do you eat dinner?					
3g	generalization					
4	When do you watch TV?					
4g	generalization					
5	When do you play?					
5g	generalization					
6	When do you take a bath?					
6g	generalization					
7	When do you go to school?					
7g	generalization					
8	When do you swim in the ocean?					
8g	generalization					
9	When does it snow?					
9g	generalization					
10	When do you put sunglasses on?					
10g	generalization					
11	When do you wear gloves?					
11g	generalization					
12	When do you build a snowman?					

12g	generalization					
13	When do you eat a snack?					
13g	generalization					
14	When do you eat lunch?					
14g	generalization					
15	When do you see your friends?					
15g	generalization					
16	When do you drink?					
16g	generalization					
17	When do you wear shorts?					
17g	generalization					
18	When do you use a vacuum cleaner?					
18g	generalization					
19	When do you see a doctor?					
19g	generalization					
20	When do you go to the mall?					
20g	generalization					
PERCENT CORRECT						

Child Name: . . . .

Answers "Where" Questions

Teaching Procedure: Present the child with the words in each step.

Prompt Hierarchy: Use the least intrusive prompt required in order for the child to be successful (gesture, faded physical, physical; faded verbal and verbal to be used **only** with verbal programs).

Materials: None.

	STEPS	date:	date:	date:	date:	date:
1	Where do you find milk?					
1g	generalization					
2	Where do you hang your coat?					
2g	generalization					
3	Where do you get a spoon?					
3g	generalization					
4	Where do you sleep?					
4g	generalization					
5	Where do you wash your face?					
5g	generalization					
6	Where do you go to the bathroom?					
6g	generalization					
7	Where do you eat dinner?					
7g	generalization					
8	Where do you watch TV?					
8g	generalization					
9	Where is your bed?					
9g	generalization					
10	Where is the couch?					
10g	generalization					
11	Where are your clothes?					
11g	generalization					
12	Where do you get ice?					

12g	generalization					
13	Where do you play?					
13g	generalization					
14	Where do you find the toilet?					
14g	generalization					
15	Where do you put sheets?					
15g	generalization					
16	Where do you heat food up?					
16g	generalization					
17	Where do you put eggs?					
17g	generalization					
18	Where do you wash clothes?					
18g	generalization					
19	Where do you find your socks?					
19g	generalization					
20	Where do you find the computer at school?					
20g	generalization					
PERCENT CORRECT						

Child Name: . . . .

Answers "Which" Questions

Teaching Procedure: Present the child with the "which" question in each step.

Prompt Hierarchy: Use the least intrusive prompt required in order for the child to be successful (gesture, faded physical, physical; faded verbal and verbal to be used **only** with verbal programs).

Materials: None.

	STEPS	date:	date:	date:	date:	date:
1	Which is an animal, cat or apple?					
1g	generalization					
2	Which is a food, dog or pizza?					
2g	generalization					
3	Which is a color, square or red?					
3g	generalization					
4	Which is a shape, circle or desk?					
4g	generalization					
5	Which is a body part, arm or phone?					
5g	generalization					
6	Which is a month, Tuesday or January?					
6g	generalization					
7	Which is clothing, watch or pants?					
7g	generalization					
8	Which is jewelry, hair or ring?					
8g	generalization					
9	Which happens in winter, snow or swimming?					
9g	generalization					
10	Which is a drink, milk or cereal?					
10g	generalization					
11	Which has a tail, dog or flower?					
11g	generalization					

12	Which has ears, plant or bunny?					
12g	generalization					
13	Which one do you sleep in, bed or car?					
13g	generalization					
14	Which goes in the sky, boat or plane?					
14g	generalization					
15	Which goes in the water, shoes or boat?					
15g	generalization					
16	Which do you read, book or pencil?					
16g	generalization					
17	Which do you write with, paper or pencil?					
17g	generalization					
18	Which do you write on, paper or door?					
18g	generalization					
19	Which do you eat with, fork or pen?					
19g	generalization					
20	Which do you cut with, napkin or scissors?					
20g	generalization					
PERCENT CORRECT						

Child Name: . . . .

Answers "Who" Questions

Teaching Procedure: Present the child with the "who" question in each step.

Prompt Hierarchy: Use the least intrusive prompt required in order for the child to be successful (gesture, faded physical, physical; faded verbal and verbal to be used **only** with verbal programs).

Materials: None.

	STEPS	date:	date:	date:	date:	date:
1	Who do you see when you are sick?					
1g	generalization					
2	Who puts out fires?					
2g	generalization					
3	Who do you go to if you are lost?					
3g	generalization					
4	Who puts you to bed at night?					
4g	generalization					
5	Whose turn is it?					
5g	generalization					
6	Whose shoe is this?					
6g	generalization					
7	Who wants a snack?					
7g	generalization					
8	Who is standing up?					
8g	generalization					
9	Who is sitting down?					
9g	generalization					
10	Who wants to go outside?					
10g	generalization					
11	Whose lunch box is this?					
11g	generalization					
12	Who is the line leader?					

12g	generalization					
13	Who wants to be my helper?					
13g	generalization					
14	Who can tell me the weather?					
14g	generalization					
15	Who delivers the mail?					
15g	generalization					
16	Who knows what color a zebra is?					
16g	generalization					
17	Who wants a drink?					
17g	generalization					
18	Who likes soccer?					
18g	generalization					
19	Who wants to sing a song?					
19g	generalization					
20	Who likes ice-cream?					
20g	generalization					
PERCENT CORRECT						

Child Name: . . . .

Answers "How" Questions

Teaching Procedure: Present the child with the "how" question in each step.

Prompt Hierarchy: Use the least intrusive prompt required in order for the child to be successful (gesture, faded physical, physical; faded verbal and verbal to be used **only** with verbal programs).

Materials: None.

	STEPS	date:	date:	date:	date:	date:
1	How do you get to school?					
1g	generalization					
2	How do you get dressed?					
2g	generalization					
3	How do you ride a bike?					
3g	generalization					
4	How do you answer a phone?					
4g	generalization					
5	How do you drink?					
5g	generalization					
6	How do you eat pasta?					
6g	generalization					
7	How do you color?					
7g	generalization					
8	How do you wash your hands?					
8g	generalization					
9	How do you sit in a movie?					
9g	generalization					
10	How do you make a sandwich?					
10g	generalization					
11	How do you cut paper?					
11g	generalization					
12	How do you throw a ball?					

12g	generalization					
13	How are you?					
13g	generalization					
14	How do you take a bath?					
14g	generalization					
15	How do you heat up soup?					
15g	generalization					
16	How do you make cookies?					
16g	generalization					
17	How do you plant flowers?					
17g	generalization					
18	How do you set the table?					
18g	generalization					
19	How do you mail a letter?					
19g	generalization					
20	How do you buy food?					
20g	generalization					
PERCENT CORRECT						

Child Name: . . . .

Answers "Why" Questions

Teaching Procedure: Present the child with the "why" question in each step.

Prompt Hierarchy: Use the least intrusive prompt required in order for the child to be successful (gesture, faded physical, physical; faded verbal and verbal to be used **only** with verbal programs).

Materials: None.

	STEPS	date:	date:	date:	date:	date:
1	Why do you sleep?					
1g	generalization					
2	Why do you wash your hands?					
2g	generalization					
3	Why do you eat?					
3g	generalization					
4	Why do you drink?					
4g	generalization					
5	Why do you take a bath?					
5g	generalization					
6	Why do you wear clothes?					
6g	generalization					
7	Why do you wear a hat?					
7g	generalization					
8	Why do you wear gloves?					
8g	generalization					
9	Why do you wear shoes?					
9g	generalization					
10	Why do you take a bus to school?					
10g	generalization					
11	Why do you go to school?					
11g	generalization					
12	Why do you use covers?					

12g	generalization					
13	Why do you talk on a phone?					
13g	generalization					
14	Why do you take a car?					
14g	generalization					
15	Why do you wear a bathing suit?					
15g	generalization					
16	Why do you read a book?					
16g	generalization					
17	Why do you say "hi" to people?					
17g	generalization					
18	Why do you watch TV?					
18g	generalization					
19	Why do you heat up soup?					
19g	generalization					
20	Why do you use an ice cube?					
20g	generalization					
PERCENT CORRECT						

Child Name:. . . . .

What Can You Do in the Community?

Teaching Procedure: Present the child with the question in each step.

Prompt Hierarchy: Use the least intrusive prompt required in order for the child to be successful (gesture, faded physical, physical; faded verbal and verbal to be used **only** with verbal programs).

Materials: None.

	STEPS	date:	date:	date:	date:	date:
1	What can you do at a restaurant?					
1g	generalization					
2	What can you do at the park?					
2g	generalization					
3	What can you do at the library?					
3g	generalization					
4	What can you do at the bank?					
4g	generalization					
5	What can you do at the supermarket?					
5g	generalization					
6	What can you do at the zoo?					
6g	generalization					
7	What can you do at the police station?					
7g	generalization					
8	What can you do at the fire station?					
8g	generalization					
9	What can you do at the hair salon?					
9g	generalization					
10	What can you do at the post office?					
10g	generalization					
11	What can you do at the airport?					
11g	generalization					
12	What can you do at the bowling alley?					

12g	generalization					
13	What can you do at the movie theater?					
13g	generalization					
14	What can you do at the gym?					
14g	generalization					
15	What can you do at the train station?					
15g	generalization					
16	What can you do at the cafeteria?					
16g	generalization					
17	What do you do at the farm?					
17g	generalization					
18	What do you do at the ice-cream store?					
18g	generalization					
19	What do you do at the mall?					
19g	generalization					
20	What do you do at school?					
20g	generalization					
PERCENT CORRECT						

Child Name: . . . .

"Tell Me About..."

Teaching Procedure: Present the child with the Sd "tell me about…" (name the item in each step). The child will need to give at least two details per item in order for it to be considered mastered.

Prompt Hierarchy: Use the least intrusive prompt required in order for the child to be successful (gesture, faded physical, physical; faded verbal and verbal to be used **only** with verbal programs).

Materials: None.

	STEPS	date:	date:	date:	date:	date:
1	cat					
1g	generalization					
2	dog					
2g	generalization					
3	pizza					
3g	generalization					
4	cereal					
4g	generalization					
5	school bus					
5g	generalization					
6	classroom					
6g	generalization					
7	house					
7g	generalization					
8	car					
8g	generalization					
9	park					
9g	generalization					
10	beach					
10g	generalization					
11	computer					
11g	generalization					
12	crayons					

12g	generalization					
13	desk					
13g	generalization					
14	refrigerator					
14g	generalization					
15	book					
15g	generalization					
16	shoes					
16g	generalization					
17	horse					
17g	generalization					
18	cow					
18g	generalization					
19	apple juice					
19g	generalization					
20	telephone					
20g	generalization					
PERCENT CORRECT						

Child Name: . . . .

Recall

Teaching Procedure: Present the child with the question in each step.

Prompt Hierarchy: Use the least intrusive prompt required in order for the child to be successful (gesture, faded physical, physical; faded verbal and verbal to be used **only** with verbal programs).

Materials: None.

	STEPS	date:	date:	date:	date:	date:
1	What did you have for breakfast today?					
1g	generalization					
2	What did you have for dinner last night?					
2g	generalization					
3	What did you do over the weekend?					
3g	generalization					
4	What did you play with during recess today?					
4g	generalization					
5	What did you do after school yesterday?					
5g	generalization					
PERCENT CORRECT						

Child Name: . . . .

Conversation Starters

Teaching Procedure: Ask the child the question in each step. The child will need to engage another person/peer in a conversation using the topics presented in each step.

Prompt Hierarchy: Use the least intrusive prompt required in order for the child to be successful (gesture, faded physical, physical; faded verbal and verbal to be used **only** with verbal programs).

Materials: None.

	STEPS	date:	date:	date:	date:	date:
1	favorite movie					
1g	generalization					
2	favorite thing to do on the weekend					
2g	generalization					
3	favorite thing to do outside					
3g	generalization					
4	tell me about your family					
4g	generalization					
5	favorite toy					
5g	generalization					
PERCENT CORRECT						

Self Help and Daily Living Skills

Child Name: . . . .

Brushes Teeth

Teaching Procedure: Present the student with the direction "brush teeth."

Prompt Hierarchy: Use the least intrusive prompt required in order for the child to be successful (gesture, faded physical, physical; faded verbal and verbal to be used **only** with verbal programs).

Materials: Toothbrush and toothpaste.

	STEPS	date:	date:	date:	date:	date:
1	gets toothbrush					
1g	generalization					
2	turns on cold water					
2g	generalization					
3	wets the toothbrush					
3g	generalization					
4	gets toothpaste					
4g	generalization					
5	puts toothpaste on the toothbrush					
5g	generalization					
6	wets the toothbrush					
6g	generalization					
7	brushes top teeth					
7g	generalization					
8	brushes bottom teeth					
8g	generalization					
9	brushes tongue					
9g	generalization					
10	spits out toothpaste					
10g	generalization					
11	rinses toothbrush under cold water					
11g	generalization					
12	puts toothbrush away					
12g	generalization					

13	turns off cold water					
13g	generalization					
14	wipes mouth					
14g	generalization					
PERCENT CORRECT						

Child Name: . . . .

Washes Face

Teaching Procedure: Present the student with the direction "wash face."

Prompt Hierarchy: Use the least intrusive prompt required in order for the child to be successful (gesture, faded physical, physical; faded verbal and verbal to be used **only** with verbal programs).

Materials: Sink, water, face soap, towel.

	STEPS	date:	date:	date:	date:	date:
1	turns on cold water					
1g	generalization					
2	wets face with water					
2g	generalization					
3	gets face soap					
3g	generalization					
4	puts soap into hands					
4g	generalization					
5	rubs hands together					
5g	generalization					
6	washes right side of face					
6g	generalization					
7	washes left side of face					
7g	generalization					
8	washes forehead					
8g	generalization					
9	rinses soap off of hands					
9g	generalization					
10	puts water into hands					
10g	generalization					
11	splashes water on face until soap is off					
11g	generalization					
12	gets a towel					

12g	generalization					
13	dries face					
13g	generalization					
PERCENT CORRECT						

Child Name: . . . .

Puts Shirt On

Teaching Procedure: Present the student with the direction "put shirt on."

Prompt Hierarchy: Use the least intrusive prompt required in order for the child to be successful (gesture, faded physical, physical; faded verbal and verbal to be used only with verbal programs).

Materials: Shirt that is on the bigger side.

	STEPS	date:	date:	date:	date:	date:
1	lays shirt on a table face down					
1g	generalization					
2	picks up the bottom back side of the shirt					
2g	generalization					
3	puts the shirt over the head					
3g	generalization					
4	takes right hand and holds bottom of the shirt while the left hand goes into the sleeve					
4g	generalization					
5	takes left hand and holds bottom of the shirt while the right hand goes into the sleeve					
5g	generalization					
6	pulls shirt down					
6g	generalization					
PERCENT CORRECT						

Child Name:. . . . .

Ties Shoes

Teaching Procedure: Present the student with the direction "tie shoes."

Prompt Hierarchy: Use the least intrusive prompt required in order for the child to be successful (gesture, faded physical, physical; faded verbal and verbal to be used **only** with verbal programs).

Materials: Shoes with laces.

	STEPS	date:	date:	date:	date:	date:
1	picks up laces					
1g	generalization					
2	crosses laces (makes an X)					
2g	generalization					
3	puts a lace in each hand					
3g	generalization					
4	puts one lace under the other lace and pulls tight					
4g	generalization					
5	makes a loop with one lace					
5g	generalization					
6	wraps the other lace around the loop					
6g	generalization					
7	pushes the lace that was wrapped around the loop through the opening (where the thumb is)					
7g	generalization					
8	pulls it through while pulling the other loop in the opposite direction at the same time					
8g	generalization					
PERCENT CORRECT						

Child Name: . . . .

Toileting

Teaching Procedure: The purpose of this program is for the student to be able to use the bathroom independently. Therefore, this program should be taught by getting the child to mand (request without being asked) for the bathroom. Once you start this program, students should be placed into underwear and no longer be in a diaper or pull-up. This will help them feel when they are wet or dry.

Prompt Hierarchy: Use the least intrusive prompt required in order for the child to be successful (gesture, faded physical, physical; faded verbal and verbal to be used **only** with verbal programs).

Materials: Toilet, toilet paper.

	STEPS	date:	date:	date:	date:	date:
1	Set a timer according to the baseline data. When the timer beeps, do not ask the child if he needs to use the bathroom; instead prompt the child to request "bathroom." This can be done through sign language, visual picture, or through verbal language. Bring the student into the bathroom and get him to take down his pants and underwear. Have him check to see if he is wet or dry. If he is dry give lots of praise. If wet, neutrally say, "you are wet, we need to go in the potty/ toilet." Then get the student to sit on/ stand at the toilet. You can run water if you think that may help him void in the toilet. Have the student stay there for two to three minutes. If he voids, give lots of praise and reinforcement, otherwise just say "good job trying." Then reset the timer.					
1g	generalization					

2	The remainder of the steps should occur in the exact same way; the only difference is you will increase the interval by 15 minutes to try and get the student to be able to last longer in between going to the bathroom. So step 2 would be every hour if you started on step 1 at every 45 minutes.					
2g	generalization					
3	The last step is for the student to independently request going to the bathroom without being prompted by a timer.					
3g	generalization					
PERCENT CORRECT						

Part II

Curriculum

Curriculum Directions

When you first start implementing this curriculum or it is the beginning of the school year, you should do a full assessment. The assessment should be conducted again in the spring time, so it should be given twice a year. The purpose of assessing in the fall is to see if skills are being maintained. We want to assess again in the spring to see the progress that was made and to help devise goals and objectives for the upcoming school year. The curriculum section is basically the student's lesson plan. Once you figure out what programs the student is going to work on, you will use those curriculum pages and follow the steps on each curriculum page. When a step or program is mastered from the curriculum section, it then becomes a mastered step or program. The mastered steps/programs should be run at least once a month.

Purpose of curriculum

The purpose of this section is to provide a task analysis for the teacher or parent to follow.

Directions of curriculum

To determine which programs you should be working on, look at the total percentages from the assessment section. If the student scored an 80 percent or lower, you should consider that a potential program to work on. However, it is recommended that you base the programs on developmental milestones when applicable. This means that if the child is three, he does not need to know how to read, so working on sight words is not developmentally appropriate. Another recommendation is to choose programs that received a lower percentage score on the assessment. Once the programs are chosen, look at the related assessments and see the highest step that the student was able to complete. For example, if the student was able to complete up to step 3G on the assessment, you will start on step 4.

Measurement

It is recommended that either probe data be collected or trial-by-trial data. Practitioners can decide which measurement procedure they would like to utilize. This can vary from program to program. A more in-depth explanation of probe data and trial-by-trial data is provided in the introduction section.

Criterion

It is recommended that the criterion be either three consecutive Independents (Y) if you are using probe as your measurement procedure or 90 percent Independent over three consecutive days if you are using trial-by-trial as your measurement. The term "consecutive" does not mean three days in a row—it is three consecutive sessions in a row. This could mean that one teacher takes data in the morning, and another teacher takes data in the afternoon. These two sessions are considered consecutive.

Prompts

This curriculum suggests that you use a least-to-most intrusive prompt hierarchy. This is so that the child does not become prompt dependent. However, if the child learns the skills by using a most-to-least intrusive prompt system, then please use that. The least-to-most intrusive prompt hierarchy means that you start with a prompt that is the most hands off. An example would be a gestural prompt. When looking at the prompts below, you will see that a physical prompt is hand over hand. Therefore, this would be the most intrusive prompt. The most important aspect of prompting is to come in with the prompt that will ensure the child will get the answer correct. It is also important to remember to fade prompts as quickly as possible so that the child does not rely on your prompt.

- *Physical Prompt*—hand-over-hand manipulation.

- *Faded Physical Prompt*—the practitioner is guiding the child.

- *Gestural Prompt*—the practitioner points to the correct response.

- *Verbal Prompt*—the answer is provided verbally for the child.

- *Faded Verbal Prompt*—the beginning part of the answer is provided for the child.

A verbal/faded verbal prompt should only be used if you require a verbal response.

Errorless Learning

It is recommended that you implement this curriculum using errorless learning. Errorless learning is a way to ensure that children understand the direct correlation between the Sd (direction) and their behavior. There are many times when you may ask a child to perform a certain task and they may not respond at all or may get the response incorrect. By utilizing errorless learning you are teaching the child that there is no room for error.

An example is: Present Sd—no response/incorrect response—immediately prompt using the least intrusive prompt that will ensure that the child gets the answer correct—immediately represent the Sd—immediately prompt. This counts as one trial.

Distractors

All programs are designed to be taught in a field of three unless otherwise specified For example, if you are working on receptive identification of coins, you will put down the coin that you are working on and then an additional two coins. The additional two coins are your distractors.

Generalization

Each program has generalization built into the task analysis. Generalization means that the step the child is on should be taught in at least three different settings, with at least three different materials, and with at least three different people. Generalization has been achieved once the child reaches the criterion.

Curriculum Section Example

Child Name: . . . . John Smith . . . .

Playground

Teaching Procedure: When presented with the Sd "go play" while on the playground, the child will engage in three different playground activities for up to 10 minutes.

Prompt Hierarchy: Use the least intrusive prompt required in order for the child to be successful (gesture, faded physical, physical; faded verbal and verbal to be used **only** with verbal programs).

Materials: Playground equipment (swing, slide, jungle gym).

	Program Started 12/5/2011	Program Mastered		
	STEPS	STARTED	MASTERED	COMMENTS
1	Present the child with the Sd "go on the slide."	12/5/2011	1/30/2012	
1g	generalization	2/5/2012	2/27/2012	
2	Present the child with the Sd "go on the jungle gym."	3/15/2012	4/10/2012	
2g	generalization	4/20/2012	4/30/2012	
3	Present the child with the Sd "go on the swing."	5/15/2012	6/2/2012	
3g	generalization	6/5/2012	6/24/2012	
4	Once the child has mastered steps 1–3 tell him to "go play." He will need to start with the slide. Once he is no longer interested in the slide, he will climb on the jungle gym, then he will go on the swing.	7/1/2012	7/16/2012	
4g	generalization	7/20/2012	7/25/2012	

Classroom and Social Skills

Child Name: . . . .

Playground

Teaching Procedure: When presented with the Sd "go play" while on the playground, the child will engage in three different playground activities for up to 10 minutes.

Prompt Hierarchy: Use the least intrusive prompt required in order for the child to be successful (gesture, faded physical, physical; faded verbal and verbal to be used **only** with verbal programs).

Materials: Playground equipment (swing, slide, jungle gym).

Program Started		Program Mastered		
	STEPS	STARTED	MASTERED	COMMENTS
1	Present the child with the Sd "go on the slide."			
1g	generalization			
2	Present the child with the Sd "go on the jungle gym."			
2g	generalization			
3	Present the child with the Sd "go on the swing."			
3g	generalization			
4	Once the child has mastered steps 1–3 tell him to "go play." He will need to start with the slide. Once he is no longer interested in the slide, he will climb on the jungle gym, then he will go on the swing.			
4g	generalization			

Child Name: . . . .

Asks a Peer to Join/Play

Teaching Procedure: Have two peers engaged in a game or activity that you want your student to play. Make sure the game or activity is motivating to your student. When you are teaching the student to ask a peer to play, have a single peer engaged in an activity by himself.

Prompt Hierarchy: Use the least intrusive prompt required in order for the child to be successful (gesture, faded physical, physical; faded verbal and verbal to be used **only** with verbal programs).

Materials: Activities or games that strongly motivate your student.

Program Started		Program Mastered		
	STEPS	**STARTED**	**MASTERED**	**COMMENTS**
1	Ask your student, "do you want to join your friends." If the student says "yes," prompt him to walk over to the peers and say "can I join you?" Make sure you speak with the other students before contriving this situation so they know they have to say "yes."			
1g	generalization			
2	Say to your student "wow ___[name] and ___ [name] are playing your favorite game, it looks like fun." Your student will need to go over and ask them to join.			
2g	generalization			
3	Your student should be able to see the peers playing and walk over without any prompt from a teacher.			
3g	generalization			

Child Name: . . . .

Winning and Losing

Teaching Procedure: Play a game that has a clear winner and loser with your student. Generalization should include peers. Make sure the game you are playing is motivating to the student.

Prompt Hierarchy: Use the least intrusive prompt required in order for the child to be successful (gesture, faded physical, physical; faded verbal and verbal to be used **only** with verbal programs).

Materials: Activities or games that strongly motivate your student and have a clear winner and loser, such as musical chairs and board games.

Program Started		Program Mastered		
	STEPS	STARTED	MASTERED	COMMENTS
1	Play a game 1:1 with your student. Make sure your student wins. You say "good game" and teach your student to say "good game."			
1g	generalization			
2	Play a game 1:1 with your student. Make sure your student loses. You say "good game" and teach your student to say "thanks, you played good too."			
2g	generalization			

Child Name: . . . .

Follows Basic Classroom Instructions

Teaching Procedure: The child will be presented with the Sd for the step you are working on.

Prompt Hierarchy: Use the least intrusive prompt required in order for the child to be successful (gesture, faded physical, physical; faded verbal and verbal to be used **only** with verbal programs).

Materials: None.

Program Started		Program Mastered		
	STEPS	STARTED	MASTERED	COMMENTS
1	Put your backpack in your cubby.			
1g	generalization			
2	Get your backpack.			
2g	generalization			
3	Put your jacket away.			
3g	generalization			
4	Get your jacket.			
4g	generalization			
5	Go line up at the door.			
5g	generalization			
6	Sit in your chair.			
6g	generalization			
7	Get your lunch.			
7g	generalization			
8	Go to the bathroom.			
8g	generalization			

Child Name: . . . .

Sits During Group Time

Teaching Procedure: Present the child with the Sd "let's go sit with the group." Generalization should include using different Sds such as "let's go to circle time."

Prompt Hierarchy: Use the least intrusive prompt required in order for the child to be successful (gesture, faded physical, physical; faded verbal and verbal to be used **only** with verbal programs).

Materials: None.

Note: It is recommended that this program be taught using backwards chaining. Therefore, the child should enter the group time activity for the last 2 minutes of the group activity. Then, once that step is mastered, the child would join the group for the last 4 minutes of the activity and so on.

Program Started		Program Mastered		
	STEPS	STARTED	MASTERED	COMMENTS
1	2 minutes			
1g	generalization			
2	4 minutes			
2g	generalization			
3	8 minutes			
3g	generalization			
4	10 minutes			
4g	generalization			
5	15 minutes			
5g	generalization			
6	20 minutes			
6g	generalization			

Child Name: . . . .

Raises Hand

Teaching Procedure: Teach this program in the natural environment during actual situations in which the child would need to raise his hand. Follow the steps below. If the child talks while teaching this skill, have the teacher non-verbally take his pointer finger and put it up to his own mouth as if he were saying quiet. Do not call on the child if he is talking/calling out while raising his hand.

Prompt Hierarchy: Use the least intrusive prompt required in order for the child to be successful (gesture, faded physical, physical; faded verbal and verbal to be used **only** with verbal programs).

Materials: None.

Program Started		Program Mastered		
	STEPS	**STARTED**	**MASTERED**	**COMMENTS**
1	One person will need to sit behind the child and when the other teacher asks "who wants to answer?" The adult sitting behind the child will physically prompt the child to raise his hand. Make sure that the child knows the answer to the question. Have the teacher leading the group say "I love the way _____ [child's name] raised his hand."			
1g	generalization			
2	One adult will need to sit behind the child and when the other adult, who is leading the group asks "who wants to answer?" The adult sitting behind the child will provide a faded physical prompt to raise his hand. Make sure that the child knows the answer to the question. Have the adult leading the group praise the child for raising his hand.			
2g	generalization			

3	One adult will need to sit behind the child and when the other adult who is leading the group asks "who wants to answer?" The adult sitting behind the child will provide a gestural prompt to raise his hand. Make sure that the child knows the answer to the question. Have the adult leading the group praise the child for raising his hand.			
3g	generalization			
4	Have the adult leading the group ask a question to which the child knows the answer. Do not provide any prompt.			
4g	generalization			

Child Name: . . . .

Weather

Teaching Procedure: Ask the child to tell you what the weather is, either using pictures or standing outside, or both.

Prompt Hierarchy: Use the least intrusive prompt required in order for the child to be successful (gesture, faded physical, physical; faded verbal and verbal to be used **only** with verbal programs).

Materials: None.

Note: Generalization should be the child identifying the weather during circle time.

Program Started		Program Mastered		
	STEPS	STARTED	MASTERED	COMMENTS
1	sunny			
1g	generalization			
2	rainy			
2g	generalization			
3	cloudy			
3g	generalization			
4	windy			
4g	generalization			
5	cold			
5g	generalization			
6	warm/hot			
6g	generalization			
7	child will state either warm/hot or cold along with either sunny, rainy, cloudy, windy			
7g	generalization			

Handwriting

Child Name: ....

Writes Lines and Shapes

Teaching Procedure: Present the child with the Sd "make a____" (state the item in the step that you are working on).

Prompt Hierarchy: Use the least intrusive prompt required in order for the child to be successful (gesture, faded physical, physical; faded verbal and verbal to be used **only** with verbal programs).

Materials: Paper, crayons, markers, pencil, shaving cream, sand.

Note: When teaching this program, make it fun! Allow the child to practice writing their lines and shapes in shaving cream, sand, etc.

Program Started		Program Mastered		
	STEPS	STARTED	MASTERED	COMMENTS
1	straight line			
1g	generalization			
2	diagonal line from right to left			
2g	generalization			
3	diagonal line from left to right			
3g	generalization			
4	circle			
4g	generalization			
5	oval			
5g	generalization			
6	square			
6g	generalization			
7	rectangle			
7g	generalization			
8	triangle			
8g	generalization			

Child Name: . . . .

Draws Pictures

Teaching Procedure: Present the child with the Sd "draw a ___" (state the item in the step that you are working on).

Prompt Hierarchy: Use the least intrusive prompt required in order for the child to be successful (gesture, faded physical, physical; faded verbal and verbal to be used **only** with verbal programs).

Materials: None.

Program Started		Program Mastered		
	STEPS	STARTED	MASTERED	COMMENTS
1	person			
1g	generalization			
2	house			
2g	generalization			
3	outside (sky, sun, grass, flower)			
3g	generalization			
4	animal			
4g	generalization			

Child Name: . . . .

Writing Upper Case Letters

Teaching Procedure: Present the child with the Sd "write the letter ___" (state the letter in the step you are working on). Make sure you state to the child that you want him to write upper case.

Prompt Hierarchy: Use the least intrusive prompt required in order for the child to be successful (gesture, faded physical, physical; faded verbal and verbal to be used **only** with verbal programs).

Materials: Paper, pencil.

Note: The child must be able to identify upper and lower case letters before starting this program. When teaching this program, make it fun! Allow the child to practice writing the letters in shaving cream, sand, etc.

Program Started		Program Mastered		
	STEPS	STARTED	MASTERED	COMMENTS
1	F			
1g	generalization			
2	E			
2g	generalization			
3	D			
3g	generalization			
4	P			
4g	generalization			
5	B			
5g	generalization			
6	R			
6g	generalization			
7	N			
7g	generalization			
8	M			
8g	generalization			
9	H			
9g	generalization			
10	K			
10g	generalization			

11	L			
11g	generalization			
12	U			
12g	generalization			
13	V			
13g	generalization			
14	W			
14g	generalization			
15	X			
15g	generalization			
16	Y			
16g	generalization			
17	Z			
17g	generalization			
18	C			
18g	generalization			
19	O			
19g	generalization			
20	Q			
20g	generalization			
21	G			
21g	generalization			
22	S			
22g	generalization			
23	A			
23g	generalization			
24	I			
24g	generalization			
25	T			
25g	generalization			
26	J			
26g	generalization			

Child Name:. . . . .

Writing Lower Case Letters

Teaching Procedure: Present the child with the Sd "write the letter ___" (state the letter in the step you are working on). Make sure you state to the child that you want him to write lower case.

Prompt Hierarchy: Use the least intrusive prompt required in order for the child to be successful (gesture, faded physical, physical; faded verbal and verbal to be used **only** with verbal programs).

Materials: Paper, pencil, shaving cream, markers, sand.

Note: The child must be able to identify upper and lower case letters before starting this program. When teaching this program, make it fun! Allow the child to practice writing the letters in shaving cream, sand, etc.

Program Started		Program Mastered		
	STEPS	STARTED	MASTERED	COMMENTS
1	c			
1g	generalization			
2	o			
2g	generalization			
3	s			
3g	generalization			
4	v			
4g	generalization			
5	w			
5g	generalization			
6	t			
6g	generalization			
7	a			
7g	generalization			
8	d			
8g	generalization			
9	g			
9g	generalization			
10	u			
10g	generalization			

11	i			
11g	generalization			
12	e			
12g	generalization			
13	l			
13g	generalization			
14	k			
14g	generalization			
15	y			
15g	generalization			
16	j			
16g	generalization			
17	p			
17g	generalization			
18	r			
18g	generalization			
19	n			
19g	generalization			
20	m			
20g	generalization			
21	h			
21g	generalization			
22	b			
22g	generalization			
23	f			
23g	generalization			
24	q			
24g	generalization			
25	x			
25g	generalization			
26	z			
26g	generalization			

Child Name:. . . . .

Writes Numbers

Teaching Procedure: Present the child with the Sd "write the number___" (state the step that you are working on).

Prompt Hierarchy: Use the least intrusive prompt required in order for the child to be successful (gesture, faded physical, physical; faded verbal and verbal to be used **only** with verbal programs).

Materials: Paper, pencil, shaving cream, sand.

Note: When teaching this program, make it fun! Allow the child to practice writing the numbers in shaving cream, sand, etc.

Program Started		Program Mastered		
	STEPS	STARTED	MASTERED	COMMENTS
1	0			
1g	generalization			
2	1			
2g	generalization			
3	2			
3g	generalization			
4	3			
4g	generalization			
5	4			
5g	generalization			
6	5			
6g	generalization			
7	6			
7g	generalization			
8	7			
8g	generalization			
9	8			
9g	generalization			
10	9			
10g	generalization			
11	10			
11g	generalization			

Reading

Child Name: . . . .

Receptively Identifies the Sounds of Letters

Teaching Procedure: In a field of three, lay down different letter cards, one of the cards showing the letter you are currently working on, and present the child with the Sd "touch/point to/show me the letter that makes the _____" (name the sound).

Prompt Hierarchy: Use the least intrusive prompt required in order for the child to be successful (gesture, faded physical, physical; faded verbal and verbal to be used **only** with verbal programs).

Materials: Letter cards.

Note: The student must be able to identify both upper and lower case letters. Generalization of this program should include using both upper case and lower case letters.

Program Started		Program Mastered		
	STEPS	STARTED	MASTERED	COMMENTS
1	A			
1g	generalization			
2	B			
2g	generalization			
3	C			
3g	generalization			
4	D			
4g	generalization			
5	E			
5g	generalization			
6	F			
6g	generalization			
7	G			
7g	generalization			
8	H			
8g	generalization			
9	I			
9g	generalization			
10	J			
10g	generalization			

11	K			
11g	generalization			
12	L			
12g	generalization			
13	M			
13g	generalization			
14	N			
14g	generalization			
15	O			
15g	generalization			
16	P			
16g	generalization			
17	Q			
17g	generalization			
18	R			
18g	generalization			
19	S			
19g	generalization			
20	T			
20g	generalization			
21	U			
21g	generalization			
22	V			
22g	generalization			
23	W			
23g	generalization			
24	X			
24g	generalization			
25	Y			
25g	generalization			
26	Z			
26g	generalization			

Child Name: . . . .

Labels Sounds

Teaching Procedure: Present the child with the Sd "tell me what sound ___ [name the letter] makes."

Prompt Hierarchy: Use the least intrusive prompt required in order for the child to be successful (gesture, faded physical, physical; faded verbal and verbal to be used **only** with verbal programs).

Materials: None.

Note: The student must be able to identify both upper and lower case letters. Generalization of this program should include using both upper case and lower case letters.

Program Started		Program Mastered		
	STEPS	**STARTED**	**MASTERED**	**COMMENTS**
1	A			
1g	generalization			
2	B			
2g	generalization			
3	C			
3g	generalization			
4	D			
4g	generalization			
5	E			
5g	generalization			
6	F			
6g	generalization			
7	G			
7g	generalization			
8	H			
8g	generalization			
9	I			
9g	generalization			
10	J			
10g	generalization			
11	K			

11g	generalization			
12	L			
12g	generalization			
13	M			
13g	generalization			
14	N			
14g	generalization			
15	O			
15g	generalization			
16	P			
16g	generalization			
17	Q			
17g	generalization			
18	R			
18g	generalization			
19	S			
19g	generalization			
20	T			
20g	generalization			
21	U			
21g	generalization			
22	V			
22g	generalization			
23	W			
23g	generalization			
24	X			
24g	generalization			
25	Y			
25g	generalization			
26	Z			
26g	generalization			

Child Name: . . . .

Match Words to Pictures

Teaching Procedure: Lay down at least three pictures. One of the pictures will be of the object in the step you are working on. Then present the child with the card that has the word written out and ask the child to match.

Prompt Hierarchy: Use the least intrusive prompt required in order for the child to be successful (gesture, faded physical, physical; faded verbal and verbal to be used **only** with verbal programs).

Materials: Cards or pieces of paper that have the words that are in each step below written out, and the related pictures.

Note: Generalization should include matching pictures to words and not just words to pictures. It should also include different fonts and sizes for the written words.

Program Started		Program Mastered		
	STEPS	**STARTED**	**MASTERED**	**COMMENTS**
1	cat			
1g	generalization			
2	dog			
2g	generalization			
3	hat			
3g	generalization			
4	bat			
4g	generalization			
5	house			
5g	generalization			
6	girl			
6g	generalization			
7	boy			
7g	generalization			
8	train			
8g	generalization			
9	car			
9g	generalization			
10	doll			

10g	generalization			
11	egg			
11g	generalization			
12	phone			
12g	generalization			
13	baby			
13g	generalization			
14	book			
14g	generalization			
15	pencil			
15g	generalization			
16	door			
16g	generalization			
17	bug			
17g	generalization			
18	desk			
18g	generalization			
19	shoe			
19g	generalization			
20	hand			
20g	generalization			

Child Name: . . . .

Match Word to Word

Teaching Procedure: Lay down at least three words. One of the words will be that in the step you are working on. Then present the child with the card that has the word written out and ask the child to match.

Prompt Hierarchy: Use the least intrusive prompt required in order for the child to be successful (gesture, faded physical, physical; faded verbal and verbal to be used **only** with verbal programs).

Materials: Cards or pieces of paper that have the words in each step below written out, and extra words to be used as distractors.

Program Started		Program Mastered		
	STEPS	STARTED	MASTERED	COMMENTS
1	cat			
1g	generalization			
2	dog			
2g	generalization			
3	hat			
3g	generalization			
4	bat			
4g	generalization			
5	house			
5g	generalization			
6	girl			
6g	generalization			
7	boy			
7g	generalization			
8	train			
8g	generalization			
9	car			
9g	generalization			
10	doll			
10g	generalization			
11	egg			

11g	generalization			
12	phone			
12g	generalization			
13	baby			
13g	generalization			
14	book			
14g	generalization			
15	pencil			
15g	generalization			
16	door			
16g	generalization			
17	bug			
17g	generalization			
18	desk			
18g	generalization			
19	shoe			
19g	generalization			
20	hand			
20g	generalization			

Child Name:. . . . .

Receptive Identification of Simple Words

Teaching Procedure: Present the child with three cards that have words written on them. One card should represent the word in the step that you are working on. Ask the child to "find/point/show you ___" (name the word in the step).

Prompt Hierarchy: Use the least intrusive prompt required in order for the child to be successful (gesture, faded physical, physical; faded verbal and verbal to be used **only** with verbal programs).

Materials: Different cards that have the words in the steps below written on them. The cards should include different background colors, different fonts, different sizes.

Program Started		Program Mastered		
	STEPS	STARTED	MASTERED	COMMENTS
1	in			
1g	generalization			
2	to			
2g	generalization			
3	the			
3g	generalization			
4	we			
4g	generalization			
5	at			
5g	generalization			
6	up			
6g	generalization			
7	go			
7g	generalization			
8	is			
8g	generalization			
9	my			
9g	generalization			
10	me			
10g	generalization			
11	of			

11g	generalization			
12	on			
12g	generalization			
13	it			
13g	generalization			
14	for			
14g	generalization			
15	you			
15g	generalization			
16	can			
16g	generalization			
17	was			
17g	generalization			
18	stop			
18g	generalization			
19	she			
19g	generalization			
20	mom			
20g	generalization			
21	dad			
21g	generalization			
22	that			
22g	generalization			
23	they			
23g	generalization			
24	had			
24g	generalization			
25	but			
25g	generalization			

Child Name: . . . .

Read Simple Words

Teaching Procedure: Hold up a card that has the word written on it and ask the child "what does it say?"

Prompt Hierarchy: Use the least intrusive prompt required in order for the child to be successful (gesture, faded physical, physical; faded verbal and verbal to be used **only** with verbal programs).

Materials: Different cards that have the words in the steps below written on them. The cards should include different background colors, different fonts, different sizes.

Program Started		Program Mastered		
	STEPS	STARTED	MASTERED	COMMENTS
1	in			
1g	generalization			
2	to			
2g	generalization			
3	the			
3g	generalization			
4	we			
4g	generalization			
5	at			
5g	generalization			
6	up			
6g	generalization			
7	go			
7g	generalization			
8	is			
8g	generalization			
9	my			
9g	generalization			
10	me			
10g	generalization			
11	of			

11g	generalization			
12	on			
12g	generalization			
13	it			
13g	generalization			
14	for			
14g	generalization			
15	you			
15g	generalization			
16	can			
16g	generalization			
17	was			
17g	generalization			
18	stop			
18g	generalization			
19	she			
19g	generalization			
20	mom			
20g	generalization			
21	dad			
21g	generalization			
22	that			
22g	generalization			
23	they			
23g	generalization			
24	had			
24g	generalization			
25	but			
25g	generalization			

Math

Child Name: . . . .

Patterns

Teaching Procedure: Start the pattern by completing two full examples and then present the direction "finish the pattern" to the child. The child will need to extend the pattern at least two more times. Example of an AAB pattern: The teacher will start the pattern by doing AAB, AAB and the child will then need to extend the pattern by doing AAB, AAB.

Prompt Hierarchy: Use the least intrusive prompt required in order for the child to be successful (gesture, faded physical, physical; faded verbal and verbal to be used **only** with verbal programs).

Materials: Anything you can make a pattern out of, such as colors, shapes, number, coins, etc.

Note: Take step 4 for example. An adult will put down on the table red, red, blue, red, red, blue and then present the child with the Sd "finish pattern."

Program Started		Program Mastered		
	STEPS	STARTED	MASTERED	COMMENTS
1	can extend an AB pattern using colors			
1g	generalization			
2	can extend an AB pattern using shapes			
2g	generalization			
3	can extend an AB pattern using anything			
3g	generalization			
4	can extend an AAB pattern using colors			
4g	generalization			
5	can extend an AAB pattern using shapes			
5g	generalization			
6	can extend an AAB pattern using anything			
6g	generalization			
7	can extend an ABB pattern using colors			
7g	generalization			

8	can extend an ABB pattern using shapes			
8g	generalization			
9	can extend an ABB pattern using anything			
9g	generalization			
10	can extend an AABB pattern using colors			
10g	generalization			
11	can extend an AABB pattern using shapes			
11g	generalization			
12	can extend an AABB pattern using anything			
12g	generalization			
13	can extend an ABC pattern			
13g	generalization			

Child Name: . . . .

Gives a Specified Amount

Teaching Procedure: When presented with the Sd "give me _____" (a specified number), the child will count out that number while leaving the remaining items where they are.

Prompt Hierarchy: Use the least intrusive prompt required in order for the child to be successful (gesture, faded physical, physical; faded verbal and verbal to be used **only** with verbal programs).

Materials: Objects that can be counted.

Note: The child will need to know how to count objects before starting this program. You also want to vary the amount of items that are being left over. For example, in step 3 the child is giving you three items. On one occasion the child should give you three items out of ten, another time it should be three items out of seven. Vary the number of distrators.

Program Started		Program Mastered		
	STEPS	STARTED	MASTERED	COMMENTS
1	1			
1g	generalization			
2	2			
2g	generalization			
3	3			
3g	generalization			
4	4			
4g	generalization			
5	5			
5g	generalization			
6	6			
6g	generalization			
7	7			
7g	generalization			
8	8			
8g	generalization			
9	9			
9g	generalization			
10	10			

10g	generalization			
11	11			
11g	generalization			
12	12			
12g	generalization			
13	13			
13g	generalization			
14	14			
14g	generalization			
15	15			
15g	generalization			
16	16			
16g	generalization			
17	17			
17g	generalization			
18	18			
18g	generalization			
19	19			
19g	generalization			
20	20			
20g	generalization			

Child Name: ....

Math Terms

Teaching Procedure: Using math manipulatives such as blocks or cubes, set up a situation that would enable the student to be able to receptively identify the step you are on. For example, in step 1 put all of the cubes on the table, then ask the student to "give me all of the cubes."

Prompt Hierarchy: Use the least intrusive prompt required in order for the child to be successful (gesture, faded physical, physical; faded verbal and verbal to be used **only** with verbal programs).

Materials: Manipulatives such as cubes and blocks.

Program Started		Program Mastered		
	STEPS	STARTED	MASTERED	COMMENTS
1	all			
1g	generalization			
2	none			
2g	generalization			
3	some			
3g	generalization			
4	more			
4g	generalization			
5	less			
5g	generalization			
6	same			
6g	generalization			
7	different			
7g	generalization			
8	greater			
8g	generalization			
9	add			
9g	generalization			
10	take away (subtract)			
10g	generalization			

Child Name: . . . .

Receptive Identification of Telling Time

Teaching Procedure: Lay down a minimum of three clocks. Make sure one of the clocks shows the time of the step that you are on. Present the child with the direction "show me/find/point to_____" (name the time for the step you are on). Example of step 1: show me 01:00."

Prompt Hierarchy: Use the least intrusive prompt required in order for the child to be successful (gesture, faded physical, physical; faded verbal and verbal to be used **only** with verbal programs).

Materials: Clocks that have adjustable minute and hour hands, or pieces of paper that have clocks drawn on them relate to the steps below.

Program Started		Program Mastered		
	STEPS	STARTED	MASTERED	COMMENTS
1	01:00			
1g	generalization			
2	02:00			
2g	generalization			
3	03:00			
3g	generalization			
4	04:00			
4g	generalization			
5	05:00			
5g	generalization			
6	06:00			
6g	generalization			
7	07:00			
7g	generalization			
8	08:00			
8g	generalization			
9	09:00			
9g	generalization			
10	10:00			
10g	generalization			
11	11:00			

11g	generalization			
12	12:00			
12g	generalization			
13	can tell to the half-hour			
13g	generalization			
14	can tell to the quarter-hour			
14g	generalization			
15	can tell to the minute			
15g	generalization			

Child Name: . . . .

Expressive Identification of Telling Time

Teaching Procedure: Hold up a picture of a clock that shows the time of the step that you are on. Present the child with the direction "what time is it?" The child will need to state the correct time.

Prompt Hierarchy: Use the least intrusive prompt required in order for the child to be successful (gesture, faded physical, physical; faded verbal and verbal to be used **only** with verbal programs).

Materials: Clocks that have adjustable minute and hour hands, or pieces of paper that have clocks drawn on that that relate to the steps below.

Note: Generalization should include the child being able to identify the correct time on an actual clock.

Program Started		Program Mastered		
	STEPS	STARTED	MASTERED	COMMENTS
1	01:00			
1g	generalization			
2	02:00			
2g	generalization			
3	03:00			
3g	generalization			
4	04:00			
4g	generalization			
5	05:00			
5g	generalization			
6	06:00			
6g	generalization			
7	07:00			
7g	generalization			
8	08:00			
8g	generalization			
9	09:00			
9g	generalization			
10	10:00			
10g	generalization			

11	11:00			
11g	generalization			
12	12:00			
12g	generalization			
13	can tell to the half-hour			
13g	generalization			
14	can tell to the quarter-hour			
14g	generalization			
15	can tell to the minute			
15g	generalization			

Child Name: . . . .

Receptive Identification of Coins

Teaching Procedure: Place the coin you are working on in each step down on a table and provide a minimum of two other coins (the distractor coins need to be different from the coin you are working on) and ask the child to "find _____" (name the coin you are on).

Prompt Hierarchy: Use the least intrusive prompt required in order for the child to be successful (gesture, faded physical, physical; faded verbal and verbal to be used **only** with verbal programs).

Materials: Quarter, dime, nickel, penny.

Notes: Please provide different language for the Sd (direction). Some other examples are "touch," "show me," "point to," etc.

Program Started		Program Mastered		
	STEPS	**STARTED**	**MASTERED**	**COMMENTS**
1	quarter			
1g	generalization			
2	dime			
2g	generalization			
3	nickel			
3g	generalization			
4	penny			
4g	generalization			

Child Name: . . . .

Expressive Identification of Coins

Teaching Procedure: Hold up the coin you are working on in each step and ask the child "what is it?" The child will name the coin.

Prompt Hierarchy: Use the least intrusive prompt required in order for the child to be successful (gesture, faded physical, physical; faded verbal and verbal to be used **only** with verbal programs).

Materials: Quarter, dime, nickel, penny.

Program Started		Program Mastered		
	STEPS	**STARTED**	**MASTERED**	**COMMENTS**
1	quarter			
1g	generalization			
2	dime			
2g	generalization			
3	nickel			
3g	generalization			
4	penny			
4g	generalization			

Child Name: . . . .

Receptive Identification of Same and Different

Teaching Procedure: Get at least two things that are either the same or different (depending on the step you are on), or pictures of them, and then at least two more pictures that are not the same and present the child with the Sd "show me which ones are_____" (name the step).

Prompt Hierarchy: Use the least intrusive prompt required in order for the child to be successful (gesture, faded physical, physical; faded verbal and verbal to be used **only** with verbal programs).

Materials: Items that are the same and items that are different.

Note: Example of same: put down on the table two bananas and then a shoe and a flower. Ask the child to find the items that are the same. Example of different: put down on the table two bananas and then a shoe and a flower. Ask the child to find the items that are different.

Program Started		Program Mastered		
	STEPS	STARTED	MASTERED	COMMENTS
1	same			
1g	generalization			
2	different			
2g	generalization			

Child Name: . . . .

Expressive Identification of Same and Different

Teaching Procedure: Get at least two things that are either the same or different (depending on the step you are on), or pictures of them, and then at least two more pictures that are not the same and present the child with the Sd "tell me which ones are _____" (name the step).

Prompt Hierarchy: Use the least intrusive prompt required in order for the child to be successful (gesture, faded physical, physical; faded verbal and verbal to be used **only** with verbal programs).

Materials: Items that are the same and items that are different.

Note: Example of same: put down on the table two bananas and then a shoe and a flower. Ask the child to tell you the items that are the same. Example of different: put down on the table two bananas and then a shoe and a flower. Ask the child to tell you the items that are different.

Program Started		Program Mastered		
	STEPS	STARTED	MASTERED	COMMENTS
1	same			
1g	generalization			
2	different			
2g	generalization			

Language Arts—Receptive Programs

Child Name: . . . .

Receptive Identification of Prepositions

Teaching Procedure: Use cards that show different prepositions and lay down a minimum of three cards. Present the child with the Sd "show me ___" (name preposition).

Prompt Hierarchy: Use the least intrusive prompt required in order for the child to be successful (gesture, faded physical, physical; faded verbal and verbal to be used **only** with verbal programs).

Materials: Cards that contain different prepositions on them; various objects that can be used to help show the different prepositions.

Note: In addition to cards, ask the child to show you the preposition/step that you are on by using an object. Example of step 1: "put the block **in** the box."

Program Started		Program Mastered		
	STEPS	STARTED	MASTERED	COMMENTS
1	in			
1g	generalization			
2	off			
2g	generalization			
3	on			
3g	generalization			
4	out			
4g	generalization			
5	under			
5g	generalization			
6	over			
6g	generalization			
7	next to			
7g	generalization			
8	behind			
8g	generalization			
9	near			
9g	generalization			
10	far			
10g	generalization			

Child Name: . . . .

Receptive Identification of Pronouns

Teaching Procedure: Using actual people or pictures, present the child with the Sd "show me ____"
(name the step that you are on).

Prompt Hierarchy: Use the least intrusive prompt required in order for the child to be successful
(gesture, faded physical, physical; faded verbal and verbal to be used **only** with verbal programs).

Materials: Pictures of pronouns, actual people.

Program Started		Program Mastered		
	STEPS	STARTED	MASTERED	COMMENTS
1	he			
1g	generalization			
2	she			
2g	generalization			
3	me			
3g	generalization			
4	we			
4g	generalization			
5	us			
5g	generalization			
6	you			
6g	generalization			
7	they			
7g	generalization			
8	hers			
8g	generalization			
9	his			
9g	generalization			
10	theirs			
10g	generalization			
11	mine			

11g	generalization			
12	I			
12g	generalization			

Child Name:. . . . .

Receptive Identification of Adjectives

Teaching Procedure: In a field of three or more, have the student identify the item when you present the direction "show me the____" (name the adjective according to the step you are on). For example, step 1 is colors—you will say "show me the blue one."

Prompt Hierarchy: Use the least intrusive prompt required in order for the child to be successful (gesture, faded physical, physical; faded verbal and verbal to be used **only** with verbal programs).

Materials: Pictures or items showing various adjectives.

Program Started		Program Mastered		
	STEPS	STARTED	MASTERED	COMMENTS
1	colors (insert various colors)			
1g	generalization			
2	tall			
2g	generalization			
3	short			
3g	generalization			
4	round			
4g	generalization			
5	big			
5g	generalization			
6	little			
6g	generalization			
7	cold			
7g	generalization			
8	hot/warm			
8g	generalization			
9	soft			
9g	generalization			
10	sharp			
10g	generalization			
11	new			

11g	generalization			
12	old			
12g	generalization			

Child Name: . . . .

Receptive Identification of Noun and Adjective

Teaching Procedure: Present the child with a minimum of two pictures/objects and ask him to "touch/find the _____" (name the step you are on).

Prompt Hierarchy: Use the least intrusive prompt required in order for the child to be successful (gesture, faded physical, physical; faded verbal and verbal to be used **only** with verbal programs).

Materials: A red ball, paper cut into a circle, a big doll, a long pencil, a wet towel, a cold drink.

Note: Example of step 1: on the table you have a picture of a red ball and a blue ball and you ask the child to "touch the red ball."

Program Started		Program Mastered		
	STEPS	**STARTED**	**MASTERED**	**COMMENTS**
1	red (ball)			
1g	generalization			
2	circle (paper)			
2g	generalization			
3	big (doll)			
3g	generalization			
4	long (pencil)			
4g	generalization			
5	wet (towel)			
5g	generalization			
6	cold (drink)			
6g	generalization			

Child Name: . . . .

Receptive Identification of Adverbs

Teaching Procedure: You will need to present an Sd that will require the child to demonstrate the adverb in the step.

Prompt Hierarchy: Use the least intrusive prompt required in order for the child to be successful (gesture, faded physical, physical; faded verbal and verbal to be used **only** with verbal programs).

Materials: None.

Note: Example of step 2: "show me how you walk quickly."

Program Started		Program Mastered		
	STEPS	STARTED	MASTERED	COMMENTS
1	softly			
1g	generalization			
2	quickly			
2g	generalization			
3	nicely			
3g	generalization			
4	quietly			
4g	generalization			
5	happily			
5g	generalization			

Child Name: . . . .

Receptive Identification of Class

Teaching Procedure: Lay down a minimum of five pictures/objects, where three of them show the step you are working on, and present the child with the Sd "show me which ones are _____" (name the class).

Prompt Hierarchy: Use the least intrusive prompt required in order for the child to be successful (gesture, faded physical, physical; faded verbal and verbal to be used **only** with verbal programs).

Materials: Clothes, animals, food, drink, toys, vehicles, or pictures of them.

Note: Example of step 1: place on the table pictures of a shirt, dog, house, shoe, pants, car and ask the child "show me/point to/touch the clothes." The child will show/touch/point to the shirt, shoe, and pants.

Program Started		Program Mastered		
	STEPS	STARTED	MASTERED	COMMENTS
1	clothes (shirt, shoes, socks, pants, shorts)			
1g	generalization			
2	animals (cat, dog, horse, pig, cow)			
2g	generalization			
3	food (pizza, cookie, sandwich, burger, soup)			
3g	generalization			
4	drink (water, soda, apple juice, milk, orange juice)			
4g	generalization			
5	toys (bubbles, puzzle, bus, shape sorter, doll)			
5g	generalization			
6	vehicle (car, train, truck)			
6g	generalization			

Child Name: . . . .

Receptive Identification of Feature

Teaching Procedure: Lay down a minimum of three pictures/objects (one of them showing the step you are working on), then present the child with the Sd "give me/show me the one that is ____" (name feature).

Prompt Hierarchy: Use the least intrusive prompt required in order for the child to be successful (gesture, faded physical, physical; faded verbal and verbal to be used **only** with verbal programs).

Materials: Pictures or items that can be identified by color, shape, having a tail, wheels, laces, pages, ears, fur, a point.

Program Started		Program Mastered		
	STEPS	**STARTED**	**MASTERED**	**COMMENTS**
1	color (e.g. "give me the one that is red")			
1g	generalization			
2	shape (e.g. "give me the one that is a circle")			
2g	generalization			
3	tail (cat, dog)			
3g	generalization			
4	wheels (car, truck)			
4g	generalization			
5	laces (shoes, boots)			
5g	generalization			
6	pages (book, magazine)			
6g	generalization			
7	ears (bunny, dog)			
7g	generalization			
8	fur (cat, bear)			
8g	generalization			
9	has a point (pencil, scissors)			
9g	generalization			

Child Name:. . . . .

Receptive Identification of Function

Teaching Procedure: Lay down a minimum of three pictures/objects (one of them showing the step you are working on), then present the child with the Sd "what do you _____?" (name function).

Prompt Hierarchy: Use the least intrusive prompt required in order for the child to be successful (gesture, faded physical, physical; faded verbal and verbal to be used **only** with verbal programs).

Materials: Pictures of or actual knife/scissors, car/truck, pencil/pen, hat/jacket, phone/cell phone, book/magazine, couch/chair, bagel/pasta/food, milk/juice/drink, pot/pan, fork/spoon, brush/comb, pool/ocean, paper/chalkboard, vacuum cleaner/broom, table/desk, cup/mug, bike/scooter, sunglasses/bathing suit, puzzles/trains, bubbles/kisses, blocks/Legos, piano/guitar, crayons/markers, drawer/closet.

Program Started		Program Mastered		
	STEPS	STARTED	MASTERED	COMMENTS
1	cut with: knife, scissors			
1g	generalization			
2	drive: car, truck			
2g	generalization			
3	write with: pencil, pen			
3g	generalization			
4	wear when it's cold: hat, jacket			
4g	generalization			
5	talk on: phone, cell phone			
5g	generalization			
6	read: book, magazine			
6g	generalization			
7	sit on: couch, chair			
7g	generalization			
8	eat: bagel, pasta, food			
8g	generalization			
9	drink: milk, juice			
9g	generalization			
10	cook with: pot, pan			

10g	generalization			
11	eat with: fork, spoon			
11g	generalization			
12	brush your hair with: brush, comb			
12g	generalization			
13	swim in: pool, ocean			
13g	generalization			
14	write on: paper, chalkboard			
14g	generalization			
15	clean with: vacuum cleaner, broom			
15g	generalization			
16	work on: table, desk			
16g	generalization			
17	drink from: cup, mug			
17g	generalization			
18	ride: bike, scooter			
18g	generalization			
19	wear when it's hot: sunglasses, bathing suit			
19g	generalization			
20	play: puzzles, trains			
20g	generalization			
21	blow: bubbles, kisses			
21g	generalization			
22	build: blocks, Legos			
22g	generalization			
23	what plays music: piano, guitar			
23g	generalization			
24	color: crayons, markers			
24g	generalization			
25	what you put clothes in: drawer, closet			
25g	generalization			

Language Arts—Expressive Programs

Child Name:. . . . .

Expressive Identification of Prepositions

Teaching Procedure: Use items such as a small ball and a cup, put the ball: in, on and below the cup and present the child with the Sd "tell me where the ball is." The child will name the preposition.

Prompt Hierarchy: Use the least intrusive prompt required in order for the child to be successful (gesture, faded physical, physical; faded verbal and verbal to be used **only** with verbal programs).

Materials: Items such as a small ball and a cup, a piece of paper and a table.

Program Started		Program Mastered		
	STEPS	STARTED	MASTERED	COMMENTS
1	in			
1g	generalization			
2	off			
2g	generalization			
3	on			
3g	generalization			
4	out			
4g	generalization			
5	under			
5g	generalization			
6	over			
6g	generalization			
7	next to			
7g	generalization			
8	behind			
8g	generalization			
9	near			
9g	generalization			
10	far			
10g	generalization			

Child Name: . . . .

Expressive Identification of Pronouns

Teaching Procedure: Ask the child a question that he would need to answer with the correct pronoun. An example of step 1 would be "tell me what that person is doing." The child would need to answer "he is jumping."

Prompt Hierarchy: Use the least intrusive prompt required in order for the child to be successful (gesture, faded physical, physical; faded verbal and verbal to be used **only** with verbal programs).

Materials: None.

Program Started		Program Mastered		
	STEPS	STARTED	MASTERED	COMMENTS
1	he			
1g	generalization			
2	she			
2g	generalization			
3	me			
3g	generalization			
4	we			
4g	generalization			
5	us			
5g	generalization			
6	you			
6g	generalization			
7	they			
7g	generalization			
8	hers			
8g	generalization			
9	his			
9g	generalization			
10	theirs			
10g	generalization			
11	mine			
11g	generalization			

12	I			
12g	generalization			

Child Name: . . . .

Expressive Identification of Adjectives

Teaching Procedure: Hold up a picture or an item and ask the student to tell you about the item. For example, hold up a picture of a red ball and ask the student "tell me about the ball." The student will say that it is red.

Prompt Hierarchy: Use the least intrusive prompt required in order for the child to be successful (gesture, faded physical, physical; faded verbal and verbal to be used **only** with verbal programs).

Materials: Pictures or items illustrating various adjectives.

Program Started		Program Mastered		
	STEPS	STARTED	MASTERED	COMMENTS
1	colors (insert various colors)			
1g	generalization			
2	tall			
2g	generalization			
3	short			
3g	generalization			
4	round			
4g	generalization			
5	big			
5g	generalization			
6	little			
6g	generalization			
7	cold			
7g	generalization			
8	hot/warm			
8g	generalization			
9	soft			
9g	generalization			
10	sharp			
10g	generalization			
11	new			
11g	generalization			

12	old			
12g	generalization			

Child Name: . . . .

Expressive Identification of Noun and Adjective

Teaching Procedure: Hold up either a picture or the actual item and present the child with the Sd "tell me about the picture/item."

Prompt Hierarchy: Use the least intrusive prompt required in order for the child to be successful (gesture, faded physical, physical; faded verbal and verbal to be used **only** with verbal programs).

Materials: A red ball, paper cut into a circle, a big doll, a long pencil, a wet towel, a cold drink.

Note: When teaching this program, you may need to hold up a comparision picture/actual item. Example of step 3: hold up a small doll and a big doll. While pointing to the big doll ask the child to "tell me about this one."

Program Started		Program Mastered		
	STEPS	**STARTED**	**MASTERED**	**COMMENTS**
1	red (ball)			
1g	generalization			
2	circle (paper)			
2g	generalization			
3	big (doll)			
3g	generalization			
4	long (pencil)			
4g	generalization			
5	wet (towel)			
5g	generalization			
6	cold (drink)			
6g	generalization			

Child Name:. . . . .

Expressive Identification of Adverbs

Teaching Procedure: Using a video, pictures, or by an actual demonstration, ask the child to "tell me how the person is ____" (name the adverb).

Prompt Hierarchy: Use the least intrusive prompt required in order for the child to be successful (gesture, faded physical, physical; faded verbal and verbal to be used **only** with verbal programs).

Materials: None.

Note: Example of step 2: demonstrate what it looks like to walk quickly. Ask the child "tell me how I am walking?" The child will say "quickly."

Program Started		Program Mastered		
	STEPS	**STARTED**	**MASTERED**	**COMMENTS**
1	softly			
1g	generalization			
2	quickly			
2g	generalization			
3	nicely			
3g	generalization			
4	quietly			
4g	generalization			
5	happily			
5g	generalization			

Child Name:. . . . .

Expressive Identification of Class

Teaching Procedure: Present the child with the Sd "tell me/name things that are _____" (name the class).

Prompt Hierarchy: Use the least intrusive prompt required in order for the child to be successful (gesture, faded physical, physical; faded verbal and verbal to be used **only** with verbal programs).

Materials: None.

Program Started		Program Mastered		
	STEPS	STARTED	MASTERED	COMMENTS
1	a type of clothing (shirt, socks)			
1g	generalization			
2	a type of animal (cat, dog)			
2g	generalization			
3	a food (pizza, cereal)			
3g	generalization			
4	a drink (milk, juice)			
4g	generalization			
5	a toy (puzzle, doll)			
5g	generalization			
6	a vehicle (car, truck)			
6g	generalization			
7	transportation (plane, train)			
7g	generalization			
8	a sport (baseball, basketball)			
8g	generalization			
9	an instrument (piano, drum)			
9g	generalization			
10	a song ("Itsy Bitsy Spider," "Mary Had a Little Lamb")			
10g	generalization			
11	a color (red, blue)			
11g	generalization			

12	a shape (square, circle)			
12g	generalization			
13	a number (1, 2)			
13g	generalization			
14	a letter (A, B)			
14g	generalization			
15	weather (rain, sun)			
15g	generalization			
16	a month (April, May)			
16g	generalization			
17	a day of the week (Monday, Tuesday)			
17g	generalization			
18	a piece of jewelry (ring, necklace)			
18g	generalization			
19	things you take to the beach (shovel, bucket)			
19g	generalization			
20	a room in a house (kitchen, bedroom)			
20g	generalization			

Child Name: . . . .

Expressive Identification of Feature

Teaching Procedure: Present the child with the Sd "tell me about a _____" (name item).

Prompt Hierarchy: Use the least intrusive prompt required in order for the child to be successful (gesture, faded physical, physical; faded verbal and verbal to be used **only** with verbal programs).

Materials: None.

Program Started		Program Mastered		
	STEPS	STARTED	MASTERED	COMMENTS
1	dog (tail, eyes)			
1g	generalization			
2	cat (fur, whiskers)			
2g	generalization			
3	car (wheels, horn)			
3g	generalization			
4	house (windows, doors)			
4g	generalization			
5	bunny (tail, nose)			
5g	generalization			
6	book (pages, pictures)			
6g	generalization			
7	phone (buttons)			
7g	generalization			
8	truck (wheels, windows)			
8g	generalization			
9	playground (slide, swing)			
9g	generalization			
10	bed (blanket, pillow)			
10g	generalization			
11	sink (faucet, soap)			
11g	generalization			
12	classroom (desks, chairs)			

12g	generalization			
13	door (knob, handle)			
13g	generalization			
14	table (legs)			
14g	generalization			
15	library (books)			
15g	generalization			
16	desk (legs)			
16g	generalization			
17	closet (clothes, hangers)			
17g	generalization			
18	family room (TV, couch)			
18g	generalization			
19	computer (monitor, mouse)			
19g	generalization			
20	sandbox (shovel, sand)			
20g	generalization			

Child Name: . . . .

Expressive Identification of Function

Teaching Procedure: Present child with the Sd "what do you ___" (name function).

Prompt Hierarchy: Use the least intrusive prompt required in order for the child to be successful (gesture, faded physical, physical; faded verbal and verbal to be used only **with** verbal programs).

Materials: None.

Program Started		Program Mastered		
	STEPS	STARTED	MASTERED	COMMENTS
1	cut with: knife, scissors			
1g	generalization			
2	drive: car, truck			
2g	generalization			
3	write with: pencil, pen			
3g	generalization			
4	wear when it's cold: hat, jacket			
4g	generalization			
5	talk on: phone, cell phone			
5g	generalization			
6	read: book, magazine			
6g	generalization			
7	sit on: couch, chair			
7g	generalization			
8	eat: bagel, pasta, food			
8g	generalization			
9	drink: milk, juice			
9g	generalization			
10	cook with: pot, pan			
10g	generalization			
11	eat with: fork, spoon			
11g	generalization			

12	brush your hair with: brush, comb			
12g	generalization			
13	swim in: pool, ocean			
13g	generalization			
14	write on: paper, chalkboard			
14g	generalization			
15	clean with: vacuum cleaner, broom			
15g	generalization			
16	work on: table, desk			
16g	generalization			
17	drink from: cup, mug			
17g	generalization			
18	ride: bike, scooter			
18g	generalization			
19	wear when it's hot: sunglasses, bathing suit			
19g	generalization			
20	play: puzzles, trains			
20g	generalization			
21	blow: bubbles, kisses			
21g	generalization			
22	build: blocks, Legos			
22g	generalization			
23	what plays music: piano, guitar			
23g	generalization			
24	color: crayons, markers			
24g	generalization			
25	what you put clothes in: drawer, closet			
25g	generalization			

Sort and Categorization

Child Name: . . . .

Receptive Identification of What Goes Together

Teaching Procedure: Lay down the objects/pictures along with at least two other objects/pictures; present the child with the remaining object/picture and present the Sd "what goes with _____?" (name the object/picture).

Prompt Hierarchy: Use the least intrusive prompt required in order for the child to be successful (gesture, faded physical, physical; faded verbal and verbal to be used **only** with verbal programs).

Materials: Objects themselves or pictures of: sock, shoe, foot, bat, ball, mitt, pillow, bed, blanket, pants, belt, leg, cup, drink, straw, plate, food, fork, toothbrush, toothpaste, teeth, refrigerator, milk, eggs, slide, swing, playground, paper, pencil, crayon.

Program Started		Program Mastered		
	STEPS	**STARTED**	**MASTERED**	**COMMENTS**
1	sock, shoe, foot			
1g	generalization			
2	bat, ball, mitt			
2g	generalization			
3	pillow, bed, blanket			
3g	generalization			
4	pants, belt, leg			
4g	generalization			
5	cup, drink, straw			
5g	generalization			
6	plate, food, fork			
6g	generalization			
7	toothbrush, toothpaste, teeth			
7g	generalization			
8	refrigerator, milk, eggs			
8g	generalization			
9	slide, swing, playground			
9g	generalization			
10	paper, pencil, crayon			
10g	generalization			

Child Name: . . . .

Expressive Identification of What Goes Together

Teaching Procedure: Present the child with the Sd "tell me what goes with ____" (name one of the items in the step that you are working on). The child will need to tell you one or two items that go with the item that you named. You can present the Sd as "tell me one thing that goes with____," or you can say, "tell me two things that go with____."

Prompt Hierarchy: Use the least intrusive prompt required in order for the child to be successful (gesture, faded physical, physical; faded verbal and verbal to be used **only** with verbal programs).

Materials: None.

Program Started		Program Mastered		
	STEPS	STARTED	MASTERED	COMMENTS
1	sock, shoe, foot			
1g	generalization			
2	bat, ball, mitt			
2g	generalization			
3	pillow, bed, blanket			
3g	generalization			
4	pants, belt, leg			
4g	generalization			
5	cup, drink, straw			
5g	generalization			
6	plate, food, fork			
6g	generalization			
7	toothbrush, toothpaste, teeth			
7g	generalization			
8	refrigerator, milk, eggs			
8g	generalization			
9	slide, swing, playground			
9g	generalization			
10	paper, pencil, crayon			
10g	generalization			

Child Name: . . . .

Categorization

Teaching Procedure: Present the child with a minimum of eight pictures/objects with at least half of the items illustrating the step the child is working on, and present the Sd "put all the _____ [name step] together."

Prompt Hierarchy: Use the least intrusive prompt required in order for the child to be successful (gesture, faded physical, physical; faded verbal and verbal to be used **only** with verbal programs).

Materials: Items that are the same color, big items, little items, items that are hot, items that are cold, items that are tall, items that are short, items that are wet, items that are dry, items that are rough, items that are soft, items that are broken, items that are sharp, items that are loud.

Program Started		Program Mastered		
	STEPS	STARTED	MASTERED	COMMENTS
1	color (all the blue ones)			
1g	generalization			
2	big			
2g	generalization			
3	little			
3g	generalization			
4	hot			
4g	generalization			
5	cold			
5g	generalization			
6	tall			
6g	generalization			
7	short			
7g	generalization			
8	wet			
8g	generalization			
9	dry			
9g	generalization			
10	rough			
10g	generalization			
11	soft			

11g	generalization			
12	broken			
12g	generalization			
13	sharp			
13g	generalization			
14	loud			
14g	generalization			

Child Name: . . . .

Receptive Identification of What is Not the Item

Teaching Procedure: Lay down at least four pictures. At least half of the pictures should be the item in the step you are working on. Present the child with the Sd "show me what is not a ____ [step name]."

Prompt Hierarchy: Use the least intrusive prompt required in order for the child to be successful (gesture, faded physical, physical; faded verbal and verbal to be used **only** with verbal programs).

Materials: Pictures that include cars, foods, shapes, colors, toys, crayons, clothes, buses, drinks.

Note: Example of step 1: lay down a picture of a phone, car, another car, and an apple. Present the Sd "show me what is not a car" and the child will identify the apple and the phone.

Program Started		Program Mastered		
	STEPS	**STARTED**	**MASTERED**	**COMMENTS**
1	car			
1g	generalization			
2	food			
2g	generalization			
3	shape			
3g	generalization			
4	color			
4g	generalization			
5	toy			
5g	generalization			
6	crayon			
6g	generalization			
7	clothes			
7g	generalization			
8	bus			
8g	generalization			
9	drink			
9g	generalization			

Child Name:. . . . .

Expressive Identification of What is Not the Item

Teaching Procedure: Present the child with the Sd "tell me what is not a ____" (name the item in the current step).

Prompt Hierarchy: Use the least intrusive prompt required in order for the child to be successful (gesture, faded physical, physical; faded verbal and verbal to be used **only** with verbal programs).

Materials: None.

Notes: Example of step 1: Present the Sd "tell me what is not a car" and the child can name anything that is not a car.

Program Started		Program Mastered		
	STEPS	STARTED	MASTERED	COMMENTS
1	car			
1g	generalization			
2	food			
2g	generalization			
3	shape			
3g	generalization			
4	color			
4g	generalization			
5	toy			
5g	generalization			
6	crayon			
6g	generalization			
7	clothes			
7g	generalization			
8	bus			
8g	generalization			
9	drink			
9g	generalization			

Child Name: . . . .

Sort by Function

Teaching Procedure: Put down a sample from each category and then hand the child the pictures and present the Sd "sort."

Prompt Hierarchy: Use the least intrusive prompt required in order for the child to be successful (gesture, faded physical, physical; faded verbal and verbal to be used **only** with verbal programs).

Materials: Pictures of things you eat (e.g. banana, cookie, pasta), things you ride in (e.g. car, truck, train), things you wear (e.g. shirt, pants, shoes), things you play with (e.g. puzzle, car, shape sorter), things you sit on (e.g. chair, sofa, bench), things you drink (e.g. juice, milk, water).

Program Started		Program Mastered		
	STEPS	**STARTED**	**MASTERED**	**COMMENTS**
1	have the child sort things you eat versus things you ride in			
1g	generalization			
2	have the child sort things you wear versus things you play with			
2g	generalization			
3	have the child sort any combination of eat, ride in, wear, play with, in a field of three			
3g	generalization			
4	have the child sort any combination of eat, ride in, wear, play with, sit on, in a field of three or more			
4g	generalization			
5	have the child sort any combination of eat, ride in, wear, play with, sit on, drink, in a field of three or more			
5g	generalization			

Child Name: . . . .

Sort by Feature

Teaching Procedure: Put down a sample from each category and then hand the child the pictures and present the child with the Sd "sort."

Prompt Hierarchy: Use the least intrusive prompt required in order for the child to be successful (gesture, faded physical, physical; faded verbal and verbal to be used **only** with verbal programs).

Materials: Pictures of things with tails (e.g. dog, horse, pig), things with wheels (e.g. bike, car, truck), things that are the same color (e.g. banana, tennis ball, lemon), things that have stripes (e.g. zebra, tiger, striped fish), things that are round (e.g. ball, coin, marble), things that are soft (e.g. rabbit, cotton ball, feather).

Program Started		Program Mastered		
	STEPS	**STARTED**	**MASTERED**	**COMMENTS**
1	have the child sort things with tails versus things with wheels			
1g	generalization			
2	have the child sort things with the same color versus things that have stripes			
2g	generalization			
3	have the child sort any combination of things with tails, wheels, same color, and stripes, in a field of three			
3g	generalization			
4	have the child sort any combination of things with tails, wheels, same color, stripes, things that are round, in a field of three or more			
4g	generalization			
5	have the child sort any combination of things with tails, wheels, same color, stripes, round, soft, in a field of three or more			
5g	generalization			

Child Name: . . . .

Sort by Class

Teaching Procedure: Put down a sample from each category and then hand the child the pictures and present the child with the Sd "sort."

Prompt Hierarchy: Use the least intrusive prompt required in order for the child to be successful (gesture, faded physical, physical; faded verbal and verbal to be used **only** with verbal programs).

Materials: Pictures of colors (e.g. blue, green, purple), food (e.g. pasta, cereal, cookie), clothes (e.g. shirt, pants, socks), animals (e.g. lion, bear, cat), shapes (e.g. triangle, circle, square), furniture (e.g. couch, table, bed), toys (e.g. puzzle, shape sorter, car).

Program Started		Program Mastered		
	STEPS	STARTED	MASTERED	COMMENTS
1	have the child sort things that are a color versus food			
1g	generalization			
2	have the child sort things that are clothes versus animals			
2g	generalization			
3	have the child sort any combination of color, food, clothes, animals, in a field of three			
3g	generalization			
4	have the child sort any combination of color, food, clothes, animals, shapes, in a field of three or more			
4g	generalization			
5	have the child sort any combination of color, food, clothes, animals, shapes, furniture, in a field of three or more			
5g	generalization			

6	have the child sort any combination of color, food, clothes, animals, shapes, furniture, toys, in a field of three or more			
6g	generalization			

Conversation and Social Skills

Child Name: . . . .

Receptively Identifies Items

Teaching Procedure: Present the child with a minimum of three pictures/objects and ask the child to "find ___" (name the item in the current step).

Prompt Hierarchy: Use the least intrusive prompt required in order for the child to be successful (gesture, faded physical, physical; faded verbal and verbal to be used **only** with verbal programs).

Materials: Pictures of animals, colors, letters, numbers, shapes, vehicles, things found at a playground (swing, slide, sandbox), things found in a home (couch, TV, kitchen), things found outside (trees, flowers, squirrels), things found in a bedroom (bed, pillow, closet).

Program Started		Program Mastered		
	STEPS	STARTED	MASTERED	COMMENTS
1	animals			
1g	generalization			
2	colors			
2g	generalization			
3	letters			
3g	generalization			
4	numbers			
4g	generalization			
5	shapes			
5g	generalization			
6	vehicles			
6g	generalization			
7	things found at a playground			
7g	generalization			
8	things found in the home			
8g	generalization			
9	things found outside			
9g	generalization			
10	things found in the bedroom			
10g	generalization			

Child Name: . . . .

Expressively Answers the Question "Name..."

Teaching Procedure: Ask the child to "name ___" (present the words in each step).

Prompt Hierarchy: Use the least intrusive prompt required in order for the child to be successful (gesture, faded physical, physical; faded verbal and verbal to be used **only** with verbal programs).

Materials: None.

Program Started		Program Mastered		
	STEPS	**STARTED**	**MASTERED**	**COMMENTS**
1	animals			
1g	generalization			
2	colors			
2g	generalization			
3	letters			
3g	generalization			
4	numbers			
4g	generalization			
5	shapes			
5g	generalization			
6	vehicles			
6g	generalization			
7	things found at a playground			
7g	generalization			
8	things found in the home			
8g	generalization			
9	things found outside			
9g	generalization			
10	things found in the bedroom			
10g	generalization			

Child Name: . . . .

Answers Questions About Items

Teaching Procedure: Present the child with the Sd, which are the words not in parentheses in each step.

Prompt Hierarchy: Use the least intrusive prompt required in order for the child to be successful (gesture, faded physical, physical; faded verbal and verbal to be used **only** with verbal programs).

Materials: None.

Program Started		Program Mastered		
	STEPS	STARTED	MASTERED	COMMENTS
1	you ride in a ___ (car)			
1g	generalization			
2	you write with a __ (pencil/ pen)			
2g	generalization			
3	you wear a ___ (a shirt, pants, shoes, etc.)			
3g	generalization			
4	you eat in a ___ (restaurant)			
4g	generalization			
5	you eat with a __ (fork)			
5g	generalization			
6	you sleep in a __ (bed)			
6g	generalization			
7	you wash your hands with __ (soap)			
7g	generalization			
8	you smell with your __ (nose)			
8g	generalization			
9	you blow __ (bubbles)			
9g	generalization			
10	you live in a __ (house)			
10g	generalization			

11	you read a __ (book)			
11g	generalization			
12	you sit on a __ (chair)			
12g	generalization			
13	you drink from a __ (cup)			
13g	generalization			
14	you see with your __ (eyes)			
14g	generalization			
15	you hear with your __ (ears)			
15g	generalization			
16	you cut with __ (scissors)			
16g	generalization			
17	you watch __ (TV)			
17g	generalization			
18	you throw a __ (ball)			
18g	generalization			
19	you listen to __ (music)			
19g	generalization			
20	you play with __ (toys)			
20g	generalization			

Child Name: . . . .

Answers "What" Questions

Teaching Procedure: Present the child with the "what" question in each step.

Prompt Hierarchy: Use the least intrusive prompt required in order for the child to be successful (gesture, faded physical, physical; faded verbal and verbal to be used **only** with verbal programs).

Materials: None.

Program Started		Program Mastered		
	STEPS	STARTED	MASTERED	COMMENTS
1	What do you see in the park?			
1g	generalization			
2	What do you see at the library?			
2g	generalization			
3	What do you see at the restaurant?			
3g	generalization			
4	What do you see at the bank?			
4g	generalization			
5	What do you see at the fire station?			
5g	generalization			
6	What do you do at the farm?			
6g	generalization			
7	What do you see at the ice-cream store?			
7g	generalization			
8	What do you get at a restaurant?			
8g	generalization			
9	What do you see in a supermarket?			
9g	generalization			
10	What do you see at the gym?			

10g	generalization			
11	What do you see at the zoo?			
11g	generalization			
12	What do you see at the mall?			
12g	generalization			
13	What do you see in the cafeteria?			
13g	generalization			
14	What do you see at the bowling ally?			
14g	generalization			
15	What do you see at the movie theater?			
15g	generalization			
16	What do you see at the post office?			
16g	generalization			
17	What do you see at the police station?			
17g	generalization			
18	What do you see at the hair salon?			
18g	generalization			
19	What do you see at an airport?			
19g	generalization			
20	What do you see at a train station?			
20g	generalization			

Child Name: . . . .

Answers "When" Questions

Teaching Procedure: Present the child with the "when" question in each step.

Prompt Hierarchy: Use the least intrusive prompt required in order for the child to be successful (gesture, faded physical, physical; faded verbal and verbal to be used **only** with verbal programs).

Materials: None.

Program Started		Program Mastered		
	STEPS	STARTED	MASTERED	COMMENTS
1	When do you sleep?			
1g	generalization			
2	When do you eat breakfast?			
2g	generalization			
3	When do you eat dinner?			
3g	generalization			
4	When do you watch TV?			
4g	generalization			
5	When do you play?			
5g	generalization			
6	When do you take a bath?			
6g	generalization			
7	When do you go to school?			
7g	generalization			
8	When do you swim in the ocean?			
8g	generalization			
9	When does it snow?			
9g	generalization			
10	When do you put sunglasses on?			
10g	generalization			
11	When do you wear gloves?			
11g	generalization			

12	When do you build a snowman?			
12g	generalization			
13	When do you eat a snack?			
13g	generalization			
14	When do you eat lunch?			
14g	generalization			
15	When do you see your friends?			
15g	generalization			
16	When do you drink?			
16g	generalization			
17	When do you wear shorts?			
17g	generalization			
18	When do you use a vacuum cleaner?			
18g	generalization			
19	When do you see a doctor?			
19g	generalization			
20	When do you go to the mall?			
20g	generalization			

Child Name: . . . .

Answers "Where" Questions

Teaching Procedure: Present the child with the words in each step.

Prompt Hierarchy: Use the least intrusive prompt required in order for the child to be successful (gesture, faded physical, physical; faded verbal and verbal to be used **only** with verbal programs).

Materials: None.

Notes: Example of step 1: Present the child with the words "where do you find milk"; the child will say "refrigerator."

Program Started		Program Mastered		
	STEPS	STARTED	MASTERED	COMMENTS
1	Where do you find milk?			
1g	generalization			
2	Where do you hang your coat?			
2g	generalization			
3	Where do you get a spoon?			
3g	generalization			
4	Where do you sleep?			
4g	generalization			
5	Where do you wash your face?			
5g	generalization			
6	Where do you go to the bathroom?			
6g	generalization			
7	Where do you eat dinner?			
7g	generalization			
8	Where do you watch TV?			
8g	generalization			
9	Where is your bed?			
9g	generalization			
10	Where is the couch?			
10g	generalization			
11	Where are your clothes?			

11g	generalization			
12	Where do you get ice?			
12g	generalization			
13	Where do you play?			
13g	generalization			
14	Where do you find the toilet?			
14g	generalization			
15	Where do you put sheets?			
15g	generalization			
16	Where do you heat food up?			
16g	generalization			
17	Where do you put eggs?			
17g	generalization			
18	Where do you wash clothes?			
18g	generalization			
19	Where do you find your socks?			
19g	generalization			
20	Where do you find the computer at school?			
20g	generalization			

Child Name: . . . .

Answers "Which" Questions

Teaching Procedure: Present the child with the "which" question in each step.

Prompt Hierarchy: Use the least intrusive prompt required in order for the child to be successful (gesture, faded physical, physical; faded verbal and verbal to be used **only** with verbal programs).

Materials: None.

Program Started		Program Mastered		
	STEPS	STARTED	MASTERED	COMMENTS
1	Which is an animal, cat or apple?			
1g	generalization			
2	Which is a food, dog or pizza?			
2g	generalization			
3	Which is a color, square or red?			
3g	generalization			
4	Which is a shape, circle or desk?			
4g	generalization			
5	Which is a body part, arm or phone?			
5g	generalization			
6	Which is a month, Tuesday or January?			
6g	generalization			
7	Which is clothing, watch or pants?			
7g	generalization			
8	Which is jewelry, hair or ring?			
8g	generalization			
9	Which happens in winter, snow or swimming?			
9g	generalization			

10	Which is a drink, milk or cereal?			
10g	generalization			
11	Which has a tail, dog or flower?			
11g	generalization			
12	Which has ears, plant or bunny?			
12g	generalization			
13	Which do you sleep in, bed or car?			
13g	generalization			
14	Which goes in the sky, boat or plane?			
14g	generalization			
15	Which goes in the water, shoes or boat?			
15g	generalization			
16	Which do you read, book or pencil?			
16g	generalization			
17	Which do you write with, paper or pencil?			
17g	generalization			
18	Which do you write on, paper or door?			
18g	generalization			
19	Which do you eat with, fork or pen?			
19g	generalization			
20	Which do you cut with, napkin or scissors?			
20g	generalization			

Child Name: . . . .

Answers "Who" Questions

Teaching Procedure: Present the child with the "who" question in each step.

Prompt Hierarchy: Use the least intrusive prompt required in order for the child to be successful (gesture, faded physical, physical; faded verbal and verbal to be used **only** with verbal programs).

Materials: None.

Note: The first 20 questions are provided; mastery is 50.

Program Started		Program Mastered		
	STEPS	STARTED	MASTERED	COMMENTS
1	Who do you see when you are sick?			
1g	generalization			
2	Who puts out fires?			
2g	generalization			
3	Who do you go to if you are lost?			
3g	generalization			
4	Who puts you to bed at night?			
4g	generalization			
5	Whose turn is it?			
5g	generalization			
6	Whose shoe is this?			
6g	generalization			
7	Who wants a snack?			
7g	generalization			
8	Who is standing up?			
8g	generalization			
9	Who is sitting down?			
9g	generalization			
10	Who wants to go outside?			
10g	generalization			
11	Whose lunch box is this?			

11g	generalization			
12	Who is the line leader?			
12g	generalization			
13	Who wants to be my helper?			
13g	generalization			
14	Who can tell me the weather?			
14g	generalization			
15	Who delivers the mail?			
15g	generalization			
16	Who knows what color a zebra is?			
16g	generalization			
17	Who wants a drink?			
17g	generalization			
18	Who likes soccer?			
18g	generalization			
19	Who wants to sing a song?			
19g	generalization			
20	Who likes ice-cream?			
20g	generalization			

Child Name: . . . .

Answers "How" Questions

Teaching Procedure: Present the child with the "how" question in each step.

Prompt Hierarchy: Use the least intrusive prompt required in order for the child to be successful (gesture, faded physical, physical; faded verbal and verbal to be used **only** with verbal programs).

Materials: None.

Program Started		Program Mastered		
	STEPS	STARTED	MASTERED	COMMENTS
1	How do you get to school?			
1g	generalization			
2	How do you get dressed?			
2g	generalization			
3	How do you ride a bike?			
3g	generalization			
4	How do you answer a phone?			
4g	generalization			
5	How do you drink?			
5g	generalization			
6	How do you eat pasta?			
6g	generalization			
7	How do you color?			
7g	generalization			
8	How do you wash your hands?			
8g	generalization			
9	How do you sit in a movie?			
9g	generalization			
10	How do you make a sandwich?			
10g	generalization			
11	How do you cut paper?			
11g	generalization			

12	How do you throw a ball?			
12g	generalization			
13	How are you?			
13g	generalization			
14	How do you take a bath?			
14g	generalization			
15	How do you heat up soup?			
15g	generalization			
16	How do you make cookies?			
16g	generalization			
17	How do you plant flowers?			
17g	generalization			
18	How do you set the table?			
18g	generalization			
19	How do you mail a letter?			
19g	generalization			
20	How do you buy food?			
20g	generalization			

Child Name: . . . .

Answers "Why" Questions

Teaching Procedure: Present the child with the "why" question in each step.

Prompt Hierarchy: Use the least intrusive prompt required in order for the child to be successful (gesture, faded physical, physical; faded verbal and verbal to be used **only** with verbal programs).

Materials: None.

Program Started		Program Mastered		
	STEPS	STARTED	MASTERED	COMMENTS
1	Why do you sleep?			
1g	generalization			
2	Why do you wash your hands?			
2g	generalization			
3	Why do you eat?			
3g	generalization			
4	Why do you drink?			
4g	generalization			
5	Why do you take a bath?			
5g	generalization			
6	Why do you wear clothes?			
6g	generalization			
7	Why do you wear a hat?			
7g	generalization			
8	Why do you wear gloves?			
8g	generalization			
9	Why do you wear shoes?			
9g	generalization			
10	Why do you take a bus to school?			
10g	generalization			
11	Why do you go to school?			
11g	generalization			

12	Why do you use covers?			
12g	generalization			
13	Why do you talk on a phone?			
13g	generalization			
14	Why do you take a car?			
14g	generalization			
15	Why do you wear a bathing suit?			
15g	generalization			
16	Why do you read a book?			
16g	generalization			
17	Why do you say "hi" to people?			
17g	generalization			
18	Why do you watch TV?			
18g	generalization			
19	Why do you heat up soup?			
19g	generalization			
20	Why do you use an ice cube?			
20g	generalization			

Child Name: . . . .

What Can You Do in the Community?

Teaching Procedure: Present the child with the question in each step.

Prompt Hierarchy: Use the least intrusive prompt required in order for the child to be successful (gesture, faded physical, physical; faded verbal and verbal to be used **only** with verbal programs).

Materials: None.

Program Started		Program Mastered		
	STEPS	**STARTED**	**MASTERED**	**COMMENTS**
1	What can you do at a restaurant?			
1g	generalization			
2	What can you do at the park?			
2g	generalization			
3	What can you do at the library?			
3g	generalization			
4	What can you do at the bank?			
4g	generalization			
5	What can you do at the supermarket?			
5g	generalization			
6	What can you do at the zoo?			
6g	generalization			
7	What can you do at the police station?			
7g	generalization			
8	What can you do at the fire station?			
8g	generalization			
9	What can you do at the hair salon?			
9g	generalization			

10	What can you do at the post office?			
10g	generalization			
11	What can you do at the airport?			
11g	generalization			
12	What can you do at the bowling alley?			
12g	generalization			
13	What can you do at the movie theater?			
13g	generalization			
14	What can you do at the gym?			
14g	generalization			
15	What can you do at the train station?			
15g	generalization			
16	What can you do at the cafeteria?			
16g	generalization			
17	What do you do at the farm?			
17g	generalization			
18	What do you do at the ice-cream store?			
18g	generalization			
19	What do you do at the mall?			
19g	generalization			
20	What do you do at school?			
20g	generalization			

Child Name: ....

"Tell Me About..."

Teaching Procedure: Present the child with the Sd "tell me about..." (name the item in each step). The child will need to give at least two details per item in order for it to be considered mastered.

Prompt Hierarchy: Use the least intrusive prompt required in order for the child to be successful (gesture, faded physical, physical; faded verbal and verbal to be used **only** with verbal programs).

Materials: None.

Note: The purpose of this program is for the child to be able to think about the item and come up with the answer without a visual. However, when first teaching this program, you may want to use visuals and then fade them out quickly. If you are going to use a visual, it is considered a prompt.

Program Started		Program Mastered		
	STEPS	STARTED	MASTERED	COMMENTS
1	cat			
1g	generalization			
2	dog			
2g	generalization			
3	pizza			
3g	generalization			
4	cereal			
4g	generalization			
5	school bus			
5g	generalization			
6	classroom			
6g	generalization			
7	house			
7g	generalization			
8	car			
8g	generalization			
9	park			
9g	generalization			
10	beach			
10g	generalization			

11	computer			
11g	generalization			
12	crayons			
12g	generalization			
13	desk			
13g	generalization			
14	refrigerator			
14g	generalization			
15	book			
15g	generalization			
16	shoes			
16g	generalization			
17	horse			
17g	generalization			
18	cow			
18g	generalization			
19	apple juice			
19g	generalization			
20	telephone			
20g	generalization			

Child Name: . . . .

Recall

Teaching Procedure: Present the child with the question in each step.

Prompt Hierarchy: Use the least intrusive prompt required in order for the child to be successful (gesture, faded physical, physical; faded verbal and verbal to be used **only** with verbal programs).

Materials: None.

Program Started		Program Mastered		
	STEPS	STARTED	MASTERED	COMMENTS
1	What did you have for breakfast today?			
1g	generalization			
2	What did you have for dinner last night?			
2g	generalization			
3	What did you do over the weekend?			
3g	generalization			
4	What did you play with during recess today?			
4g	generalization			
5	What did you do after school yesterday?			
5g	generalization			

Child Name:. . . . .

Conversation Starters

Teaching Procedure: Ask the child the question in each step. The child will need to engage another person/peer in a conversation using the topics presented in each step.

Prompt Hierarchy: Use the least intrusive prompt required in order for the child to be successful (gesture, faded physical, physical; faded verbal and verbal to be used **only** with verbal programs).

Materials: None.

Note: Example of step 1: an adult says "what is your favorite movie?" The child says "I like *Toy Story*, what is your favorite movie?" The adult replies "I like *The Little Mermaid*." It is important to note that shaping the child's answer is going to be essential when teaching this program.

Program Started		Program Mastered		
	STEPS	**STARTED**	**MASTERED**	**COMMENTS**
1	favorite movie			
1g	generalization			
2	favorite thing to do on the weekend			
2g	generalization			
3	favorite thing to do outside			
3g	generalization			
4	tell me about your family			
4g	generalization			
5	favorite toy			
5g	generalization			

Self Help and Daily Living Skills

Child Name:. . . . .

Brushes Teeth

Teaching Procedure: Present the student with the direction "brush teeth."

Prompt Hierarchy: Use the least intrusive prompt required in order for the child to be successful (gesture, faded physical, physical; faded verbal and verbal to be used **only** with verbal programs).

Materials: Toothbrush and toothpaste.

Note: This program should be taught using backward chaining. For example, the teacher will prompt the student through steps 1–13 and 14 would be the step you take data on (can the student perform step 14 independently?). Once the student has mastered steps 14 and 14g, the teacher will prompt him through steps 1–12 and take data on whether he can complete steps 13 and 14 independently.

Program Started		Program Mastered		
	STEPS	STARTED	MASTERED	COMMENTS
1	gets toothbrush			
1g	generalization			
2	turns on cold water			
2g	generalization			
3	wets the toothbrush			
3g	generalization			
4	gets toothpaste			
4g	generalization			
5	puts toothpaste on the toothbrush			
5g	generalization			
6	wets the toothbrush			
6g	generalization			
7	brushes top teeth			
7g	generalization			
8	brushes bottom teeth			
8g	generalization			
9	brushes tongue			
9g	generalization			
10	spits out toothpaste			

10g	generalization			
11	rinses toothbrush under cold water			
11g	generalization			
12	puts toothbrush away			
12g	generalization			
13	turns off cold water			
13g	generalization			
14	wipes mouth			
14g	generalization			

Child Name:. . . . .

Washes Face

Teaching Procedure: Present the student with the direction "wash face."

Prompt Hierarchy: Use the least intrusive prompt required in order for the child to be successful (gesture, faded physical, physical; faded verbal and verbal to be used **only** with verbal programs).

Materials: Sink, water, face soap, towel.

Note: This program should be taught using backward chaining. For example, the teacher will prompt the student through steps 1–12 and 13 would be the step you take data on (can the student perform step 13 independently?). Once the student has mastered steps 13 and 13g, the teacher will prompt him through steps 1–11 and take data on whether he can complete steps 12 and 13 independently.

Program Started		Program Mastered		
	STEPS	STARTED	MASTERED	COMMENTS
1	turns on cold water			
1g	generalization			
2	wets face with water			
2g	generalization			
3	gets face soap			
3g	generalization			
4	puts soap into hands			
4g	generalization			
5	rubs hands together			
5g	generalization			
6	washes right side of face			
6g	generalization			
7	washes left side of face			
7g	generalization			
8	washes forehead			
8g	generalization			
9	rinses soap off of hands			
9g	generalization			
10	puts water into hands			

10g	generalization			
11	splashes water on face until soap is off			
11g	generalization			
12	gets a towel			
12g	generalization			
13	dries face			
13g	generalization			

Child Name: . . . .

Puts Shirt On

Teaching Procedure: Present the student with the direction "put shirt on."

Prompt Hierarchy: Use the least intrusive prompt required in order for the child to be successful (gesture, faded physical, physical; faded verbal and verbal to be used **only** with verbal programs).

Materials: Shirt that is on the bigger side.

Note: This program should be taught using backward chaining. For example, the teacher will prompt the student through steps 1–5 and 6 would be the step you take data on (can the student perform step 6 independently?). Once the student has mastered steps 6 and 6g, the teacher will prompt him through steps 1–4 and take data on whether he can complete steps 5 and 6 independently.

Program Started		Program Mastered		
	STEPS	STARTED	MASTERED	COMMENTS
1	lays shirt on a table face down			
1g	generalization			
2	picks up the bottom back side of the shirt			
2g	generalization			
3	puts the shirt over the head			
3g	generalization			
4	takes right hand and holds bottom of the shirt while the left hand goes into the sleeve			
4g	generalization			
5	takes left hand and holds bottom of the shirt while the right hand goes into the sleeve			
5g	generalization			
6	pulls shirt down			
6g	generalization			

Child Name: . . . .

Ties Shoes

Teaching Procedure: Present the student with the direction "tie shoes."

Prompt Hierarchy: Use the least intrusive prompt required in order for the child to be successful (gesture, faded physical, physical; faded verbal and verbal to be used only with verbal programs).

Materials: Shoes with laces.

Note: This program should be taught using backward chaining. For example, the teacher will prompt the student through steps 1–7 and 8 would be the step you take data on (can the student perform step 8 independently?). Once the student has mastered steps 8 and 8g, the teacher will prompt him through steps 1–6 and take data on whether he can complete steps 7 and 8 independently..

Program Started		Program Mastered		
	STEPS	STARTED	MASTERED	COMMENTS
1	picks up laces			
1g	generalization			
2	crosses laces (makes an X)			
2g	generalization			
3	puts a lace in each hand			
3g	generalization			
4	puts one lace under the other lace and pull tight			
4g	generalization			
5	makes a loop with one lace			
5g	generalization			
6	wraps the other lace around the loop			
6g	generalization			
7	pushes the lace that was wrapped around the loop through the opening (where the thumb is)			
7g	generalization			
8	pulls it through while pulling the other loop in the opposite direction at the same time			
8g	generalization			

Child Name:..

Toileting

Teaching Procedure: The purpose of this program is for the student to be able to use the bathroom independently. Therefore, this program should be taught by getting the child to mand (request without being asked) for the bathroom. Once you start this program, students should be placed into underwear and no longer be in a diaper or pull-up. This will help them feel when they are wet or dry.

Prompt Hierarchy: Use the least intrusive prompt required in order for the child to be successful (gesture, faded physical, physical; faded verbal and verbal to be used **only** with verbal programs).

Materials: Toilet, toilet paper.

Note: Take baseline data (this means take data to see when the student urinates). This will require frequent checks of his/her diaper/pull-up. If the student is wet approximately every hour, then the program should start with taking him/her to the bathroom every 45 minutes. If the student is wet every 45 minutes, then the program should start with taking him/her to the bathroom every 30 minutes.

Program Started		Program Mastered		
	STEPS	STARTED	MASTERED	COMMENTS
1	Set a timer according to the baseline data. When the timer beeps, do not ask the child if he needs to use the bathroom; instead prompt the child to request "bathroom." This can be done through sign language, visual picture, or through verbal language. Bring the student into the bathroom and get him to take down his pants and underwear. Have him check to see if he is wet or dry. If he is dry give lots of praise. If wet, neutrally say, "you are wet, we need to go in the potty/toilet." Then get the student to sit on/stand at the toilet. You can run water if you think that may help him void in the toilet. Have the student stay there for two to three minutes.			

	If he voids, give lots of praise and reinforcement, otherwise just say "good job trying." Then reset the timer.			
1g	generalization			
2	The remainder of the steps should occur in the exact same way; the only difference is you will increase the interval by 15 minutes to try and get the student to be able to last longer in between going to the bathroom. So step 2 would be every hour if you started on step 1 at every 45 minutes.			
2g	generalization			
3	The last step is for the student to independently request going to the bathroom without being prompted by a timer.			
3g	generalization			

Part III

Mastered Programs

Mastered Directions

Purpose

The purpose of the mastered section is to provide an accurate way of keeping continuous and ongoing data after the student has achieved mastery of either a step or the entire program. Making sure the student retains the skills is an essential component to ensuring generalization and maintenance of the mastered skills. Therefore, this section plays a large role in staying up to date with the student's mastered programs so we can easily track whether the skills are being maintained.

Directions for the mastered section

Once the child achieves mastery on any step in the program, that step is considered mastered. Ongoing data should be collected to ensure the child does not lose that skill. It is suggested that mastery data be collected at least once a month.

This section is set up using probe data. This means that you assess the skill and if the child was able to do the task independently then you circle the Y. If the child was not able to retain the skill, you circle the N. If the child scored a N, probe the step/program again the next day. If the child receives two consecutive days of N, that step/program goes back into the daily programs until the child reaches the mastered criterion again.

Generalization in the mastered section

Generalization is included in the steps of the mastered program. It is suggested that this is the step that you collect mastered data on. For example, if the child mastered steps 3 and 3G, take mastered data on just 3G. This is because once the skill/program has been mastered we really want to make sure that it is being retained in the natural environment. Therefore, taking data on the generalization step will ensure that the skill is being tested in the natural environment.

Mastered Section Example

Child Name: . . . . John Smith . . . .

Playground

Teaching Procedure: When presented with the Sd "go play" while on the playground, the child will engage in three different playground activities for up to ten minutes.

Prompt Hierarchy: Use the least intrusive prompt required in order for the child to be successful (gesture, faded physical, physical; faded verbal and verbal to be used **only** with verbal programs).

Materials: Playground equipment (swing, slide, jungle gym).

	STEPS	date:	date:	date:	date:	date:
1	Present the child with the Sd "go on the slide."	3/20/12 Ⓨ/N	4/15/12 Ⓨ/N	5/15/12 Ⓨ/N	6/15/12 Ⓨ/N	Y/N
1g	generalization	3/20/12 Ⓨ/N	4/15/12 Ⓨ/N	5/15/12 Ⓨ/N	6/15/12 Ⓨ/N	Y/N
2	Present the child with the Sd "go on the jungle gym."	5/15/12 Ⓨ/N	6/15/12 Ⓨ/N	7/10/12 Ⓨ/N	8/20/12 Ⓨ/N	Y/N
2g	generalization	5/15/12 Ⓨ/N	6/15/12 Ⓨ/N	7/10/12 Ⓨ/N	8/20/12 Ⓨ/N	Y/N
3	Present the child with the Sd "go on the swing."	7/10/12 Ⓨ/N	8/20/12 Ⓨ/N	Y/N	Y/N	Y/N
3g	generalization	7/10/12 Ⓨ/N	8/20/12 Ⓨ/N	Y/N	Y/N	Y/N
4	Once the child has mastered steps 1–3 tell him to "go play." He will need to start with the slide. Once he is no longer interested in the slide, he will climb on the jungle gym, then he will go on the swing.	8/20/12 Ⓨ/N	Y/N	Y/N	Y/N	Y/N
4g	generalization	8/20/12 Ⓨ/N	Y/N	Y/N	Y/N	Y/N

Classroom and Social Skills

Child Name: . . . .

Playground

Teaching Procedure: When presented with the Sd "go play" while on the playground, the child will engage in three different playground activities for up to ten minutes.

Prompt Hierarchy: Use the least intrusive prompt required in order for the child to be successful (gesture, faded physical, physical; faded verbal and verbal to be used **only** with verbal programs).

Materials: Playground equipment (swing, slide, jungle gym).

	STEPS	date:	date:	date:	date:	date:
1	Present the child with the Sd "go on the slide."	Y/N	Y/N	Y/N	Y/N	Y/N
1g	generalization	Y/N	Y/N	Y/N	Y/N	Y/N
2	Present the child with the Sd "go on the jungle gym."	Y/N	Y/N	Y/N	Y/N	Y/N
2g	generalization	Y/N	Y/N	Y/N	Y/N	Y/N
3	Present the child with the Sd "go on the swing."	Y/N	Y/N	Y/N	Y/N	Y/N
3g	generalization	Y/N	Y/N	Y/N	Y/N	Y/N
4	Once the child has mastered steps 1–3 tell him to "go play." He will need to start with the slide. Once he is no longer interested in the slide, he will climb on the jungle gym, then he will go on the swing.	Y/N	Y/N	Y/N	Y/N	Y/N
4g	generalization	Y/N	Y/N	Y/N	Y/N	Y/N

Child Name: . . . .

Asks a Peer to Join/Play

Teaching Procedure: Have two peers engaged in a game or activity that you want your student to play. Make sure the game or activity is motivating to your student. When you are teaching the student to ask a peer to play, have a single peer engaged in an activity by themself.

Prompt Hierarchy: Use the least intrusive prompt required in order for the child to be successful (gesture, faded physical, physical; faded verbal and verbal to be used **only** with verbal programs).

Materials: Activities or games that strongly motivate your student.

	STEPS	date:	date:	date:	date:	date:
1	Ask your student, "do you want to join your friends?" If the student says "yes," prompt him to walk over to the peers and say "can I join you?" Make sure you speak with the other students before contriving this situation so they know they have to say "yes."	Y/N	Y/N	Y/N	Y/N	Y/N
1g	generalization	Y/N	Y/N	Y/N	Y/N	Y/N
2	Say to your student "wow, ___[name] and ___[name] are playing your favorite game, it looks like fun." Your student will need to go over and ask them to join.	Y/N	Y/N	Y/N	Y/N	Y/N
2g	generalization	Y/N	Y/N	Y/N	Y/N	Y/N
3	Your student should be able to see the peers playing and walk over without any prompt from a teacher.	Y/N	Y/N	Y/N	Y/N	Y/N
3g	generalization	Y/N	Y/N	Y/N	Y/N	Y/N

Child Name: . . . .

Winning and Losing

Teaching Procedure: Play a game that has a clear winner and loser with your student. Generalization should include peers. Make sure the game you are playing is motivating to the student.

Prompt Hierarchy: Use the least intrusive prompt required in order for the child to be successful (gesture, faded physical, physical; faded verbal and verbal to be used **only** with verbal programs).

Materials: Activities or games that strongly motivate your student and have a clear winner and loser, such as musical chairs and board games.

	STEPS	date:	date:	date:	date:	date:
1	Play a game 1:1 with your student. Make sure your student wins. You say "good game" and teach your student to say "good game."	Y/N	Y/N	Y/N	Y/N	Y/N
1g	generalization	Y/N	Y/N	Y/N	Y/N	Y/N
2	Play a game 1:1 with your student. Make sure your student loses. You say "good game" and teach your student to say "thanks, you played good too."	Y/N	Y/N	Y/N	Y/N	Y/N
2g	generalization	Y/N	Y/N	Y/N	Y/N	Y/N

Child Name:. . . . .

Follows Basic Classroom Instructions

Teaching Procedure: The child will be presented with the Sd for the step you are working on.

Prompt Hierarchy: Use the least intrusive prompt required in order for the child to be successful (gesture, faded physical, physical; faded verbal and verbal to be used **only** with verbal programs).

Materials: None.

	STEPS	date:	date:	date:	date:	date:
1	Put your backpack in your cubby.	Y/N	Y/N	Y/N	Y/N	Y/N
1g	generalization	Y/N	Y/N	Y/N	Y/N	Y/N
2	Get your backpack.	Y/N	Y/N	Y/N	Y/N	Y/N
2g	generalization	Y/N	Y/N	Y/N	Y/N	Y/N
3	Put your jacket away.	Y/N	Y/N	Y/N	Y/N	Y/N
3g	generalization	Y/N	Y/N	Y/N	Y/N	Y/N
4	Get your jacket.	Y/N	Y/N	Y/N	Y/N	Y/N
4g	generalization	Y/N	Y/N	Y/N	Y/N	Y/N
5	Go line up at the door.	Y/N	Y/N	Y/N	Y/N	Y/N
5g	generalization	Y/N	Y/N	Y/N	Y/N	Y/N
6	Sit in your chair.	Y/N	Y/N	Y/N	Y/N	Y/N
6g	generalization	Y/N	Y/N	Y/N	Y/N	Y/N
7	Get your lunch.	Y/N	Y/N	Y/N	Y/N	Y/N
7g	generalization	Y/N	Y/N	Y/N	Y/N	Y/N
8	Go to the bathroom.	Y/N	Y/N	Y/N	Y/N	Y/N
8g	generalization	Y/N	Y/N	Y/N	Y/N	Y/N

Child Name: . . . .

Sits During Group Time

Teaching Procedure: Present the child with the Sd "let's go sit with the group." Generalization should include using different Sds such as "let's go to circle time."

Prompt Hierarchy: Use the least intrusive prompt required in order for the child to be successful (gesture, faded physical, physical; faded verbal and verbal to be used **only** with verbal programs).

Materials: None.

	STEPS	date:	date:	date:	date:	date:
1	2 minutes	Y/N	Y/N	Y/N	Y/N	Y/N
1g	generalization	Y/N	Y/N	Y/N	Y/N	Y/N
2	4 minutes	Y/N	Y/N	Y/N	Y/N	Y/N
2g	generalization	Y/N	Y/N	Y/N	Y/N	Y/N
3	8 minutes	Y/N	Y/N	Y/N	Y/N	Y/N
3g	generalization	Y/N	Y/N	Y/N	Y/N	Y/N
4	10 minutes	Y/N	Y/N	Y/N	Y/N	Y/N
4g	generalization	Y/N	Y/N	Y/N	Y/N	Y/N
5	15 minutes	Y/N	Y/N	Y/N	Y/N	Y/N
5g	generalization	Y/N	Y/N	Y/N	Y/N	Y/N
6	20 minutes	Y/N	Y/N	Y/N	Y/N	Y/N
6g	generalization	Y/N	Y/N	Y/N	Y/N	Y/N

Child Name: . . . .

Raises Hand

Teaching Procedure: Teach this program in the natural environment during actual situations in which the child would need to raise his hand. Follow the steps below. If the child talks while teaching this skill, have the teacher non-verbally take his pointer finger and put it up to his own mouth as if he were saying quiet. Do not call on the child if he is talking/calling out while raising his hand.

Prompt Hierarchy: Use the least intrusive prompt required in order for the child to be successful (gesture, faded physical, physical; faded verbal and verbal to be used **only** with verbal programs).

Materials: None.

	STEPS	date:	date:	date:	date:	date:
1	One adult will need to sit behind the child and when the other teacher asks "who wants to answer?" The adult sitting behind the child will physically prompt the child to raise his hand. Make sure that the child knows the answer to the question. Have the teacher leading the group say "I love the way _____ [child's name] raised his hand."	Y/N	Y/N	Y/N	Y/N	Y/N
1g	generalization	Y/N	Y/N	Y/N	Y/N	Y/N
2	One adult will need to sit behind the child and when the other adult, who is leading the group asks "who wants to answer?" The adult sitting behind the child will provide a faded physical prompt to raise his hand. Make sure that the child knows the answer to the question. Have the adult leading the group praise the child for raising his hand.	Y/N	Y/N	Y/N	Y/N	Y/N
2g	generalization	Y/N	Y/N	Y/N	Y/N	Y/N

3	One adult will need to sit behind the child and when the other adult, who is leading the group asks "who wants to answer?" The adult sitting behind the child will provide a gestural prompt to raise his hand. Make sure that the child knows the answer to the question. Have the adult leading the group praise the child for raising his hand.	Y/N	Y/N	Y/N	Y/N	Y/N
3g	generalization	Y/N	Y/N	Y/N	Y/N	Y/N
4	Have the adult leading the group ask a question to which the child knows the answer. Do not provide any prompt.	Y/N	Y/N	Y/N	Y/N	Y/N
4g	generalization	Y/N	Y/N	Y/N	Y/N	Y/N

Child Name: . . . .

Weather

Teaching Procedure: Ask the child to tell you what the weather is, either using pictures, or standing outside, or both.

Prompt Hierarchy: Use the least intrusive prompt required in order for the child to be successful (gesture, faded physical, physical; faded verbal and verbal to be used **only** with verbal programs).

Materials: None.

	STEPS	date:	date:	date:	date:	date:
1	sunny	Y/N	Y/N	Y/N	Y/N	Y/N
1g	generalization	Y/N	Y/N	Y/N	Y/N	Y/N
2	rainy	Y/N	Y/N	Y/N	Y/N	Y/N
2g	generalization	Y/N	Y/N	Y/N	Y/N	Y/N
3	cloudy	Y/N	Y/N	Y/N	Y/N	Y/N
3g	generalization	Y/N	Y/N	Y/N	Y/N	Y/N
4	windy	Y/N	Y/N	Y/N	Y/N	Y/N
4g	generalization	Y/N	Y/N	Y/N	Y/N	Y/N
5	cold	Y/N	Y/N	Y/N	Y/N	Y/N
5g	generalization	Y/N	Y/N	Y/N	Y/N	Y/N
6	warm/hot	Y/N	Y/N	Y/N	Y/N	Y/N
6g	generalization	Y/N	Y/N	Y/N	Y/N	Y/N
7	child will state either warm/hot or cold along with either sunny, rainy, cloudy, windy	Y/N	Y/N	Y/N	Y/N	Y/N
7g	generalization	Y/N	Y/N	Y/N	Y/N	Y/N

Handwriting

Child Name: . . . .

Writes Lines and Shapes

Teaching Procedure: Present the child with the Sd "make a___" (state the item in the step that you are working on).

Prompt Hierarchy: Use the least intrusive prompt required in order for the child to be successful (gesture, faded physical, physical; faded verbal and verbal to be used **only** with verbal programs).

Materials: Paper, crayons, markers, pencil, shaving cream, sand.

	STEPS	date:	date:	date:	date:	date:
1	straight line	Y/N	Y/N	Y/N	Y/N	Y/N
1g	generalization	Y/N	Y/N	Y/N	Y/N	Y/N
2	diagonal line from right to left	Y/N	Y/N	Y/N	Y/N	Y/N
2g	generalization	Y/N	Y/N	Y/N	Y/N	Y/N
3	diagonal line from left to right	Y/N	Y/N	Y/N	Y/N	Y/N
3g	generalization	Y/N	Y/N	Y/N	Y/N	Y/N
4	circle	Y/N	Y/N	Y/N	Y/N	Y/N
4g	generalization	Y/N	Y/N	Y/N	Y/N	Y/N
5	oval	Y/N	Y/N	Y/N	Y/N	Y/N
5g	generalization	Y/N	Y/N	Y/N	Y/N	Y/N
6	square	Y/N	Y/N	Y/N	Y/N	Y/N
6g	generalization	Y/N	Y/N	Y/N	Y/N	Y/N
7	rectangle	Y/N	Y/N	Y/N	Y/N	Y/N
7g	generalization	Y/N	Y/N	Y/N	Y/N	Y/N
8	triangle	Y/N	Y/N	Y/N	Y/N	Y/N
8g	generalization	Y/N	Y/N	Y/N	Y/N	Y/N

Child Name: . . . .

Draws Pictures

Teaching Procedure: Present the child with the Sd "draw a ____" (state the item in the step that you are working on)

Prompt Hierarchy: Use the least intrusive prompt required in order for the child to be successful (gesture, faded physical, physical; faded verbal and verbal to be used **only** with verbal programs).

Materials: None.

	STEPS	date:	date:	date:	date:	date:
1	person	Y/N	Y/N	Y/N	Y/N	Y/N
1g	generalization	Y/N	Y/N	Y/N	Y/N	Y/N
2	house	Y/N	Y/N	Y/N	Y/N	Y/N
2g	generalization	Y/N	Y/N	Y/N	Y/N	Y/N
3	outside (sky, sun, grass, flower)	Y/N	Y/N	Y/N	Y/N	Y/N
3g	generalization	Y/N	Y/N	Y/N	Y/N	Y/N
4	animal	Y/N	Y/N	Y/N	Y/N	Y/N
4g	generalization	Y/N	Y/N	Y/N	Y/N	Y/N

Child Name: ....

Writing Upper Case Letters

Teaching Procedure: Present the child with the Sd "write the letter ___" (state the letter in the step you are working on). Make sure you state to the child that you want him to write upper case.

Prompt Hierarchy: Use the least intrusive prompt required in order for the child to be successful (gesture, faded physical, physical; faded verbal and verbal to be used **only** with verbal programs).

Materials: Paper, pencil.

	STEPS	date:	date:	date:	date:	date:
1	F	Y/N	Y/N	Y/N	Y/N	Y/N
1g	generalization	Y/N	Y/N	Y/N	Y/N	Y/N
2	E	Y/N	Y/N	Y/N	Y/N	Y/N
2g	generalization	Y/N	Y/N	Y/N	Y/N	Y/N
3	D	Y/N	Y/N	Y/N	Y/N	Y/N
3g	generalization	Y/N	Y/N	Y/N	Y/N	Y/N
4	P	Y/N	Y/N	Y/N	Y/N	Y/N
4g	generalization	Y/N	Y/N	Y/N	Y/N	Y/N
5	B	Y/N	Y/N	Y/N	Y/N	Y/N
5g	generalization	Y/N	Y/N	Y/N	Y/N	Y/N
6	R	Y/N	Y/N	Y/N	Y/N	Y/N
6g	generalization	Y/N	Y/N	Y/N	Y/N	Y/N
7	N	Y/N	Y/N	Y/N	Y/N	Y/N
7g	generalization	Y/N	Y/N	Y/N	Y/N	Y/N
8	M	Y/N	Y/N	Y/N	Y/N	Y/N
8g	generalization	Y/N	Y/N	Y/N	Y/N	Y/N
9	H	Y/N	Y/N	Y/N	Y/N	Y/N
9g	generalization	Y/N	Y/N	Y/N	Y/N	Y/N
10	K	Y/N	Y/N	Y/N	Y/N	Y/N
10g	generalization	Y/N	Y/N	Y/N	Y/N	Y/N
11	L	Y/N	Y/N	Y/N	Y/N	Y/N
11g	generalization	Y/N	Y/N	Y/N	Y/N	Y/N
12	U	Y/N	Y/N	Y/N	Y/N	Y/N

12g	generalization	Y/N	Y/N	Y/N	Y/N	Y/N
13	V	Y/N	Y/N	Y/N	Y/N	Y/N
13g	generalization	Y/N	Y/N	Y/N	Y/N	Y/N
14	W	Y/N	Y/N	Y/N	Y/N	Y/N
14g	generalization	Y/N	Y/N	Y/N	Y/N	Y/N
15	X	Y/N	Y/N	Y/N	Y/N	Y/N
15g	generalization	Y/N	Y/N	Y/N	Y/N	Y/N
16	Y	Y/N	Y/N	Y/N	Y/N	Y/N
16g	generalization	Y/N	Y/N	Y/N	Y/N	Y/N
17	Z	Y/N	Y/N	Y/N	Y/N	Y/N
17g	generalization	Y/N	Y/N	Y/N	Y/N	Y/N
18	C	Y/N	Y/N	Y/N	Y/N	Y/N
18g	generalization	Y/N	Y/N	Y/N	Y/N	Y/N
19	O	Y/N	Y/N	Y/N	Y/N	Y/N
19g	generalization	Y/N	Y/N	Y/N	Y/N	Y/N
20	Q	Y/N	Y/N	Y/N	Y/N	Y/N
20g	generalization	Y/N	Y/N	Y/N	Y/N	Y/N
21	G	Y/N	Y/N	Y/N	Y/N	Y/N
21g	generalization	Y/N	Y/N	Y/N	Y/N	Y/N
22	S	Y/N	Y/N	Y/N	Y/N	Y/N
22g	generalization	Y/N	Y/N	Y/N	Y/N	Y/N
23	A	Y/N	Y/N	Y/N	Y/N	Y/N
23g	generalization	Y/N	Y/N	Y/N	Y/N	Y/N
24	I	Y/N	Y/N	Y/N	Y/N	Y/N
24g	generalization	Y/N	Y/N	Y/N	Y/N	Y/N
25	T	Y/N	Y/N	Y/N	Y/N	Y/N
25g	generalization	Y/N	Y/N	Y/N	Y/N	Y/N
26	J	Y/N	Y/N	Y/N	Y/N	Y/N
26g	generalization	Y/N	Y/N	Y/N	Y/N	Y/N

Child Name:. . . . .

Writing Lower Case Letters

Teaching Procedure: Present the child with the Sd "write the letter ____" (state the letter in the step you are working on). Make sure you state to the child that you want him to write lower case.

Prompt Hierarchy: Use the least intrusive prompt required in order for the child to be successful (gesture, faded physical, physical; faded verbal and verbal to be used **only** with verbal programs).

Materials: Paper, pencil, shaving cream, markers, sand.

	STEPS	date:	date:	date:	date:	date:
1	c	Y/N	Y/N	Y/N	Y/N	Y/N
1g	generalization	Y/N	Y/N	Y/N	Y/N	Y/N
2	o	Y/N	Y/N	Y/N	Y/N	Y/N
2g	generalization	Y/N	Y/N	Y/N	Y/N	Y/N
3	s	Y/N	Y/N	Y/N	Y/N	Y/N
3g	generalization	Y/N	Y/N	Y/N	Y/N	Y/N
4	v	Y/N	Y/N	Y/N	Y/N	Y/N
4g	generalization	Y/N	Y/N	Y/N	Y/N	Y/N
5	w	Y/N	Y/N	Y/N	Y/N	Y/N
5g	generalization	Y/N	Y/N	Y/N	Y/N	Y/N
6	t	Y/N	Y/N	Y/N	Y/N	Y/N
6g	generalization	Y/N	Y/N	Y/N	Y/N	Y/N
7	a	Y/N	Y/N	Y/N	Y/N	Y/N
7g	generalization	Y/N	Y/N	Y/N	Y/N	Y/N
8	d	Y/N	Y/N	Y/N	Y/N	Y/N
8g	generalization	Y/N	Y/N	Y/N	Y/N	Y/N
9	g	Y/N	Y/N	Y/N	Y/N	Y/N
9g	generalization	Y/N	Y/N	Y/N	Y/N	Y/N
10	u	Y/N	Y/N	Y/N	Y/N	Y/N
10g	generalization	Y/N	Y/N	Y/N	Y/N	Y/N
11	i	Y/N	Y/N	Y/N	Y/N	Y/N
11g	generalization	Y/N	Y/N	Y/N	Y/N	Y/N
12	e	Y/N	Y/N	Y/N	Y/N	Y/N

12g	generalization	Y/N	Y/N	Y/N	Y/N	Y/N
13	l	Y/N	Y/N	Y/N	Y/N	Y/N
13g	generalization	Y/N	Y/N	Y/N	Y/N	Y/N
14	k	Y/N	Y/N	Y/N	Y/N	Y/N
14g	generalization	Y/N	Y/N	Y/N	Y/N	Y/N
15	y	Y/N	Y/N	Y/N	Y/N	Y/N
15g	generalization	Y/N	Y/N	Y/N	Y/N	Y/N
16	j	Y/N	Y/N	Y/N	Y/N	Y/N
16g	generalization	Y/N	Y/N	Y/N	Y/N	Y/N
17	p	Y/N	Y/N	Y/N	Y/N	Y/N
17g	generalization	Y/N	Y/N	Y/N	Y/N	Y/N
18	r	Y/N	Y/N	Y/N	Y/N	Y/N
18g	generalization	Y/N	Y/N	Y/N	Y/N	Y/N
19	n	Y/N	Y/N	Y/N	Y/N	Y/N
19g	generalization	Y/N	Y/N	Y/N	Y/N	Y/N
20	m	Y/N	Y/N	Y/N	Y/N	Y/N
20g	generalization	Y/N	Y/N	Y/N	Y/N	Y/N
21	h	Y/N	Y/N	Y/N	Y/N	Y/N
21g	generalization	Y/N	Y/N	Y/N	Y/N	Y/N
22	b	Y/N	Y/N	Y/N	Y/N	Y/N
22g	generalization	Y/N	Y/N	Y/N	Y/N	Y/N
23	f	Y/N	Y/N	Y/N	Y/N	Y/N
23g	generalization	Y/N	Y/N	Y/N	Y/N	Y/N
24	q	Y/N	Y/N	Y/N	Y/N	Y/N
24g	generalization	Y/N	Y/N	Y/N	Y/N	Y/N
25	x	Y/N	Y/N	Y/N	Y/N	Y/N
25g	generalization	Y/N	Y/N	Y/N	Y/N	Y/N
26	z	Y/N	Y/N	Y/N	Y/N	Y/N
26g	generalization	Y/N	Y/N	Y/N	Y/N	Y/N

Child Name: . . . .

Writes Numbers

Teaching Procedure: Present the child with the Sd "write the number____" (state the step that you are working on).

Prompt Hierarchy: Use the least intrusive prompt required in order for the child to be successful (gesture, faded physical, physical; faded verbal and verbal to be used **only** with verbal programs).

Materials: Paper, pencil, shaving cream, sand.

	STEPS	date:	date:	date:	date:	date:
1	0	Y/N	Y/N	Y/N	Y/N	Y/N
1g	generalization	Y/N	Y/N	Y/N	Y/N	Y/N
2	1	Y/N	Y/N	Y/N	Y/N	Y/N
2g	generalization	Y/N	Y/N	Y/N	Y/N	Y/N
3	2	Y/N	Y/N	Y/N	Y/N	Y/N
3g	generalization	Y/N	Y/N	Y/N	Y/N	Y/N
4	3	Y/N	Y/N	Y/N	Y/N	Y/N
4g	generalization	Y/N	Y/N	Y/N	Y/N	Y/N
5	4	Y/N	Y/N	Y/N	Y/N	Y/N
5g	generalization	Y/N	Y/N	Y/N	Y/N	Y/N
6	5	Y/N	Y/N	Y/N	Y/N	Y/N
6g	generalization	Y/N	Y/N	Y/N	Y/N	Y/N
7	6	Y/N	Y/N	Y/N	Y/N	Y/N
7g	generalization	Y/N	Y/N	Y/N	Y/N	Y/N
8	7	Y/N	Y/N	Y/N	Y/N	Y/N
8g	generalization	Y/N	Y/N	Y/N	Y/N	Y/N
9	8	Y/N	Y/N	Y/N	Y/N	Y/N
9g	generalization	Y/N	Y/N	Y/N	Y/N	Y/N
10	9	Y/N	Y/N	Y/N	Y/N	Y/N
10g	generalization	Y/N	Y/N	Y/N	Y/N	Y/N
11	10	Y/N	Y/N	Y/N	Y/N	Y/N
11g	generalization	Y/N	Y/N	Y/N	Y/N	Y/N

Reading

Child Name: . . . .

Receptively Identifies the Sounds of Letters

Teaching Procedure: In a field of three, lay down different letter cards, one of the cards showing the letter you are currently working on, and present the child with the Sd "touch/point to/show me the letter that makes the _____" (name the sound).

Prompt Hierarchy: Use the least intrusive prompt required in order for the child to be successful (gesture, faded physical, physical; faded verbal and verbal to be used **only** with verbal programs).

Materials: Letter cards.

	STEPS	date:	date:	date:	date:	date:
1	A	Y/N	Y/N	Y/N	Y/N	Y/N
1g	generalization	Y/N	Y/N	Y/N	Y/N	Y/N
2	B	Y/N	Y/N	Y/N	Y/N	Y/N
2g	generalization	Y/N	Y/N	Y/N	Y/N	Y/N
3	C	Y/N	Y/N	Y/N	Y/N	Y/N
3g	generalization	Y/N	Y/N	Y/N	Y/N	Y/N
4	D	Y/N	Y/N	Y/N	Y/N	Y/N
4g	generalization	Y/N	Y/N	Y/N	Y/N	Y/N
5	E	Y/N	Y/N	Y/N	Y/N	Y/N
5g	generalization	Y/N	Y/N	Y/N	Y/N	Y/N
6	F	Y/N	Y/N	Y/N	Y/N	Y/N
6g	generalization	Y/N	Y/N	Y/N	Y/N	Y/N
7	G	Y/N	Y/N	Y/N	Y/N	Y/N
7g	generalization	Y/N	Y/N	Y/N	Y/N	Y/N
8	H	Y/N	Y/N	Y/N	Y/N	Y/N
8g	generalization	Y/N	Y/N	Y/N	Y/N	Y/N
9	I	Y/N	Y/N	Y/N	Y/N	Y/N
9g	generalization	Y/N	Y/N	Y/N	Y/N	Y/N
10	J	Y/N	Y/N	Y/N	Y/N	Y/N
10g	generalization	Y/N	Y/N	Y/N	Y/N	Y/N
11	K	Y/N	Y/N	Y/N	Y/N	Y/N
11g	generalization	Y/N	Y/N	Y/N	Y/N	Y/N

12	L	Y/N	Y/N	Y/N	Y/N	Y/N
12g	generalization	Y/N	Y/N	Y/N	Y/N	Y/N
13	M	Y/N	Y/N	Y/N	Y/N	Y/N
13g	generalization	Y/N	Y/N	Y/N	Y/N	Y/N
14	N	Y/N	Y/N	Y/N	Y/N	Y/N
14g	generalization	Y/N	Y/N	Y/N	Y/N	Y/N
15	O	Y/N	Y/N	Y/N	Y/N	Y/N
15g	generalization	Y/N	Y/N	Y/N	Y/N	Y/N
16	P	Y/N	Y/N	Y/N	Y/N	Y/N
16g	generalization	Y/N	Y/N	Y/N	Y/N	Y/N
17	Q	Y/N	Y/N	Y/N	Y/N	Y/N
17g	generalization	Y/N	Y/N	Y/N	Y/N	Y/N
18	R	Y/N	Y/N	Y/N	Y/N	Y/N
18g	generalization	Y/N	Y/N	Y/N	Y/N	Y/N
19	S	Y/N	Y/N	Y/N	Y/N	Y/N
19g	generalization	Y/N	Y/N	Y/N	Y/N	Y/N
20	T	Y/N	Y/N	Y/N	Y/N	Y/N
20g	generalization	Y/N	Y/N	Y/N	Y/N	Y/N
21	U	Y/N	Y/N	Y/N	Y/N	Y/N
21g	generalization	Y/N	Y/N	Y/N	Y/N	Y/N
22	V	Y/N	Y/N	Y/N	Y/N	Y/N
22g	generalization	Y/N	Y/N	Y/N	Y/N	Y/N
23	W	Y/N	Y/N	Y/N	Y/N	Y/N
23g	generalization	Y/N	Y/N	Y/N	Y/N	Y/N
24	X	Y/N	Y/N	Y/N	Y/N	Y/N
24g	generalization	Y/N	Y/N	Y/N	Y/N	Y/N
25	Y	Y/N	Y/N	Y/N	Y/N	Y/N
25g	generalization	Y/N	Y/N	Y/N	Y/N	Y/N
26	Z	Y/N	Y/N	Y/N	Y/N	Y/N
26g	generalization	Y/N	Y/N	Y/N	Y/N	Y/N

Child Name:. . . . .

Labels Sounds

Teaching Procedure: Present the child with the Sd "tell me what sound ___" [name the letter] makes."

Prompt Hierarchy: Use the least intrusive prompt required in order for the child to be successful (gesture, faded physical, physical; faded verbal and verbal to be used **only** with verbal programs).

Materials: None.

	STEPS	date:	date:	date:	date:	date:
1	A	Y/N	Y/N	Y/N	Y/N	Y/N
1g	generalization	Y/N	Y/N	Y/N	Y/N	Y/N
2	B	Y/N	Y/N	Y/N	Y/N	Y/N
2g	generalization	Y/N	Y/N	Y/N	Y/N	Y/N
3	C	Y/N	Y/N	Y/N	Y/N	Y/N
3g	generalization	Y/N	Y/N	Y/N	Y/N	Y/N
4	D	Y/N	Y/N	Y/N	Y/N	Y/N
4g	generalization	Y/N	Y/N	Y/N	Y/N	Y/N
5	E	Y/N	Y/N	Y/N	Y/N	Y/N
5g	generalization	Y/N	Y/N	Y/N	Y/N	Y/N
6	F	Y/N	Y/N	Y/N	Y/N	Y/N
6g	generalization	Y/N	Y/N	Y/N	Y/N	Y/N
7	G	Y/N	Y/N	Y/N	Y/N	Y/N
7g	generalization	Y/N	Y/N	Y/N	Y/N	Y/N
8	H	Y/N	Y/N	Y/N	Y/N	Y/N
8g	generalization	Y/N	Y/N	Y/N	Y/N	Y/N
9	I	Y/N	Y/N	Y/N	Y/N	Y/N
9g	generalization	Y/N	Y/N	Y/N	Y/N	Y/N
10	J	Y/N	Y/N	Y/N	Y/N	Y/N
10g	generalization	Y/N	Y/N	Y/N	Y/N	Y/N
11	K	Y/N	Y/N	Y/N	Y/N	Y/N
11g	generalization	Y/N	Y/N	Y/N	Y/N	Y/N
12	L	Y/N	Y/N	Y/N	Y/N	Y/N
12g	generalization	Y/N	Y/N	Y/N	Y/N	Y/N

13	M	Y/N	Y/N	Y/N	Y/N	Y/N
13g	generalization	Y/N	Y/N	Y/N	Y/N	Y/N
14	N	Y/N	Y/N	Y/N	Y/N	Y/N
14g	generalization	Y/N	Y/N	Y/N	Y/N	Y/N
15	O	Y/N	Y/N	Y/N	Y/N	Y/N
15g	generalization	Y/N	Y/N	Y/N	Y/N	Y/N
16	P	Y/N	Y/N	Y/N	Y/N	Y/N
16g	generalization	Y/N	Y/N	Y/N	Y/N	Y/N
17	Q	Y/N	Y/N	Y/N	Y/N	Y/N
17g	generalization	Y/N	Y/N	Y/N	Y/N	Y/N
18	R	Y/N	Y/N	Y/N	Y/N	Y/N
18g	generalization	Y/N	Y/N	Y/N	Y/N	Y/N
19	S	Y/N	Y/N	Y/N	Y/N	Y/N
19g	generalization	Y/N	Y/N	Y/N	Y/N	Y/N
20	T	Y/N	Y/N	Y/N	Y/N	Y/N
20g	generalization	Y/N	Y/N	Y/N	Y/N	Y/N
21	U	Y/N	Y/N	Y/N	Y/N	Y/N
21g	generalization	Y/N	Y/N	Y/N	Y/N	Y/N
22	V	Y/N	Y/N	Y/N	Y/N	Y/N
22g	generalization	Y/N	Y/N	Y/N	Y/N	Y/N
23	W	Y/N	Y/N	Y/N	Y/N	Y/N
23g	generalization	Y/N	Y/N	Y/N	Y/N	Y/N
24	X	Y/N	Y/N	Y/N	Y/N	Y/N
24g	generalization	Y/N	Y/N	Y/N	Y/N	Y/N
25	Y	Y/N	Y/N	Y/N	Y/N	Y/N
25g	generalization	Y/N	Y/N	Y/N	Y/N	Y/N
26	Z	Y/N	Y/N	Y/N	Y/N	Y/N
26g	generalization	Y/N	Y/N	Y/N	Y/N	Y/N

Child Name: . . . .

Match Words to Pictures

Teaching Procedure: Lay down at least three pictures. One of the pictures will be of the object in the step you are working on. Then present the child with the card that has the word written out and ask the child to match.

Prompt Hierarchy: Use the least intrusive prompt required in order for the child to be successful (gesture, faded physical, physical; faded verbal and verbal to be used **only** with verbal programs).

Materials: Cards or pieces of paper that have the words that are in each step below written out, and the related pictures.

	STEPS	date:	date:	date:	date:	date:
1	cat	Y/N	Y/N	Y/N	Y/N	Y/N
1g	generalization	Y/N	Y/N	Y/N	Y/N	Y/N
2	dog	Y/N	Y/N	Y/N	Y/N	Y/N
2g	generalization	Y/N	Y/N	Y/N	Y/N	Y/N
3	hat	Y/N	Y/N	Y/N	Y/N	Y/N
3g	generalization	Y/N	Y/N	Y/N	Y/N	Y/N
4	bat	Y/N	Y/N	Y/N	Y/N	Y/N
4g	generalization	Y/N	Y/N	Y/N	Y/N	Y/N
5	house	Y/N	Y/N	Y/N	Y/N	Y/N
5g	generalization	Y/N	Y/N	Y/N	Y/N	Y/N
6	girl	Y/N	Y/N	Y/N	Y/N	Y/N
6g	generalization	Y/N	Y/N	Y/N	Y/N	Y/N
7	boy	Y/N	Y/N	Y/N	Y/N	Y/N
7g	generalization	Y/N	Y/N	Y/N	Y/N	Y/N
8	train	Y/N	Y/N	Y/N	Y/N	Y/N
8g	generalization	Y/N	Y/N	Y/N	Y/N	Y/N
9	car	Y/N	Y/N	Y/N	Y/N	Y/N
9g	generalization	Y/N	Y/N	Y/N	Y/N	Y/N
10	doll	Y/N	Y/N	Y/N	Y/N	Y/N
10g	generalization	Y/N	Y/N	Y/N	Y/N	Y/N
11	egg	Y/N	Y/N	Y/N	Y/N	Y/N
11g	generalization	Y/N	Y/N	Y/N	Y/N	Y/N

12	phone	Y/N	Y/N	Y/N	Y/N	Y/N
12g	generalization	Y/N	Y/N	Y/N	Y/N	Y/N
13	baby	Y/N	Y/N	Y/N	Y/N	Y/N
13g	generalization	Y/N	Y/N	Y/N	Y/N	Y/N
14	book	Y/N	Y/N	Y/N	Y/N	Y/N
14g	generalization	Y/N	Y/N	Y/N	Y/N	Y/N
15	pencil	Y/N	Y/N	Y/N	Y/N	Y/N
15g	generalization	Y/N	Y/N	Y/N	Y/N	Y/N
16	door	Y/N	Y/N	Y/N	Y/N	Y/N
16g	generalization	Y/N	Y/N	Y/N	Y/N	Y/N
17	bug	Y/N	Y/N	Y/N	Y/N	Y/N
17g	generalization	Y/N	Y/N	Y/N	Y/N	Y/N
18	desk	Y/N	Y/N	Y/N	Y/N	Y/N
18g	generalization	Y/N	Y/N	Y/N	Y/N	Y/N
19	shoe	Y/N	Y/N	Y/N	Y/N	Y/N
19g	generalization	Y/N	Y/N	Y/N	Y/N	Y/N
20	hand	Y/N	Y/N	Y/N	Y/N	Y/N
20g	generalization	Y/N	Y/N	Y/N	Y/N	Y/N

Child Name: . . . .

Match Word to Word

Teaching Procedure: Lay down at least three words. One of the words will be that in the step you are working on. Then present the child with the card that has the word written out and ask the child to match.

Prompt Hierarchy: Use the least intrusive prompt required in order for the child to be successful (gesture, faded physical, physical; faded verbal and verbal to be used **only** with verbal programs).

Materials: Cards or pieces of paper that have the words in each step below written out, and extra words to be used as distractors.

	STEPS	date:	date:	date:	date:	date:
1	cat	Y/N	Y/N	Y/N	Y/N	Y/N
1g	generalization	Y/N	Y/N	Y/N	Y/N	Y/N
2	dog	Y/N	Y/N	Y/N	Y/N	Y/N
2g	generalization	Y/N	Y/N	Y/N	Y/N	Y/N
3	hat	Y/N	Y/N	Y/N	Y/N	Y/N
3g	generalization	Y/N	Y/N	Y/N	Y/N	Y/N
4	bat	Y/N	Y/N	Y/N	Y/N	Y/N
4g	generalization	Y/N	Y/N	Y/N	Y/N	Y/N
5	house	Y/N	Y/N	Y/N	Y/N	Y/N
5g	generalization	Y/N	Y/N	Y/N	Y/N	Y/N
6	girl	Y/N	Y/N	Y/N	Y/N	Y/N
6g	generalization	Y/N	Y/N	Y/N	Y/N	Y/N
7	boy	Y/N	Y/N	Y/N	Y/N	Y/N
7g	generalization	Y/N	Y/N	Y/N	Y/N	Y/N
8	train	Y/N	Y/N	Y/N	Y/N	Y/N
8g	generalization	Y/N	Y/N	Y/N	Y/N	Y/N
9	car	Y/N	Y/N	Y/N	Y/N	Y/N
9g	generalization	Y/N	Y/N	Y/N	Y/N	Y/N
10	doll	Y/N	Y/N	Y/N	Y/N	Y/N
10g	generalization	Y/N	Y/N	Y/N	Y/N	Y/N
11	egg	Y/N	Y/N	Y/N	Y/N	Y/N
11g	generalization	Y/N	Y/N	Y/N	Y/N	Y/N

12	phone	Y/N	Y/N	Y/N	Y/N	Y/N
12g	generalization	Y/N	Y/N	Y/N	Y/N	Y/N
13	baby	Y/N	Y/N	Y/N	Y/N	Y/N
13g	generalization	Y/N	Y/N	Y/N	Y/N	Y/N
14	book	Y/N	Y/N	Y/N	Y/N	Y/N
14g	generalization	Y/N	Y/N	Y/N	Y/N	Y/N
15	pencil	Y/N	Y/N	Y/N	Y/N	Y/N
15g	generalization	Y/N	Y/N	Y/N	Y/N	Y/N
16	door	Y/N	Y/N	Y/N	Y/N	Y/N
16g	generalization	Y/N	Y/N	Y/N	Y/N	Y/N
17	bug	Y/N	Y/N	Y/N	Y/N	Y/N
17g	generalization	Y/N	Y/N	Y/N	Y/N	Y/N
18	desk	Y/N	Y/N	Y/N	Y/N	Y/N
18g	generalization	Y/N	Y/N	Y/N	Y/N	Y/N
19	shoe	Y/N	Y/N	Y/N	Y/N	Y/N
19g	generalization	Y/N	Y/N	Y/N	Y/N	Y/N
20	hand	Y/N	Y/N	Y/N	Y/N	Y/N
20g	generalization	Y/N	Y/N	Y/N	Y/N	Y/N

Child Name: . . . .

Receptive Identification of Simple Words

Teaching Procedure: Present the child with three cards that have words written on them. One card should represent the word in the step that you are working on. Ask the child to "find/point/show you ___" (name the word in the step).

Prompt Hierarchy: Use the least intrusive prompt required in order for the child to be successful (gesture, faded physical, physical; faded verbal and verbal to be used **only** with verbal programs).

Materials: Different cards that have the words in the steps below written on them. The cards should include different background colors, different fonts, different sizes.

	STEPS	date:	date:	date:	date:	date:
1	in	Y/N	Y/N	Y/N	Y/N	Y/N
1g	generalization	Y/N	Y/N	Y/N	Y/N	Y/N
2	to	Y/N	Y/N	Y/N	Y/N	Y/N
2g	generalization	Y/N	Y/N	Y/N	Y/N	Y/N
3	the	Y/N	Y/N	Y/N	Y/N	Y/N
3g	generalization	Y/N	Y/N	Y/N	Y/N	Y/N
4	we	Y/N	Y/N	Y/N	Y/N	Y/N
4g	generalization	Y/N	Y/N	Y/N	Y/N	Y/N
5	at	Y/N	Y/N	Y/N	Y/N	Y/N
5g	generalization	Y/N	Y/N	Y/N	Y/N	Y/N
6	up	Y/N	Y/N	Y/N	Y/N	Y/N
6g	generalization	Y/N	Y/N	Y/N	Y/N	Y/N
7	go	Y/N	Y/N	Y/N	Y/N	Y/N
7g	generalization	Y/N	Y/N	Y/N	Y/N	Y/N
8	is	Y/N	Y/N	Y/N	Y/N	Y/N
8g	generalization	Y/N	Y/N	Y/N	Y/N	Y/N
9	my	Y/N	Y/N	Y/N	Y/N	Y/N
9g	generalization	Y/N	Y/N	Y/N	Y/N	Y/N
10	me	Y/N	Y/N	Y/N	Y/N	Y/N
10g	generalization	Y/N	Y/N	Y/N	Y/N	Y/N
11	of	Y/N	Y/N	Y/N	Y/N	Y/N
11g	generalization	Y/N	Y/N	Y/N	Y/N	Y/N

12	on	Y/N	Y/N	Y/N	Y/N	Y/N
12g	generalization	Y/N	Y/N	Y/N	Y/N	Y/N
13	it	Y/N	Y/N	Y/N	Y/N	Y/N
13g	generalization	Y/N	Y/N	Y/N	Y/N	Y/N
14	for	Y/N	Y/N	Y/N	Y/N	Y/N
14g	generalization	Y/N	Y/N	Y/N	Y/N	Y/N
15	you	Y/N	Y/N	Y/N	Y/N	Y/N
15g	generalization	Y/N	Y/N	Y/N	Y/N	Y/N
16	can	Y/N	Y/N	Y/N	Y/N	Y/N
16g	generalization	Y/N	Y/N	Y/N	Y/N	Y/N
17	was	Y/N	Y/N	Y/N	Y/N	Y/N
17g	generalization	Y/N	Y/N	Y/N	Y/N	Y/N
18	stop	Y/N	Y/N	Y/N	Y/N	Y/N
18g	generalization	Y/N	Y/N	Y/N	Y/N	Y/N
19	she	Y/N	Y/N	Y/N	Y/N	Y/N
19g	generalization	Y/N	Y/N	Y/N	Y/N	Y/N
20	mom	Y/N	Y/N	Y/N	Y/N	Y/N
20g	generalization	Y/N	Y/N	Y/N	Y/N	Y/N
21	dad	Y/N	Y/N	Y/N	Y/N	Y/N
21g	generalization	Y/N	Y/N	Y/N	Y/N	Y/N
22	that	Y/N	Y/N	Y/N	Y/N	Y/N
22g	generalization	Y/N	Y/N	Y/N	Y/N	Y/N
23	they	Y/N	Y/N	Y/N	Y/N	Y/N
23g	generalization	Y/N	Y/N	Y/N	Y/N	Y/N
24	had	Y/N	Y/N	Y/N	Y/N	Y/N
24g	generalization	Y/N	Y/N	Y/N	Y/N	Y/N
25	but	Y/N	Y/N	Y/N	Y/N	Y/N
25g	generalization	Y/N	Y/N	Y/N	Y/N	Y/N

Child Name: . . . .

Read Simple Words

Teaching Procedure: Hold up a card that has the word written on it and ask the child "what does it say?"

Prompt Hierarchy: Use the least intrusive prompt required in order for the child to be successful (gesture, faded physical, physical; faded verbal and verbal to be used **only** with verbal programs).

Materials: Different cards that have the words in the steps below written on them. The cards should include different background colors, different fonts, different sizes.

	STEPS	date:	date:	date:	date:	date:
1	in	Y/N	Y/N	Y/N	Y/N	Y/N
1g	generalization	Y/N	Y/N	Y/N	Y/N	Y/N
2	to	Y/N	Y/N	Y/N	Y/N	Y/N
2g	generalization	Y/N	Y/N	Y/N	Y/N	Y/N
3	the	Y/N	Y/N	Y/N	Y/N	Y/N
3g	generalization	Y/N	Y/N	Y/N	Y/N	Y/N
4	we	Y/N	Y/N	Y/N	Y/N	Y/N
4g	generalization	Y/N	Y/N	Y/N	Y/N	Y/N
5	at	Y/N	Y/N	Y/N	Y/N	Y/N
5g	generalization	Y/N	Y/N	Y/N	Y/N	Y/N
6	up	Y/N	Y/N	Y/N	Y/N	Y/N
6g	generalization	Y/N	Y/N	Y/N	Y/N	Y/N
7	go	Y/N	Y/N	Y/N	Y/N	Y/N
7g	generalization	Y/N	Y/N	Y/N	Y/N	Y/N
8	is	Y/N	Y/N	Y/N	Y/N	Y/N
8g	generalization	Y/N	Y/N	Y/N	Y/N	Y/N
9	my	Y/N	Y/N	Y/N	Y/N	Y/N
9g	generalization	Y/N	Y/N	Y/N	Y/N	Y/N
10	me	Y/N	Y/N	Y/N	Y/N	Y/N
10g	generalization	Y/N	Y/N	Y/N	Y/N	Y/N
11	of	Y/N	Y/N	Y/N	Y/N	Y/N
11g	generalization	Y/N	Y/N	Y/N	Y/N	Y/N

12	on	Y/N	Y/N	Y/N	Y/N	Y/N
12g	generalization	Y/N	Y/N	Y/N	Y/N	Y/N
13	it	Y/N	Y/N	Y/N	Y/N	Y/N
13g	generalization	Y/N	Y/N	Y/N	Y/N	Y/N
14	for	Y/N	Y/N	Y/N	Y/N	Y/N
14g	generalization	Y/N	Y/N	Y/N	Y/N	Y/N
15	you	Y/N	Y/N	Y/N	Y/N	Y/N
15g	generalization	Y/N	Y/N	Y/N	Y/N	Y/N
16	can	Y/N	Y/N	Y/N	Y/N	Y/N
16g	generalization	Y/N	Y/N	Y/N	Y/N	Y/N
17	was	Y/N	Y/N	Y/N	Y/N	Y/N
17g	generalization	Y/N	Y/N	Y/N	Y/N	Y/N
18	stop	Y/N	Y/N	Y/N	Y/N	Y/N
18g	generalization	Y/N	Y/N	Y/N	Y/N	Y/N
19	she	Y/N	Y/N	Y/N	Y/N	Y/N
19g	generalization	Y/N	Y/N	Y/N	Y/N	Y/N
20	mom	Y/N	Y/N	Y/N	Y/N	Y/N
20g	generalization	Y/N	Y/N	Y/N	Y/N	Y/N
21	dad	Y/N	Y/N	Y/N	Y/N	Y/N
21g	generalization	Y/N	Y/N	Y/N	Y/N	Y/N
22	that	Y/N	Y/N	Y/N	Y/N	Y/N
22g	generalization	Y/N	Y/N	Y/N	Y/N	Y/N
23	they	Y/N	Y/N	Y/N	Y/N	Y/N
23g	generalization	Y/N	Y/N	Y/N	Y/N	Y/N
24	had	Y/N	Y/N	Y/N	Y/N	Y/N
24g	generalization	Y/N	Y/N	Y/N	Y/N	Y/N
25	but	Y/N	Y/N	Y/N	Y/N	Y/N
25g	generalization	Y/N	Y/N	Y/N	Y/N	Y/N

Math

Child Name:. . . . .

Patterns

Teaching Procedure: Start the pattern by completing two full examples and then present the direction "finish the pattern" to the child. The child will need to extend the pattern at least two more times. Example of an AAB pattern: The teacher will start the pattern by doing AAB, AAB and the child will then need to extend the pattern by doing AAB, AAB.

Prompt Hierarchy: Use the least intrusive prompt required in order for the child to be successful (gesture, faded physical, physical; faded verbal and verbal to be used **only** with verbal programs).

Materials: Anything you can make a pattern out of, such as colors, shapes, number, coins, etc.

	STEPS	date:	date:	date:	date:	date:
1	can extend an AB pattern using colors	Y/N	Y/N	Y/N	Y/N	Y/N
1g	generalization	Y/N	Y/N	Y/N	Y/N	Y/N
2	can extend an AB pattern using shapes	Y/N	Y/N	Y/N	Y/N	Y/N
2g	generalization	Y/N	Y/N	Y/N	Y/N	Y/N
3	can extend an AB pattern using anything	Y/N	Y/N	Y/N	Y/N	Y/N
3g	generalization	Y/N	Y/N	Y/N	Y/N	Y/N
4	can extend an AAB pattern using colors	Y/N	Y/N	Y/N	Y/N	Y/N
4g	generalization	Y/N	Y/N	Y/N	Y/N	Y/N
5	can extend an AAB pattern using shapes	Y/N	Y/N	Y/N	Y/N	Y/N
5g	generalization	Y/N	Y/N	Y/N	Y/N	Y/N
6	can extend an AAB pattern using anything	Y/N	Y/N	Y/N	Y/N	Y/N
6g	generalization	Y/N	Y/N	Y/N	Y/N	Y/N
7	can extend an ABB pattern using colors	Y/N	Y/N	Y/N	Y/N	Y/N
7g	generalization	Y/N	Y/N	Y/N	Y/N	Y/N
8	can extend an ABB pattern using shapes	Y/N	Y/N	Y/N	Y/N	Y/N
8g	generalization	Y/N	Y/N	Y/N	Y/N	Y/N
9	can extend an ABB pattern using anything	Y/N	Y/N	Y/N	Y/N	Y/N
9g	generalization	Y/N	Y/N	Y/N	Y/N	Y/N

10	can extend an AABB pattern using colors	Y/N	Y/N	Y/N	Y/N	Y/N
10g	generalization	Y/N	Y/N	Y/N	Y/N	Y/N
11	can extend an AABB pattern using shapes	Y/N	Y/N	Y/N	Y/N	Y/N
11g	generalization	Y/N	Y/N	Y/N	Y/N	Y/N
12	can extend an AABB pattern using anything	Y/N	Y/N	Y/N	Y/N	Y/N
12g	generalization	Y/N	Y/N	Y/N	Y/N	Y/N
13	can extend an ABC pattern	Y/N	Y/N	Y/N	Y/N	Y/N
13g	generalization	Y/N	Y/N	Y/N	Y/N	Y/N

Child Name: . . . .

Gives a Specified Amount

Teaching Procedure: When presented with the Sd "give me _____" (a specified number), the child will count out that number while leaving the remaining items where they are.

Prompt Hierarchy: Use the least intrusive prompt required in order for the child to be successful (gesture, faded physical, physical; faded verbal and verbal to be used **only** with verbal programs).

Materials: Objects that can be counted.

	STEPS	date:	date:	date:	date:	date:
1	1	Y/N	Y/N	Y/N	Y/N	Y/N
1g	generalization	Y/N	Y/N	Y/N	Y/N	Y/N
2	2	Y/N	Y/N	Y/N	Y/N	Y/N
2g	generalization	Y/N	Y/N	Y/N	Y/N	Y/N
3	3	Y/N	Y/N	Y/N	Y/N	Y/N
3g	generalization	Y/N	Y/N	Y/N	Y/N	Y/N
4	4	Y/N	Y/N	Y/N	Y/N	Y/N
4g	generalization	Y/N	Y/N	Y/N	Y/N	Y/N
5	5	Y/N	Y/N	Y/N	Y/N	Y/N
5g	generalization	Y/N	Y/N	Y/N	Y/N	Y/N
6	6	Y/N	Y/N	Y/N	Y/N	Y/N
6g	generalization	Y/N	Y/N	Y/N	Y/N	Y/N
7	7	Y/N	Y/N	Y/N	Y/N	Y/N
7g	generalization	Y/N	Y/N	Y/N	Y/N	Y/N
8	8	Y/N	Y/N	Y/N	Y/N	Y/N
8g	generalization	Y/N	Y/N	Y/N	Y/N	Y/N
9	9	Y/N	Y/N	Y/N	Y/N	Y/N
9g	generalization	Y/N	Y/N	Y/N	Y/N	Y/N
10	10	Y/N	Y/N	Y/N	Y/N	Y/N
10g	generalization	Y/N	Y/N	Y/N	Y/N	Y/N
11	11	Y/N	Y/N	Y/N	Y/N	Y/N
11g	generalization	Y/N	Y/N	Y/N	Y/N	Y/N
12	12	Y/N	Y/N	Y/N	Y/N	Y/N

12g	generalization	Y/N	Y/N	Y/N	Y/N	Y/N
13	13	Y/N	Y/N	Y/N	Y/N	Y/N
13g	generalization	Y/N	Y/N	Y/N	Y/N	Y/N
14	14	Y/N	Y/N	Y/N	Y/N	Y/N
14g	generalization	Y/N	Y/N	Y/N	Y/N	Y/N
15	15	Y/N	Y/N	Y/N	Y/N	Y/N
15g	generalization	Y/N	Y/N	Y/N	Y/N	Y/N
16	16	Y/N	Y/N	Y/N	Y/N	Y/N
16g	generalization	Y/N	Y/N	Y/N	Y/N	Y/N
17	17	Y/N	Y/N	Y/N	Y/N	Y/N
17g	generalization	Y/N	Y/N	Y/N	Y/N	Y/N
18	18	Y/N	Y/N	Y/N	Y/N	Y/N
18g	generalization	Y/N	Y/N	Y/N	Y/N	Y/N
19	19	Y/N	Y/N	Y/N	Y/N	Y/N
19g	generalization	Y/N	Y/N	Y/N	Y/N	Y/N
20	20	Y/N	Y/N	Y/N	Y/N	Y/N
20g	generalization	Y/N	Y/N	Y/N	Y/N	Y/N

Child Name:. . . . .

Math Terms

Teaching Procedure: Using math manipulatives such as blocks or cubes, set up a situation that would enable the student to be able to receptively identify the step you are on. For example, in step 1 put all of the cubes on the table, then ask the student to "give me all of the cubes."

Prompt Hierarchy: Use the least intrusive prompt required in order for the child to be successful (gesture, faded physical, physical; faded verbal and verbal to be used **only** with verbal programs).

Materials: Manipulatives such as cubes and blocks.

	STEPS	date:	date:	date:	date:	date:
1	all	Y/N	Y/N	Y/N	Y/N	Y/N
1g	generalization	Y/N	Y/N	Y/N	Y/N	Y/N
2	none	Y/N	Y/N	Y/N	Y/N	Y/N
2g	generalization	Y/N	Y/N	Y/N	Y/N	Y/N
3	some	Y/N	Y/N	Y/N	Y/N	Y/N
3g	generalization	Y/N	Y/N	Y/N	Y/N	Y/N
4	more	Y/N	Y/N	Y/N	Y/N	Y/N
4g	generalization	Y/N	Y/N	Y/N	Y/N	Y/N
5	less	Y/N	Y/N	Y/N	Y/N	Y/N
5g	generalization	Y/N	Y/N	Y/N	Y/N	Y/N
6	same	Y/N	Y/N	Y/N	Y/N	Y/N
6g	generalization	Y/N	Y/N	Y/N	Y/N	Y/N
7	different	Y/N	Y/N	Y/N	Y/N	Y/N
7g	generalization	Y/N	Y/N	Y/N	Y/N	Y/N
8	greater	Y/N	Y/N	Y/N	Y/N	Y/N
8g	generalization	Y/N	Y/N	Y/N	Y/N	Y/N
9	add	Y/N	Y/N	Y/N	Y/N	Y/N
9g	generalization	Y/N	Y/N	Y/N	Y/N	Y/N
10	take away (subtract)	Y/N	Y/N	Y/N	Y/N	Y/N
10g	generalization	Y/N	Y/N	Y/N	Y/N	Y/N

Child Name: . . . .

Receptive Identification of Telling Time

Teaching Procedure: Lay down a minimum of three clocks. Make sure one of the clocks shows the time of the step that you are on. Present the child with the direction "show me/find/point to_____" (name the time for the step you are on). Example of step 1: "show me 01:00."

Prompt Hierarchy: Use the least intrusive prompt required in order for the child to be successful (gesture, faded physical, physical; faded verbal and verbal to be used **only** with verbal programs).

Materials: Clocks that have adjustable minute and hour hands, or pieces of paper that have clocks drawn on them that relate to the steps below.

	STEPS	date:	date:	date:	date:	date:
1	01:00	Y/N	Y/N	Y/N	Y/N	Y/N
1g	generalization	Y/N	Y/N	Y/N	Y/N	Y/N
2	02:00	Y/N	Y/N	Y/N	Y/N	Y/N
2g	generalization	Y/N	Y/N	Y/N	Y/N	Y/N
3	03:00	Y/N	Y/N	Y/N	Y/N	Y/N
3g	generalization	Y/N	Y/N	Y/N	Y/N	Y/N
4	04:00	Y/N	Y/N	Y/N	Y/N	Y/N
4g	generalization	Y/N	Y/N	Y/N	Y/N	Y/N
5	05:00	Y/N	Y/N	Y/N	Y/N	Y/N
5g	generalization	Y/N	Y/N	Y/N	Y/N	Y/N
6	06:00	Y/N	Y/N	Y/N	Y/N	Y/N
6g	generalization	Y/N	Y/N	Y/N	Y/N	Y/N
7	07:00	Y/N	Y/N	Y/N	Y/N	Y/N
7g	generalization	Y/N	Y/N	Y/N	Y/N	Y/N
8	08:00	Y/N	Y/N	Y/N	Y/N	Y/N
8g	generalization	Y/N	Y/N	Y/N	Y/N	Y/N
9	09:00	Y/N	Y/N	Y/N	Y/N	Y/N
9g	generalization	Y/N	Y/N	Y/N	Y/N	Y/N
10	10:00	Y/N	Y/N	Y/N	Y/N	Y/N
10g	generalization	Y/N	Y/N	Y/N	Y/N	Y/N
11	11:00	Y/N	Y/N	Y/N	Y/N	Y/N
11g	generalization	Y/N	Y/N	Y/N	Y/N	Y/N

12	12:00	Y/N	Y/N	Y/N	Y/N	Y/N
12g	generalization	Y/N	Y/N	Y/N	Y/N	Y/N
13	can tell to the half-hour	Y/N	Y/N	Y/N	Y/N	Y/N
13g	generalization	Y/N	Y/N	Y/N	Y/N	Y/N
14	can tell to the quarter-hour	Y/N	Y/N	Y/N	Y/N	Y/N
14g	generalization	Y/N	Y/N	Y/N	Y/N	Y/N
15	can tell to the minute	Y/N	Y/N	Y/N	Y/N	Y/N
15g	generalization	Y/N	Y/N	Y/N	Y/N	Y/N

Child Name: . . . .

Expressive Identification of Telling Time

Teaching Procedure: Hold up a picture of a clock that shows the time of the step that you are on. Present the child with the direction "what time is it?" The child will need to state the correct time.

Prompt Hierarchy: Use the least intrusive prompt required in order for the child to be successful (gesture, faded physical, physical; faded verbal and verbal to be used **only** with verbal programs).

Materials: Clocks that have adjustable minute and hour hands, or pieces of paper that have clocks drawn on them that relate to the steps below.

	STEPS	date:	date:	date:	date:	date:
1	01:00	Y/N	Y/N	Y/N	Y/N	Y/N
1g	generalization	Y/N	Y/N	Y/N	Y/N	Y/N
2	02:00	Y/N	Y/N	Y/N	Y/N	Y/N
2g	generalization	Y/N	Y/N	Y/N	Y/N	Y/N
3	03:00	Y/N	Y/N	Y/N	Y/N	Y/N
3g	generalization	Y/N	Y/N	Y/N	Y/N	Y/N
4	04:00	Y/N	Y/N	Y/N	Y/N	Y/N
4g	generalization	Y/N	Y/N	Y/N	Y/N	Y/N
5	05:00	Y/N	Y/N	Y/N	Y/N	Y/N
5g	generalization	Y/N	Y/N	Y/N	Y/N	Y/N
6	06:00	Y/N	Y/N	Y/N	Y/N	Y/N
6g	generalization	Y/N	Y/N	Y/N	Y/N	Y/N
7	07:00	Y/N	Y/N	Y/N	Y/N	Y/N
7g	generalization	Y/N	Y/N	Y/N	Y/N	Y/N
8	08:00	Y/N	Y/N	Y/N	Y/N	Y/N
8g	generalization	Y/N	Y/N	Y/N	Y/N	Y/N
9	09:00	Y/N	Y/N	Y/N	Y/N	Y/N
9g	generalization	Y/N	Y/N	Y/N	Y/N	Y/N
10	10:00	Y/N	Y/N	Y/N	Y/N	Y/N
10g	generalization	Y/N	Y/N	Y/N	Y/N	Y/N
11	11:00	Y/N	Y/N	Y/N	Y/N	Y/N
11g	generalization	Y/N	Y/N	Y/N	Y/N	Y/N

12	12:00	Y/N	Y/N	Y/N	Y/N	Y/N
12g	generalization	Y/N	Y/N	Y/N	Y/N	Y/N
13	can tell to the half-hour	Y/N	Y/N	Y/N	Y/N	Y/N
13g	generalization	Y/N	Y/N	Y/N	Y/N	Y/N
14	can tell to the quarter-hour	Y/N	Y/N	Y/N	Y/N	Y/N
14g	generalization	Y/N	Y/N	Y/N	Y/N	Y/N
15	can tell to the minute	Y/N	Y/N	Y/N	Y/N	Y/N
15g	generalization	Y/N	Y/N	Y/N	Y/N	Y/N

Child Name: . . . .

Receptive Identification of Coins

Teaching Procedure: Place the coin you are working on in each step down on a table and provide a minimum of two other coins (the distractor coins need to be different from the coin you are working on) and ask the child to "find _____" (name the coin you are on).

Prompt Hierarchy: Use the least intrusive prompt required in order for the child to be successful (gesture, faded physical, physical; faded verbal and verbal to be used **only** with verbal programs).

Materials: Quarter, dime, nickel, penny.

	STEPS	date:	date:	date:	date:	date:
1	quarter	Y/N	Y/N	Y/N	Y/N	Y/N
1g	generalization	Y/N	Y/N	Y/N	Y/N	Y/N
2	dime	Y/N	Y/N	Y/N	Y/N	Y/N
2g	generalization	Y/N	Y/N	Y/N	Y/N	Y/N
3	nickel	Y/N	Y/N	Y/N	Y/N	Y/N
3g	generalization	Y/N	Y/N	Y/N	Y/N	Y/N
4	penny	Y/N	Y/N	Y/N	Y/N	Y/N
4g	generalization	Y/N	Y/N	Y/N	Y/N	Y/N

Child Name: . . . .

Expressive Identification of Coins

Teaching Procedure: Hold up the coin you are working on in each step and ask the child "what is it?" The child will name the coin.

Prompt Hierarchy: Use the least intrusive prompt required in order for the child to be successful (gesture, faded physical, physical; faded verbal and verbal to be used **only** with verbal programs).

Materials: Quarter, dime, nickel, penny.

	STEPS	date:	date:	date:	date:	date:
1	quarter	Y/N	Y/N	Y/N	Y/N	Y/N
1g	generalization	Y/N	Y/N	Y/N	Y/N	Y/N
2	dime	Y/N	Y/N	Y/N	Y/N	Y/N
2g	generalization	Y/N	Y/N	Y/N	Y/N	Y/N
3	nickel	Y/N	Y/N	Y/N	Y/N	Y/N
3g	generalization	Y/N	Y/N	Y/N	Y/N	Y/N
4	penny	Y/N	Y/N	Y/N	Y/N	Y/N
4g	generalization	Y/N	Y/N	Y/N	Y/N	Y/N

Child Name: . . . .

Receptive Identification of Same and Different

Teaching Procedure: Get at least two things that are either the same or different (depending on the step you are on), or pictures of them, and then at least two more pictures that are not the same and present the child with the Sd "show me which ones are_____" (name the step).

Prompt Hierarchy: Use the least intrusive prompt required in order for the child to be successful (gesture, faded physical, physical; faded verbal and verbal to be used **only** with verbal programs).

Materials: Items that are the same and items that are different.

	STEPS	date:	date:	date:	date:	date:
1	same	Y/N	Y/N	Y/N	Y/N	Y/N
1g	generalization	Y/N	Y/N	Y/N	Y/N	Y/N
2	different	Y/N	Y/N	Y/N	Y/N	Y/N
2g	generalization	Y/N	Y/N	Y/N	Y/N	Y/N

Child Name:. . . . .

Expressive Identification of Same and Different

Teaching Procedure: Get at least two things that are either the same or different (depending on the step you are on), or pictures of them, and then at least two more pictures that are not the same and present the child with the Sd "tell me which ones are _____" (name the step).

Prompt Hierarchy: Use the least intrusive prompt required in order for the child to be successful (gesture, faded physical, physical; faded verbal and verbal to be used **only** with verbal programs).

Materials: Items that are the same and items that are different.

	STEPS	date:	date:	date:	date:	date:
1	same	Y/N	Y/N	Y/N	Y/N	Y/N
1g	generalization	Y/N	Y/N	Y/N	Y/N	Y/N
2	different	Y/N	Y/N	Y/N	Y/N	Y/N
2g	generalization	Y/N	Y/N	Y/N	Y/N	Y/N

Language Arts—Receptive Programs

Child Name: . . . .

Receptive Identification of Prepositions

Teaching Procedure: Use cards that show different prepositions and lay down a minimum of three cards. Present the child with the Sd "show me ___" (name preposition).

Prompt Hierarchy: Use the least intrusive prompt required in order for the child to be successful (gesture, faded physical, physical; faded verbal and verbal to be used **only** with verbal programs).

Materials: Cards that contain different prepositions on them; various objects can be used to help show the different prepositions.

	STEPS	date:	date:	date:	date:	date:
1	in	Y/N	Y/N	Y/N	Y/N	Y/N
1g	generalization	Y/N	Y/N	Y/N	Y/N	Y/N
2	off	Y/N	Y/N	Y/N	Y/N	Y/N
2g	generalization	Y/N	Y/N	Y/N	Y/N	Y/N
3	on	Y/N	Y/N	Y/N	Y/N	Y/N
3g	generalization	Y/N	Y/N	Y/N	Y/N	Y/N
4	out	Y/N	Y/N	Y/N	Y/N	Y/N
4g	generalization	Y/N	Y/N	Y/N	Y/N	Y/N
5	under	Y/N	Y/N	Y/N	Y/N	Y/N
5g	generalization	Y/N	Y/N	Y/N	Y/N	Y/N
6	over	Y/N	Y/N	Y/N	Y/N	Y/N
6g	generalization	Y/N	Y/N	Y/N	Y/N	Y/N
7	next to	Y/N	Y/N	Y/N	Y/N	Y/N
7g	generalization	Y/N	Y/N	Y/N	Y/N	Y/N
8	behind	Y/N	Y/N	Y/N	Y/N	Y/N
8g	generalization	Y/N	Y/N	Y/N	Y/N	Y/N
9	near	Y/N	Y/N	Y/N	Y/N	Y/N
9g	generalization	Y/N	Y/N	Y/N	Y/N	Y/N
10	far	Y/N	Y/N	Y/N	Y/N	Y/N
10g	generalization	Y/N	Y/N	Y/N	Y/N	Y/N

Child Name: . . . .

Receptive Identification of Pronouns

Teaching Procedure: Using actual people or pictures, present the child with the Sd "show me ___"
(name the step that you are on).

Prompt Hierarchy: Use the least intrusive prompt required in order for the child to be successful
(gesture, faded physical, physical; faded verbal and verbal to be used **only** with verbal programs).

Materials: Pictures of pronouns, actual people.

	STEPS	date:	date:	date:	date:	date:
1	he	Y/N	Y/N	Y/N	Y/N	Y/N
1g	generalization	Y/N	Y/N	Y/N	Y/N	Y/N
2	she	Y/N	Y/N	Y/N	Y/N	Y/N
2g	generalization	Y/N	Y/N	Y/N	Y/N	Y/N
3	me	Y/N	Y/N	Y/N	Y/N	Y/N
3g	generalization	Y/N	Y/N	Y/N	Y/N	Y/N
4	we	Y/N	Y/N	Y/N	Y/N	Y/N
4g	generalization	Y/N	Y/N	Y/N	Y/N	Y/N
5	us	Y/N	Y/N	Y/N	Y/N	Y/N
5g	generalization	Y/N	Y/N	Y/N	Y/N	Y/N
6	you	Y/N	Y/N	Y/N	Y/N	Y/N
6g	generalization	Y/N	Y/N	Y/N	Y/N	Y/N
7	they	Y/N	Y/N	Y/N	Y/N	Y/N
7g	generalization	Y/N	Y/N	Y/N	Y/N	Y/N
8	hers	Y/N	Y/N	Y/N	Y/N	Y/N
8g	generalization	Y/N	Y/N	Y/N	Y/N	Y/N
9	his	Y/N	Y/N	Y/N	Y/N	Y/N
9g	generalization	Y/N	Y/N	Y/N	Y/N	Y/N
10	theirs	Y/N	Y/N	Y/N	Y/N	Y/N
10g	generalization	Y/N	Y/N	Y/N	Y/N	Y/N
11	mine	Y/N	Y/N	Y/N	Y/N	Y/N
11g	generalization	Y/N	Y/N	Y/N	Y/N	Y/N
12	I	Y/N	Y/N	Y/N	Y/N	Y/N
12g	generalization	Y/N	Y/N	Y/N	Y/N	Y/N

Child Name: . . . .

Receptive Identification of Adjectives

Teaching Procedure: In a field of three or more, have the student identify the item when you present the direction "show me the____" (name the adjective according to the step you are on). For example, step 1 is colors—you will say "show me the blue one."

Prompt Hierarchy: Use the least intrusive prompt required in order for the child to be successful (gesture, faded physical, physical; faded verbal and verbal to be used **only** with verbal programs).

Materials: Pictures or items of various adjectives.

	STEPS	date:	date:	date:	date:	date:
1	colors (insert various colors)	Y/N	Y/N	Y/N	Y/N	Y/N
1g	generalization	Y/N	Y/N	Y/N	Y/N	Y/N
2	tall	Y/N	Y/N	Y/N	Y/N	Y/N
2g	generalization	Y/N	Y/N	Y/N	Y/N	Y/N
3	short	Y/N	Y/N	Y/N	Y/N	Y/N
3g	generalization	Y/N	Y/N	Y/N	Y/N	Y/N
4	round	Y/N	Y/N	Y/N	Y/N	Y/N
4g	generalization	Y/N	Y/N	Y/N	Y/N	Y/N
5	big	Y/N	Y/N	Y/N	Y/N	Y/N
5g	generalization	Y/N	Y/N	Y/N	Y/N	Y/N
6	little	Y/N	Y/N	Y/N	Y/N	Y/N
6g	generalization	Y/N	Y/N	Y/N	Y/N	Y/N
7	cold	Y/N	Y/N	Y/N	Y/N	Y/N
7g	generalization	Y/N	Y/N	Y/N	Y/N	Y/N
8	hot/warm	Y/N	Y/N	Y/N	Y/N	Y/N
8g	generalization	Y/N	Y/N	Y/N	Y/N	Y/N
9	soft	Y/N	Y/N	Y/N	Y/N	Y/N
9g	generalization	Y/N	Y/N	Y/N	Y/N	Y/N
10	sharp	Y/N	Y/N	Y/N	Y/N	Y/N
10g	generalization	Y/N	Y/N	Y/N	Y/N	Y/N
11	new	Y/N	Y/N	Y/N	Y/N	Y/N
11g	generalization	Y/N	Y/N	Y/N	Y/N	Y/N
12	old	Y/N	Y/N	Y/N	Y/N	Y/N
12g	generalization	Y/N	Y/N	Y/N	Y/N	Y/N

Child Name:..

Receptive Identification of Noun and Adjective

Teaching Procedure: Present the child with a minimum of two pictures/objects and ask him to "touch/find the _____" (name the step you are on).

Prompt Hierarchy: Use the least intrusive prompt required in order for the child to be successful (gesture, faded physical, physical; faded verbal and verbal to be used **only** with verbal programs).

Materials: A red ball, paper cut into a circle, a big doll, a long pencil, a wet towel, a cold drink.

	STEPS	date:	date:	date:	date:	date:
1	red (ball)	Y/N	Y/N	Y/N	Y/N	Y/N
1g	generalization	Y/N	Y/N	Y/N	Y/N	Y/N
2	circle (paper)	Y/N	Y/N	Y/N	Y/N	Y/N
2g	generalization	Y/N	Y/N	Y/N	Y/N	Y/N
3	big (doll)	Y/N	Y/N	Y/N	Y/N	Y/N
3g	generalization	Y/N	Y/N	Y/N	Y/N	Y/N
4	long (pencil)	Y/N	Y/N	Y/N	Y/N	Y/N
4g	generalization	Y/N	Y/N	Y/N	Y/N	Y/N
5	wet (towel)	Y/N	Y/N	Y/N	Y/N	Y/N
5g	generalization	Y/N	Y/N	Y/N	Y/N	Y/N
6	cold (drink)	Y/N	Y/N	Y/N	Y/N	Y/N
6g	generalization	Y/N	Y/N	Y/N	Y/N	Y/N

Child Name: . . . .

Receptive Identification of Adverbs

Teaching Procedure: You will need to present an Sd that will require the child to demonstrate the adverb in the step.

Prompt Hierarchy: Use the least intrusive prompt required in order for the child to be successful (gesture, faded physical, physical; faded verbal and verbal to be used **only** with verbal programs).

Materials: None.

	STEPS	date:	date:	date:	date:	date:
1	softly	Y/N	Y/N	Y/N	Y/N	Y/N
1g	generalization	Y/N	Y/N	Y/N	Y/N	Y/N
2	quickly	Y/N	Y/N	Y/N	Y/N	Y/N
2g	generalization	Y/N	Y/N	Y/N	Y/N	Y/N
3	nicely	Y/N	Y/N	Y/N	Y/N	Y/N
3g	generalization	Y/N	Y/N	Y/N	Y/N	Y/N
4	quietly	Y/N	Y/N	Y/N	Y/N	Y/N
4g	generalization	Y/N	Y/N	Y/N	Y/N	Y/N
5	happily	Y/N	Y/N	Y/N	Y/N	Y/N
5g	generalization	Y/N	Y/N	Y/N	Y/N	Y/N

Child Name: . . . .

Receptive Identification of Class

Teaching Procedure: Lay down a minimum of five pictures/objects, where three of them show the step you are working on, and present the child with the Sd "show me which ones are _____" (name the class).

Prompt Hierarchy: Use the least intrusive prompt required in order for the child to be successful (gesture, faded physical, physical; faded verbal and verbal to be used **only** with verbal programs).

Materials: Clothes, animals, food, drink, toys, vehicles or pictures of them.

	STEPS	date:	date:	date:	date:	date:
1	clothes (shirt, shoes, socks, pants, shorts)	Y/N	Y/N	Y/N	Y/N	Y/N
1g	generalization	Y/N	Y/N	Y/N	Y/N	Y/N
2	animals (cat, dog, horse, pig, cow)	Y/N	Y/N	Y/N	Y/N	Y/N
2g	generalization	Y/N	Y/N	Y/N	Y/N	Y/N
3	food (pizza, cookie, sandwich, burger, soup)	Y/N	Y/N	Y/N	Y/N	Y/N
3g	generalization	Y/N	Y/N	Y/N	Y/N	Y/N
4	drink (water, soda, apple juice, milk, orange juice)	Y/N	Y/N	Y/N	Y/N	Y/N
4g	generalization	Y/N	Y/N	Y/N	Y/N	Y/N
5	toys (bubbles, puzzle, bus, shape sorter, doll)	Y/N	Y/N	Y/N	Y/N	Y/N
5g	generalization	Y/N	Y/N	Y/N	Y/N	Y/N
6	vehicle (car, train, truck)	Y/N	Y/N	Y/N	Y/N	Y/N
6g	generalization	Y/N	Y/N	Y/N	Y/N	Y/N

Child Name: . . . .

Receptive Identification of Feature

Teaching Procedure: Lay down a minimum of three pictures/objects (one of them showing the step you are working on), then present the child with the Sd "give me/show me the one that is _____" (name feature).

Prompt Hierarchy: Use the least intrusive prompt required in order for the child to be successful (gesture, faded physical, physical; faded verbal and verbal to be used **only** with verbal programs).

Materials: Pictures or items that can be identified by color, shape, having a tail, wheels, laces, pages, ears, fur, a point.

	STEPS	date:	date:	date:	date:	date:
1	color (e.g. "give me the one that is red")	Y/N	Y/N	Y/N	Y/N	Y/N
1g	generalization	Y/N	Y/N	Y/N	Y/N	Y/N
2	shape (e.g. "give me the one that is a circle")	Y/N	Y/N	Y/N	Y/N	Y/N
2g	generalization	Y/N	Y/N	Y/N	Y/N	Y/N
3	tail (cat, dog)	Y/N	Y/N	Y/N	Y/N	Y/N
3g	generalization	Y/N	Y/N	Y/N	Y/N	Y/N
4	wheels (car, truck)	Y/N	Y/N	Y/N	Y/N	Y/N
4g	generalization	Y/N	Y/N	Y/N	Y/N	Y/N
5	laces (shoes, boots)	Y/N	Y/N	Y/N	Y/N	Y/N
5g	generalization	Y/N	Y/N	Y/N	Y/N	Y/N
6	pages (book, magazine)	Y/N	Y/N	Y/N	Y/N	Y/N
6g	generalization	Y/N	Y/N	Y/N	Y/N	Y/N
7	ears (bunny, dog)	Y/N	Y/N	Y/N	Y/N	Y/N
7g	generalization	Y/N	Y/N	Y/N	Y/N	Y/N
8	fur (cat, bear)	Y/N	Y/N	Y/N	Y/N	Y/N
8g	generalization	Y/N	Y/N	Y/N	Y/N	Y/N
9	has a point (pencil, scissors)	Y/N	Y/N	Y/N	Y/N	Y/N
9g	generalization	Y/N	Y/N	Y/N	Y/N	Y/N

Child Name:. . . . .

Receptive Identification of Function

Teaching Procedure: Lay down a minimum of three pictures/objects (one of them showing the step you are working on), then present the child with the Sd "what do you _____?" (name function).

Prompt Hierarchy: Use the least intrusive prompt required in order for the child to be successful (gesture, faded physical, physical; faded verbal and verbal to be used **only** with verbal programs).

Materials: Pictures of or actual knife/scissors, car/truck, pencil/pen, hat/jacket, phone/cell phone, book/magazine, couch/chair, bagel/pasta/food, milk/juice/drink, pot/pan, fork/spoon, brush/comb, pool/ocean, paper/chalkboard, vacuum cleaner/broom, table/desk, cup/mug, bike/scooter, sunglasses/bathing suit, puzzles/trains, bubbles/kisses, blocks/Legos, piano/guitar, crayons/markers, drawer/closet.

	STEPS	date:	date:	date:	date:	date:
1	cut with: knife, scissors	Y/N	Y/N	Y/N	Y/N	Y/N
1g	generalization	Y/N	Y/N	Y/N	Y/N	Y/N
2	drive: car, truck	Y/N	Y/N	Y/N	Y/N	Y/N
2g	generalization	Y/N	Y/N	Y/N	Y/N	Y/N
3	write with: pencil, pen	Y/N	Y/N	Y/N	Y/N	Y/N
3g	generalization	Y/N	Y/N	Y/N	Y/N	Y/N
4	wear when it's cold: hat, jacket	Y/N	Y/N	Y/N	Y/N	Y/N
4g	generalization	Y/N	Y/N	Y/N	Y/N	Y/N
5	talk on: phone, cell phone	Y/N	Y/N	Y/N	Y/N	Y/N
5g	generalization	Y/N	Y/N	Y/N	Y/N	Y/N
6	read: book, magazine	Y/N	Y/N	Y/N	Y/N	Y/N
6g	generalization	Y/N	Y/N	Y/N	Y/N	Y/N
7	sit on: couch, chair	Y/N	Y/N	Y/N	Y/N	Y/N
7g	generalization	Y/N	Y/N	Y/N	Y/N	Y/N
8	eat: bagel, pasta, food	Y/N	Y/N	Y/N	Y/N	Y/N
8g	generalization	Y/N	Y/N	Y/N	Y/N	Y/N
9	drink: milk, juice	Y/N	Y/N	Y/N	Y/N	Y/N
9g	generalization	Y/N	Y/N	Y/N	Y/N	Y/N
10	cook with: pot, pan	Y/N	Y/N	Y/N	Y/N	Y/N
10g	generalization	Y/N	Y/N	Y/N	Y/N	Y/N

11	eat with: fork, spoon	Y/N	Y/N	Y/N	Y/N	Y/N
11g	generalization	Y/N	Y/N	Y/N	Y/N	Y/N
12	brush your hair with: brush, comb	Y/N	Y/N	Y/N	Y/N	Y/N
12g	generalization	Y/N	Y/N	Y/N	Y/N	Y/N
13	swim in: pool, ocean	Y/N	Y/N	Y/N	Y/N	Y/N
13g	generalization	Y/N	Y/N	Y/N	Y/N	Y/N
14	write on: paper, chalkboard	Y/N	Y/N	Y/N	Y/N	Y/N
14g	generalization	Y/N	Y/N	Y/N	Y/N	Y/N
15	clean with: vacuum cleaner, broom	Y/N	Y/N	Y/N	Y/N	Y/N
15g	generalization	Y/N	Y/N	Y/N	Y/N	Y/N
16	work on: table, desk	Y/N	Y/N	Y/N	Y/N	Y/N
16g	generalization	Y/N	Y/N	Y/N	Y/N	Y/N
17	drink from: cup, mug	Y/N	Y/N	Y/N	Y/N	Y/N
17g	generalization	Y/N	Y/N	Y/N	Y/N	Y/N
18	ride: bike, scooter	Y/N	Y/N	Y/N	Y/N	Y/N
18g	generalization	Y/N	Y/N	Y/N	Y/N	Y/N
19	wear when it's hot: sunglasses, bathing suit	Y/N	Y/N	Y/N	Y/N	Y/N
19g	generalization	Y/N	Y/N	Y/N	Y/N	Y/N
20	play: puzzles, trains	Y/N	Y/N	Y/N	Y/N	Y/N
20g	generalization	Y/N	Y/N	Y/N	Y/N	Y/N
21	blow: bubbles, kisses	Y/N	Y/N	Y/N	Y/N	Y/N
21g	generalization	Y/N	Y/N	Y/N	Y/N	Y/N
22	build: blocks, Legos	Y/N	Y/N	Y/N	Y/N	Y/N
22g	generalization	Y/N	Y/N	Y/N	Y/N	Y/N
23	what plays music: piano, guitar	Y/N	Y/N	Y/N	Y/N	Y/N
23g	generalization	Y/N	Y/N	Y/N	Y/N	Y/N
24	color: crayons, markers	Y/N	Y/N	Y/N	Y/N	Y/N
24g	generalization	Y/N	Y/N	Y/N	Y/N	Y/N
25	what you put clothes in: drawer, closet	Y/N	Y/N	Y/N	Y/N	Y/N
25g	generalization	Y/N	Y/N	Y/N	Y/N	Y/N

Language Arts—Expressive Programs

Child Name: . . . .

Expressive Identification of Prepositions

Teaching Procedure: Use items such as a small ball and a cup, put the ball: in, on, and below the cup and present the child with the Sd "tell me where the ball is." The child will name the preposition.

Prompt Hierarchy: Use the least intrusive prompt required in order for the child to be successful (gesture, faded physical, physical; faded verbal and verbal to be used **only** with verbal programs).

Materials: Items such as a small ball and a cup, a piece of paper and a table.

	STEPS	date:	date:	date:	date:	date:
1	in	Y/N	Y/N	Y/N	Y/N	Y/N
1g	generalization	Y/N	Y/N	Y/N	Y/N	Y/N
2	off	Y/N	Y/N	Y/N	Y/N	Y/N
2g	generalization	Y/N	Y/N	Y/N	Y/N	Y/N
3	on	Y/N	Y/N	Y/N	Y/N	Y/N
3g	generalization	Y/N	Y/N	Y/N	Y/N	Y/N
4	out	Y/N	Y/N	Y/N	Y/N	Y/N
4g	generalization	Y/N	Y/N	Y/N	Y/N	Y/N
5	under	Y/N	Y/N	Y/N	Y/N	Y/N
5g	generalization	Y/N	Y/N	Y/N	Y/N	Y/N
6	over	Y/N	Y/N	Y/N	Y/N	Y/N
6g	generalization	Y/N	Y/N	Y/N	Y/N	Y/N
7	next to	Y/N	Y/N	Y/N	Y/N	Y/N
7g	generalization	Y/N	Y/N	Y/N	Y/N	Y/N
8	behind	Y/N	Y/N	Y/N	Y/N	Y/N
8g	generalization	Y/N	Y/N	Y/N	Y/N	Y/N
9	near	Y/N	Y/N	Y/N	Y/N	Y/N
9g	generalization	Y/N	Y/N	Y/N	Y/N	Y/N
10	far	Y/N	Y/N	Y/N	Y/N	Y/N
10g	generalization	Y/N	Y/N	Y/N	Y/N	Y/N

Child Name: . . . .

Expressive Identification of Pronouns

Teaching Procedure: Ask the child a question that he would need to answer with the correct pronoun. An example of step 1 would be "tell me what that person is doing." The child would need to answer "he is jumping."

Prompt Hierarchy: Use the least intrusive prompt required in order for the child to be successful (gesture, faded physical, physical; faded verbal and verbal to be used **only** with verbal programs).

Materials: None.

	STEPS	date:	date:	date:	date:	date:
1	he	Y/N	Y/N	Y/N	Y/N	Y/N
1g	generalization	Y/N	Y/N	Y/N	Y/N	Y/N
2	she	Y/N	Y/N	Y/N	Y/N	Y/N
2g	generalization	Y/N	Y/N	Y/N	Y/N	Y/N
3	me	Y/N	Y/N	Y/N	Y/N	Y/N
3g	generalization	Y/N	Y/N	Y/N	Y/N	Y/N
4	we	Y/N	Y/N	Y/N	Y/N	Y/N
4g	generalization	Y/N	Y/N	Y/N	Y/N	Y/N
5	us	Y/N	Y/N	Y/N	Y/N	Y/N
5g	generalization	Y/N	Y/N	Y/N	Y/N	Y/N
6	you	Y/N	Y/N	Y/N	Y/N	Y/N
6g	generalization	Y/N	Y/N	Y/N	Y/N	Y/N
7	they	Y/N	Y/N	Y/N	Y/N	Y/N
7g	generalization	Y/N	Y/N	Y/N	Y/N	Y/N
8	hers	Y/N	Y/N	Y/N	Y/N	Y/N
8g	generalization	Y/N	Y/N	Y/N	Y/N	Y/N
9	his	Y/N	Y/N	Y/N	Y/N	Y/N
9g	generalization	Y/N	Y/N	Y/N	Y/N	Y/N
10	theirs	Y/N	Y/N	Y/N	Y/N	Y/N
10g	generalization	Y/N	Y/N	Y/N	Y/N	Y/N
11	mine	Y/N	Y/N	Y/N	Y/N	Y/N
11g	generalization	Y/N	Y/N	Y/N	Y/N	Y/N
12	I	Y/N	Y/N	Y/N	Y/N	Y/N
12g	generalization	Y/N	Y/N	Y/N	Y/N	Y/N

Child Name: ....

Expressive Identification of Adjectives

Teaching Procedure: Hold up a picture or an item and ask the student to tell you about the item. For example, hold up a picture of a red ball and ask the student "tell me about the ball." The student will say that it is red.

Prompt Hierarchy: Use the least intrusive prompt required in order for the child to be successful (gesture, faded physical, physical; faded verbal and verbal to be used **only** with verbal programs).

Materials: Pictures or items illustrating various adjectives.

	STEPS	date:	date:	date:	date:	date:
1	colors (insert various colors)	Y/N	Y/N	Y/N	Y/N	Y/N
1g	generalization	Y/N	Y/N	Y/N	Y/N	Y/N
2	tall	Y/N	Y/N	Y/N	Y/N	Y/N
2g	generalization	Y/N	Y/N	Y/N	Y/N	Y/N
3	short	Y/N	Y/N	Y/N	Y/N	Y/N
3g	generalization	Y/N	Y/N	Y/N	Y/N	Y/N
4	round	Y/N	Y/N	Y/N	Y/N	Y/N
4g	generalization	Y/N	Y/N	Y/N	Y/N	Y/N
5	big	Y/N	Y/N	Y/N	Y/N	Y/N
5g	generalization	Y/N	Y/N	Y/N	Y/N	Y/N
6	little	Y/N	Y/N	Y/N	Y/N	Y/N
6g	generalization	Y/N	Y/N	Y/N	Y/N	Y/N
7	cold	Y/N	Y/N	Y/N	Y/N	Y/N
7g	generalization	Y/N	Y/N	Y/N	Y/N	Y/N
8	hot/warm	Y/N	Y/N	Y/N	Y/N	Y/N
8g	generalization	Y/N	Y/N	Y/N	Y/N	Y/N
9	soft	Y/N	Y/N	Y/N	Y/N	Y/N
9g	generalization	Y/N	Y/N	Y/N	Y/N	Y/N
10	sharp	Y/N	Y/N	Y/N	Y/N	Y/N
10g	generalization	Y/N	Y/N	Y/N	Y/N	Y/N
11	new	Y/N	Y/N	Y/N	Y/N	Y/N
11g	generalization	Y/N	Y/N	Y/N	Y/N	Y/N
12	old	Y/N	Y/N	Y/N	Y/N	Y/N
12g	generalization	Y/N	Y/N	Y/N	Y/N	Y/N

Child Name: . . . .

Expressive Identification of Noun and Adjective

Teaching Procedure: Hold up either a picture or the actual item and present the child with the Sd "tell me about the picture/item."

Prompt Hierarchy: Use the least intrusive prompt required in order for the child to be successful (gesture, faded physical, physical; faded verbal and verbal to be used **only** with verbal programs).

Materials: A red ball, paper cut into a circle, a big doll, a long pencil, a wet towel, a cold drink.

	STEPS	date:	date:	date:	date:	date:
1	red (ball)	Y/N	Y/N	Y/N	Y/N	Y/N
1g	generalization	Y/N	Y/N	Y/N	Y/N	Y/N
2	circle (paper)	Y/N	Y/N	Y/N	Y/N	Y/N
2g	generalization	Y/N	Y/N	Y/N	Y/N	Y/N
3	big (doll)	Y/N	Y/N	Y/N	Y/N	Y/N
3g	generalization	Y/N	Y/N	Y/N	Y/N	Y/N
4	long (pencil)	Y/N	Y/N	Y/N	Y/N	Y/N
4g	generalization	Y/N	Y/N	Y/N	Y/N	Y/N
5	wet (towel)	Y/N	Y/N	Y/N	Y/N	Y/N
5g	generalization	Y/N	Y/N	Y/N	Y/N	Y/N
6	cold (drink)	Y/N	Y/N	Y/N	Y/N	Y/N
6g	generalization	Y/N	Y/N	Y/N	Y/N	Y/N

Child Name: . . . .

Expressive Identification of Adverbs

Teaching Procedure: Using a video, pictures, or by an actual demonstration, ask the child to "tell me how the person is _____" (name the adverb).

Prompt Hierarchy: Use the least intrusive prompt required in order for the child to be successful (gesture, faded physical, physical; faded verbal and verbal to be used **only** with verbal programs).

Materials: None.

	STEPS	date:	date:	date:	date:	date:
1	softly	Y/N	Y/N	Y/N	Y/N	Y/N
1g	generalization	Y/N	Y/N	Y/N	Y/N	Y/N
2	quickly	Y/N	Y/N	Y/N	Y/N	Y/N
2g	generalization	Y/N	Y/N	Y/N	Y/N	Y/N
3	nicely	Y/N	Y/N	Y/N	Y/N	Y/N
3g	generalization	Y/N	Y/N	Y/N	Y/N	Y/N
4	quietly	Y/N	Y/N	Y/N	Y/N	Y/N
4g	generalization	Y/N	Y/N	Y/N	Y/N	Y/N
5	happily	Y/N	Y/N	Y/N	Y/N	Y/N
5g	generalization	Y/N	Y/N	Y/N	Y/N	Y/N

Child Name: . . . .

Expressive Identification of Class

Teaching Procedure: Present the child with the Sd "tell me/name things that are ____" (name the class).

Prompt Hierarchy: Use the least intrusive prompt required in order for the child to be successful (gesture, faded physical, physical; faded verbal and verbal to be used **only** with verbal programs).

Materials: None.

	STEPS	date:	date:	date:	date:	date:
1	a type of clothing (shirt, socks)	Y/N	Y/N	Y/N	Y/N	Y/N
1g	generalization	Y/N	Y/N	Y/N	Y/N	Y/N
2	a type of animal (cat, dog)	Y/N	Y/N	Y/N	Y/N	Y/N
2g	generalization	Y/N	Y/N	Y/N	Y/N	Y/N
3	a food (pizza, cereal)	Y/N	Y/N	Y/N	Y/N	Y/N
3g	generalization	Y/N	Y/N	Y/N	Y/N	Y/N
4	a drink (milk, juice)	Y/N	Y/N	Y/N	Y/N	Y/N
4g	generalization	Y/N	Y/N	Y/N	Y/N	Y/N
5	a toy (puzzle, doll)	Y/N	Y/N	Y/N	Y/N	Y/N
5g	generalization	Y/N	Y/N	Y/N	Y/N	Y/N
6	a vehicle (car, truck)	Y/N	Y/N	Y/N	Y/N	Y/N
6g	generalization	Y/N	Y/N	Y/N	Y/N	Y/N
7	transportation (plane, train)	Y/N	Y/N	Y/N	Y/N	Y/N
7g	generalization	Y/N	Y/N	Y/N	Y/N	Y/N
8	a sport (baseball, basketball)	Y/N	Y/N	Y/N	Y/N	Y/N
8g	generalization	Y/N	Y/N	Y/N	Y/N	Y/N
9	an instrument is (piano, drum)	Y/N	Y/N	Y/N	Y/N	Y/N
9g	generalization	Y/N	Y/N	Y/N	Y/N	Y/N
10	a song ("Itsy Bitsy Spider," "Mary Had a Little Lamb")	Y/N	Y/N	Y/N	Y/N	Y/N
10g	generalization	Y/N	Y/N	Y/N	Y/N	Y/N
11	a color is (red, blue)	Y/N	Y/N	Y/N	Y/N	Y/N
11g	generalization	Y/N	Y/N	Y/N	Y/N	Y/N

12	a shape (square, circle)	Y/N	Y/N	Y/N	Y/N	Y/N
12g	generalization	Y/N	Y/N	Y/N	Y/N	Y/N
13	a number (1, 2)	Y/N	Y/N	Y/N	Y/N	Y/N
13g	generalization	Y/N	Y/N	Y/N	Y/N	Y/N
14	a letter (A, B)	Y/N	Y/N	Y/N	Y/N	Y/N
14g	generalization	Y/N	Y/N	Y/N	Y/N	Y/N
15	weather (rain, sun)	Y/N	Y/N	Y/N	Y/N	Y/N
15g	generalization	Y/N	Y/N	Y/N	Y/N	Y/N
16	a month (April, May)	Y/N	Y/N	Y/N	Y/N	Y/N
16g	generalization	Y/N	Y/N	Y/N	Y/N	Y/N
17	a day of the week (Monday, Tuesday)	Y/N	Y/N	Y/N	Y/N	Y/N
17g	generalization	Y/N	Y/N	Y/N	Y/N	Y/N
18	a piece of jewelry (ring, necklace)	Y/N	Y/N	Y/N	Y/N	Y/N
18g	generalization	Y/N	Y/N	Y/N	Y/N	Y/N
19	things you take to the beach (shovel, bucket)	Y/N	Y/N	Y/N	Y/N	Y/N
19g	generalization	Y/N	Y/N	Y/N	Y/N	Y/N
20	a room in a house (kitchen, bedroom)	Y/N	Y/N	Y/N	Y/N	Y/N
20g	generalization	Y/N	Y/N	Y/N	Y/N	Y/N

Child Name: . . . .

Expressive Identification of Feature

Teaching Procedure: Present the child with the Sd "tell me about a _____" (name item).

Prompt Hierarchy: Use the least intrusive prompt required in order for the child to be successful (gesture, faded physical, physical; faded verbal and verbal to be used **only** with verbal programs).

Materials: None.

	STEPS	date:	date:	date:	date:	date:
1	dog (tail, eyes)	Y/N	Y/N	Y/N	Y/N	Y/N
1g	generalization	Y/N	Y/N	Y/N	Y/N	Y/N
2	cat (fur, whiskers)	Y/N	Y/N	Y/N	Y/N	Y/N
2g	generalization	Y/N	Y/N	Y/N	Y/N	Y/N
3	car (wheels, horn)	Y/N	Y/N	Y/N	Y/N	Y/N
3g	generalization	Y/N	Y/N	Y/N	Y/N	Y/N
4	house (windows, doors)	Y/N	Y/N	Y/N	Y/N	Y/N
4g	generalization	Y/N	Y/N	Y/N	Y/N	Y/N
5	bunny (tail, nose)	Y/N	Y/N	Y/N	Y/N	Y/N
5g	generalization	Y/N	Y/N	Y/N	Y/N	Y/N
6	book (pages, pictures)	Y/N	Y/N	Y/N	Y/N	Y/N
6g	generalization	Y/N	Y/N	Y/N	Y/N	Y/N
7	phone (buttons)	Y/N	Y/N	Y/N	Y/N	Y/N
7g	generalization	Y/N	Y/N	Y/N	Y/N	Y/N
8	truck (wheels, windows)	Y/N	Y/N	Y/N	Y/N	Y/N
8g	generalization	Y/N	Y/N	Y/N	Y/N	Y/N
9	playground (slide, swing)	Y/N	Y/N	Y/N	Y/N	Y/N
9g	generalization	Y/N	Y/N	Y/N	Y/N	Y/N
10	bed (blanket, pillow)	Y/N	Y/N	Y/N	Y/N	Y/N
10g	generalization	Y/N	Y/N	Y/N	Y/N	Y/N
11	sink (faucet, soap)	Y/N	Y/N	Y/N	Y/N	Y/N
11g	generalization	Y/N	Y/N	Y/N	Y/N	Y/N
12	classroom (desk, chairs)	Y/N	Y/N	Y/N	Y/N	Y/N
12g	generalization	Y/N	Y/N	Y/N	Y/N	Y/N

13	door (knob, handle)	Y/N	Y/N	Y/N	Y/N	Y/N
13g	generalization	Y/N	Y/N	Y/N	Y/N	Y/N
14	table (legs)	Y/N	Y/N	Y/N	Y/N	Y/N
14g	generalization	Y/N	Y/N	Y/N	Y/N	Y/N
15	library (books)	Y/N	Y/N	Y/N	Y/N	Y/N
15g	generalization	Y/N	Y/N	Y/N	Y/N	Y/N
16	desk (legs)	Y/N	Y/N	Y/N	Y/N	Y/N
16g	generalization	Y/N	Y/N	Y/N	Y/N	Y/N
17	closet (clothes, hangers)	Y/N	Y/N	Y/N	Y/N	Y/N
17g	generalization	Y/N	Y/N	Y/N	Y/N	Y/N
18	family room (TV, couch)	Y/N	Y/N	Y/N	Y/N	Y/N
18g	generalization	Y/N	Y/N	Y/N	Y/N	Y/N
19	computer (monitor, mouse)	Y/N	Y/N	Y/N	Y/N	Y/N
19g	generalization	Y/N	Y/N	Y/N	Y/N	Y/N
20	sandbox (shovel, sand)	Y/N	Y/N	Y/N	Y/N	Y/N
20g	generalization	Y/N	Y/N	Y/N	Y/N	Y/N

Child Name: . . . .

Expressive Identification of Function

Teaching Procedure: Present child with the Sd "what do you ___" (name function).

Prompt Hierarchy: Use the least intrusive prompt required in order for the child to be successful (gesture, faded physical, physical; faded verbal and verbal to be used **only** with verbal programs).

Materials: None.

	STEPS	date:	date:	date:	date:	date:
1	cut with: knife, scissors	Y/N	Y/N	Y/N	Y/N	Y/N
1g	generalization	Y/N	Y/N	Y/N	Y/N	Y/N
2	drive: car, truck	Y/N	Y/N	Y/N	Y/N	Y/N
2g	generalization	Y/N	Y/N	Y/N	Y/N	Y/N
3	write with: pencil, pen	Y/N	Y/N	Y/N	Y/N	Y/N
3g	generalization	Y/N	Y/N	Y/N	Y/N	Y/N
4	wear when it's cold: hat, jacket	Y/N	Y/N	Y/N	Y/N	Y/N
4g	generalization	Y/N	Y/N	Y/N	Y/N	Y/N
5	talk on: phone, cell phone	Y/N	Y/N	Y/N	Y/N	Y/N
5g	generalization	Y/N	Y/N	Y/N	Y/N	Y/N
6	read: book, magazine	Y/N	Y/N	Y/N	Y/N	Y/N
6g	generalization	Y/N	Y/N	Y/N	Y/N	Y/N
7	sit on: couch, chair	Y/N	Y/N	Y/N	Y/N	Y/N
7g	generalization	Y/N	Y/N	Y/N	Y/N	Y/N
8	eat: bagel, pasta, food	Y/N	Y/N	Y/N	Y/N	Y/N
8g	generalization	Y/N	Y/N	Y/N	Y/N	Y/N
9	drink: milk, juice	Y/N	Y/N	Y/N	Y/N	Y/N
9g	generalization	Y/N	Y/N	Y/N	Y/N	Y/N
10	cook with: pot, pan	Y/N	Y/N	Y/N	Y/N	Y/N
10g	generalization	Y/N	Y/N	Y/N	Y/N	Y/N
11	eat with: fork, spoon	Y/N	Y/N	Y/N	Y/N	Y/N
11g	generalization	Y/N	Y/N	Y/N	Y/N	Y/N
12	brush your hair with: brush, comb	Y/N	Y/N	Y/N	Y/N	Y/N
12g	generalization	Y/N	Y/N	Y/N	Y/N	Y/N

13	swim in: pool, ocean	Y/N	Y/N	Y/N	Y/N	Y/N
13g	generalization	Y/N	Y/N	Y/N	Y/N	Y/N
14	write on: paper, chalkboard	Y/N	Y/N	Y/N	Y/N	Y/N
14g	generalization	Y/N	Y/N	Y/N	Y/N	Y/N
15	clean with: vacuum cleaner, broom	Y/N	Y/N	Y/N	Y/N	Y/N
15g	generalization	Y/N	Y/N	Y/N	Y/N	Y/N
16	work on: table, desk	Y/N	Y/N	Y/N	Y/N	Y/N
16g	generalization	Y/N	Y/N	Y/N	Y/N	Y/N
17	drink from: cup, mug	Y/N	Y/N	Y/N	Y/N	Y/N
17g	generalization	Y/N	Y/N	Y/N	Y/N	Y/N
18	ride: bike, scooter	Y/N	Y/N	Y/N	Y/N	Y/N
18g	generalization	Y/N	Y/N	Y/N	Y/N	Y/N
19	wear when it's hot: sunglasses, bathing suit	Y/N	Y/N	Y/N	Y/N	Y/N
19g	generalization	Y/N	Y/N	Y/N	Y/N	Y/N
20	play: puzzles, trains	Y/N	Y/N	Y/N	Y/N	Y/N
20g	generalization	Y/N	Y/N	Y/N	Y/N	Y/N
21	blow: bubbles, kisses	Y/N	Y/N	Y/N	Y/N	Y/N
21g	generalization	Y/N	Y/N	Y/N	Y/N	Y/N
22	build: blocks, Legos	Y/N	Y/N	Y/N	Y/N	Y/N
22g	generalization	Y/N	Y/N	Y/N	Y/N	Y/N
23	what plays music: piano, guitar	Y/N	Y/N	Y/N	Y/N	Y/N
23g	generalization	Y/N	Y/N	Y/N	Y/N	Y/N
24	color: crayons, markers	Y/N	Y/N	Y/N	Y/N	Y/N
24g	generalization	Y/N	Y/N	Y/N	Y/N	Y/N
25	what you put clothes in: drawer, closet	Y/N	Y/N	Y/N	Y/N	Y/N
25g	generalization	Y/N	Y/N	Y/N	Y/N	Y/N

Sort and Categorization

Child Name: . . . .

Receptive Identification of What Goes Together

Teaching Procedure: Lay down the objects/pictures along with at least two other objects/pictures; present the child with the remaining object/picture and present the Sd "what goes with ____" (name the object/picture).

Prompt Hierarchy: Use the least intrusive prompt required in order for the child to be successful (gesture, faded physical, physical; faded verbal and verbal to be used **only** with verbal programs).

Materials: Objects themselves or pictures of: sock, shoe, foot, bat, ball, mitt, pillow, bed, blanket, pants, belt, leg, cup, drink, straw, plate, food, fork, toothbrush, toothpaste, teeth, refrigerator, milk, eggs, slide, swing, playground, paper, pencil, crayon.

	STEPS	date:	date:	date:	date:	date:
1	sock, shoe, foot	Y/N	Y/N	Y/N	Y/N	Y/N
1g	generalization	Y/N	Y/N	Y/N	Y/N	Y/N
2	bat, ball, mitt	Y/N	Y/N	Y/N	Y/N	Y/N
2g	generalization	Y/N	Y/N	Y/N	Y/N	Y/N
3	pillow, bed, blanket	Y/N	Y/N	Y/N	Y/N	Y/N
3g	generalization	Y/N	Y/N	Y/N	Y/N	Y/N
4	pants, belt, leg	Y/N	Y/N	Y/N	Y/N	Y/N
4g	generalization	Y/N	Y/N	Y/N	Y/N	Y/N
5	cup, drink, straw	Y/N	Y/N	Y/N	Y/N	Y/N
5g	generalization	Y/N	Y/N	Y/N	Y/N	Y/N
6	plate, food, fork	Y/N	Y/N	Y/N	Y/N	Y/N
6g	generalization	Y/N	Y/N	Y/N	Y/N	Y/N
7	toothbrush, toothpaste, teeth	Y/N	Y/N	Y/N	Y/N	Y/N
7g	generalization	Y/N	Y/N	Y/N	Y/N	Y/N
8	refrigerator, milk, eggs	Y/N	Y/N	Y/N	Y/N	Y/N
8g	generalization	Y/N	Y/N	Y/N	Y/N	Y/N
9	slide, swing, playground	Y/N	Y/N	Y/N	Y/N	Y/N
9g	generalization	Y/N	Y/N	Y/N	Y/N	Y/N
10	paper, pencil, crayon	Y/N	Y/N	Y/N	Y/N	Y/N
10g	generalization	Y/N	Y/N	Y/N	Y/N	Y/N

Child Name:...

Expressive Identification of What Goes Together

Teaching Procedure: Present the child with the Sd "tell me what goes with _____" (name one of the items in the step that you are working on). The child will need to tell you one or two items that go with the item that you named. You can present the Sd as "tell me one thing that goes with_____," or you can say, "tell me two things that go with_____."

Prompt Hierarchy: Use the least intrusive prompt required in order for the child to be successful (gesture, faded physical, physical; faded verbal and verbal to be used **only** with verbal programs).

Materials: None.

	STEPS	date:	date:	date:	date:	date:
1	sock, shoe, foot	Y/N	Y/N	Y/N	Y/N	Y/N
1g	generalization	Y/N	Y/N	Y/N	Y/N	Y/N
2	bat, ball, mitt	Y/N	Y/N	Y/N	Y/N	Y/N
2g	generalization	Y/N	Y/N	Y/N	Y/N	Y/N
3	pillow, bed, blanket	Y/N	Y/N	Y/N	Y/N	Y/N
3g	generalization	Y/N	Y/N	Y/N	Y/N	Y/N
4	pants, belt, leg	Y/N	Y/N	Y/N	Y/N	Y/N
4g	generalization	Y/N	Y/N	Y/N	Y/N	Y/N
5	cup, drink, straw	Y/N	Y/N	Y/N	Y/N	Y/N
5g	generalization	Y/N	Y/N	Y/N	Y/N	Y/N
6	plate, food, fork	Y/N	Y/N	Y/N	Y/N	Y/N
6g	generalization	Y/N	Y/N	Y/N	Y/N	Y/N
7	toothbrush, toothpaste, teeth	Y/N	Y/N	Y/N	Y/N	Y/N
7g	generalization	Y/N	Y/N	Y/N	Y/N	Y/N
8	refrigerator, milk, eggs	Y/N	Y/N	Y/N	Y/N	Y/N
8g	generalization	Y/N	Y/N	Y/N	Y/N	Y/N
9	slide, swing, playground	Y/N	Y/N	Y/N	Y/N	Y/N
9g	generalization	Y/N	Y/N	Y/N	Y/N	Y/N
10	paper, pencil, crayon	Y/N	Y/N	Y/N	Y/N	Y/N
10g	generalization	Y/N	Y/N	Y/N	Y/N	Y/N

Child Name:. . . . .

Categorization

Teaching Procedure: Present the child with a minimum of eight pictures/objects with at least half of the items illustrating the step the child is working on, and present the Sd "put all the _____ [name step] together."

Prompt Hierarchy: Use the least intrusive prompt required in order for the child to be successful (gesture, faded physical, physical; faded verbal and verbal to be used **only** with verbal programs).

Materials: Items that are the same color, big items, little items, items that are hot, items that are cold, items that are tall, items that are short, items that are wet, items that are dry, items that are rough, items that are soft, items that are broken, items that are sharp, items that are loud.

	STEPS	date:	date:	date:	date:	date:
1	color (all the blue ones)	Y/N	Y/N	Y/N	Y/N	Y/N
1g	generalization	Y/N	Y/N	Y/N	Y/N	Y/N
2	big	Y/N	Y/N	Y/N	Y/N	Y/N
2g	generalization	Y/N	Y/N	Y/N	Y/N	Y/N
3	little	Y/N	Y/N	Y/N	Y/N	Y/N
3g	generalization	Y/N	Y/N	Y/N	Y/N	Y/N
4	hot	Y/N	Y/N	Y/N	Y/N	Y/N
4g	generalization	Y/N	Y/N	Y/N	Y/N	Y/N
5	cold	Y/N	Y/N	Y/N	Y/N	Y/N
5g	generalization	Y/N	Y/N	Y/N	Y/N	Y/N
6	tall	Y/N	Y/N	Y/N	Y/N	Y/N
6g	generalization	Y/N	Y/N	Y/N	Y/N	Y/N
7	short	Y/N	Y/N	Y/N	Y/N	Y/N
7g	generalization	Y/N	Y/N	Y/N	Y/N	Y/N
8	wet	Y/N	Y/N	Y/N	Y/N	Y/N
8g	generalization	Y/N	Y/N	Y/N	Y/N	Y/N
9	dry	Y/N	Y/N	Y/N	Y/N	Y/N
9g	generalization	Y/N	Y/N	Y/N	Y/N	Y/N
10	rough	Y/N	Y/N	Y/N	Y/N	Y/N
10g	generalization	Y/N	Y/N	Y/N	Y/N	Y/N
11	soft	Y/N	Y/N	Y/N	Y/N	Y/N

11g	generalization	Y/N	Y/N	Y/N	Y/N	Y/N
12	broken	Y/N	Y/N	Y/N	Y/N	Y/N
12g	generalization	Y/N	Y/N	Y/N	Y/N	Y/N
13	sharp	Y/N	Y/N	Y/N	Y/N	Y/N
13g	generalization	Y/N	Y/N	Y/N	Y/N	Y/N
14	loud	Y/N	Y/N	Y/N	Y/N	Y/N
14g	generalization	Y/N	Y/N	Y/N	Y/N	Y/N

Child Name:. . . . .

Receptive Identification of What is Not the Item

Teaching Procedure: Lay down at least four pictures. At least half of the pictures should be the item in the step you are working on, and present the child with the Sd "show me what is not a ____ [step name]."

Prompt Hierarchy: Use the least intrusive prompt required in order for the child to be successful (gesture, faded physical, physical; faded verbal and verbal to be used **only** with verbal programs).

Materials: Pictures that include cars, foods, shapes, colors, toys, crayons, clothes, buses, drinks.

	STEPS	date:	date:	date:	date:	date:
1	car	Y/N	Y/N	Y/N	Y/N	Y/N
1g	generalization	Y/N	Y/N	Y/N	Y/N	Y/N
2	food	Y/N	Y/N	Y/N	Y/N	Y/N
2g	generalization	Y/N	Y/N	Y/N	Y/N	Y/N
3	shape	Y/N	Y/N	Y/N	Y/N	Y/N
3g	generalization	Y/N	Y/N	Y/N	Y/N	Y/N
4	color	Y/N	Y/N	Y/N	Y/N	Y/N
4g	generalization	Y/N	Y/N	Y/N	Y/N	Y/N
5	toy	Y/N	Y/N	Y/N	Y/N	Y/N
5g	generalization	Y/N	Y/N	Y/N	Y/N	Y/N
6	crayon	Y/N	Y/N	Y/N	Y/N	Y/N
6g	generalization	Y/N	Y/N	Y/N	Y/N	Y/N
7	clothes	Y/N	Y/N	Y/N	Y/N	Y/N
7g	generalization	Y/N	Y/N	Y/N	Y/N	Y/N
8	bus	Y/N	Y/N	Y/N	Y/N	Y/N
8g	generalization	Y/N	Y/N	Y/N	Y/N	Y/N
9	drink	Y/N	Y/N	Y/N	Y/N	Y/N
9g	generalization	Y/N	Y/N	Y/N	Y/N	Y/N

Child Name:. . . . .

Expressive Identification of What is Not the Item

Teaching Procedure: Present the child with the Sd "tell me what is not a ___" (name the item in the current step).

Prompt Hierarchy: Use the least intrusive prompt required in order for the child to be successful (gesture, faded physical, physical; faded verbal and verbal to be used **only** with verbal programs).

Materials: None.

	STEPS	date:	date:	date:	date:	date:
1	car	Y/N	Y/N	Y/N	Y/N	Y/N
1g	generalization	Y/N	Y/N	Y/N	Y/N	Y/N
2	food	Y/N	Y/N	Y/N	Y/N	Y/N
2g	generalization	Y/N	Y/N	Y/N	Y/N	Y/N
3	shape	Y/N	Y/N	Y/N	Y/N	Y/N
3g	generalization	Y/N	Y/N	Y/N	Y/N	Y/N
4	color	Y/N	Y/N	Y/N	Y/N	Y/N
4g	generalization	Y/N	Y/N	Y/N	Y/N	Y/N
5	toy	Y/N	Y/N	Y/N	Y/N	Y/N
5g	generalization	Y/N	Y/N	Y/N	Y/N	Y/N
6	crayon	Y/N	Y/N	Y/N	Y/N	Y/N
6g	generalization	Y/N	Y/N	Y/N	Y/N	Y/N
7	clothes	Y/N	Y/N	Y/N	Y/N	Y/N
7g	generalization	Y/N	Y/N	Y/N	Y/N	Y/N
8	bus	Y/N	Y/N	Y/N	Y/N	Y/N
8g	generalization	Y/N	Y/N	Y/N	Y/N	Y/N
9	drink	Y/N	Y/N	Y/N	Y/N	Y/N
9g	generalization	Y/N	Y/N	Y/N	Y/N	Y/N

Child Name:. . . . .

Sort By Function

Teaching Procedure: Put down a sample from each category and then hand the child the pictures and present the Sd "sort."

Prompt Hierarchy: Use the least intrusive prompt required in order for the child to be successful (gesture, faded physical, physical; faded verbal and verbal to be used **only** with verbal programs).

Materials: Pictures of things you eat (e.g. banana, cookie, pasta), things you ride in (e.g. car, truck, train), things you wear (e.g. shirt, pants, shoes), things you play with (e.g. puzzle, car, shape sorter), things you sit on (e.g. chair, sofa, bench), things you drink (e.g. juice, milk, water).

	STEPS	date:	date:	date:	date:	date:
1	have the child sort things you eat versus things you ride in	Y/N	Y/N	Y/N	Y/N	Y/N
1g	generalization	Y/N	Y/N	Y/N	Y/N	Y/N
2	have the child sort things you wear versus things you play with	Y/N	Y/N	Y/N	Y/N	Y/N
2g	generalization	Y/N	Y/N	Y/N	Y/N	Y/N
3	have the child sort any combination of eat, ride in, wear, play with, in a field of three	Y/N	Y/N	Y/N	Y/N	Y/N
3g	generalization	Y/N	Y/N	Y/N	Y/N	Y/N
4	have the child sort any combination of eat, ride in, wear, play with, sit on, in a field of three or more	Y/N	Y/N	Y/N	Y/N	Y/N
4g	generalization	Y/N	Y/N	Y/N	Y/N	Y/N
5	have the child sort any combination of eat, ride in, wear, play with, sit on, drink, in a field of three or more	Y/N	Y/N	Y/N	Y/N	Y/N
5g	generalization	Y/N	Y/N	Y/N	Y/N	Y/N

Child Name: . . . .

Sort by Feature

Teaching Procedure: Put down a sample from each category and then hand the child the pictures and present the child with the Sd "sort."

Prompt Hierarchy: Use the least intrusive prompt required in order for the child to be successful (gesture, faded physical, physical; faded verbal and verbal to be used **only** with verbal programs).

Materials: Pictures of things with tails (e.g. dog, horse, pig), things with wheels (e.g. bike, car, truck), things that are the same color (e.g. banana, tennis ball, lemon), things that have stripes (e.g. zebra, tiger, striped fish), things that are round (e.g. ball, coin, marble), things that are soft (e.g. rabbit, cotton ball, feather).

	STEPS	date:	date:	date:	date:	date:
1	have the child sort things with tails versus things with wheels	Y/N	Y/N	Y/N	Y/N	Y/N
1g	generalization	Y/N	Y/N	Y/N	Y/N	Y/N
2	have the child sort things with the same color versus things that have stripes	Y/N	Y/N	Y/N	Y/N	Y/N
2g	generalization	Y/N	Y/N	Y/N	Y/N	Y/N
3	have the child sort any combination of things with tails, wheels, same color, and stripes, in a field of three	Y/N	Y/N	Y/N	Y/N	Y/N
3g	generalization	Y/N	Y/N	Y/N	Y/N	Y/N
4	have the child sort any combination of things with tails, wheels, same color, stripes, things that are round, in a field of three or more	Y/N	Y/N	Y/N	Y/N	Y/N
4g	generalization	Y/N	Y/N	Y/N	Y/N	Y/N
5	have the child sort any combination of things with tails, wheels, same color, stripes, round, soft, in a field of three or more	Y/N	Y/N	Y/N	Y/N	Y/N
5g	generalization	Y/N	Y/N	Y/N	Y/N	Y/N

Child Name:. . . . .

Sort by Class

Teaching Procedure: Put down a sample from each category and then hand the child the pictures and present the child with the Sd "sort."

Prompt Hierarchy: Use the least intrusive prompt required in order for the child to be successful (gesture, faded physical, physical; faded verbal and verbal to be used **only** with verbal programs).

Materials: Pictures of colors (e.g. blue, green, purple), food (e.g. pasta, cereal, cookie), clothes (e.g. shirt, pants, socks), animals (e.g. lion, bear, cat), shapes (e.g. triangle, circle, square), furniture (e.g. couch, table, bed), toys (e.g. puzzle, shape sorter, car).

	STEPS	date:	date:	date:	date:	date:
1	have the child sort things that are a color versus food	Y/N	Y/N	Y/N	Y/N	Y/N
1g	generalization	Y/N	Y/N	Y/N	Y/N	Y/N
2	have the child sort things that are clothes versus animals	Y/N	Y/N	Y/N	Y/N	Y/N
2g	generalization	Y/N	Y/N	Y/N	Y/N	Y/N
3	have the child sort any combination of color, food, clothes, animals, in a field of three	Y/N	Y/N	Y/N	Y/N	Y/N
3g	generalization	Y/N	Y/N	Y/N	Y/N	Y/N
4	have the child sort any combination of color, food, clothes, animals, shapes, in a field of three or more	Y/N	Y/N	Y/N	Y/N	Y/N
4g	generalization	Y/N	Y/N	Y/N	Y/N	Y/N
5	have the child sort any combination of color, food, clothes, animals, shapes, furniture, in a field of three or more	Y/N	Y/N	Y/N	Y/N	Y/N
5g	generalization	Y/N	Y/N	Y/N	Y/N	Y/N
6	have the child sort any combination of color, food, clothes, animals, shapes, furniture, toys, in a field of three or more	Y/N	Y/N	Y/N	Y/N	Y/N
6g	generalization	Y/N	Y/N	Y/N	Y/N	Y/N

Conversation and Social Skills

Child Name: . . . .

Receptively Identifies Items

Teaching Procedure: Present the child with a minimum of three pictures/objects and ask the child to "find ___" (name the item in the current step).

Prompt Hierarchy: Use the least intrusive prompt required in order for the child to be successful (gesture, faded physical, physical; faded verbal and verbal to be used **only** with verbal programs).

Materials: Pictures of animals, colors, letters, numbers, shapes, vehicles, things found at a playground (swing, slide, sandbox), things found in a home (couch, TV, kitchen), things found outside (trees, flowers, squirrels), things found in a bedroom (bed, pillow, closet).

	STEPS	date:	date:	date:	date:	date:
1	animals	Y/N	Y/N	Y/N	Y/N	Y/N
1g	generalization	Y/N	Y/N	Y/N	Y/N	Y/N
2	colors	Y/N	Y/N	Y/N	Y/N	Y/N
2g	generalization	Y/N	Y/N	Y/N	Y/N	Y/N
3	letters	Y/N	Y/N	Y/N	Y/N	Y/N
3g	generalization	Y/N	Y/N	Y/N	Y/N	Y/N
4	numbers	Y/N	Y/N	Y/N	Y/N	Y/N
4g	generalization	Y/N	Y/N	Y/N	Y/N	Y/N
5	shapes	Y/N	Y/N	Y/N	Y/N	Y/N
5g	generalization	Y/N	Y/N	Y/N	Y/N	Y/N
6	vehicles	Y/N	Y/N	Y/N	Y/N	Y/N
6g	generalization	Y/N	Y/N	Y/N	Y/N	Y/N
7	things found at a playground	Y/N	Y/N	Y/N	Y/N	Y/N
7g	generalization	Y/N	Y/N	Y/N	Y/N	Y/N
8	things found in the home	Y/N	Y/N	Y/N	Y/N	Y/N
8g	generalization	Y/N	Y/N	Y/N	Y/N	Y/N
9	things found outside	Y/N	Y/N	Y/N	Y/N	Y/N
9g	generalization	Y/N	Y/N	Y/N	Y/N	Y/N
10	things found in the bedroom	Y/N	Y/N	Y/N	Y/N	Y/N
10g	generalization	Y/N	Y/N	Y/N	Y/N	Y/N

Child Name: . . . .

Expressively Answers the Question "Name..."

Teaching Procedure: Ask the child to "name ___" (present the words in each step).

Prompt Hierarchy: Use the least intrusive prompt required in order for the child to be successful (gesture, faded physical, physical; faded verbal and verbal to be used **only** with verbal programs).

Materials: None.

	STEPS	date:	date:	date:	date:	date:
1	animals	Y/N	Y/N	Y/N	Y/N	Y/N
1g	generalization	Y/N	Y/N	Y/N	Y/N	Y/N
2	colors	Y/N	Y/N	Y/N	Y/N	Y/N
2g	generalization	Y/N	Y/N	Y/N	Y/N	Y/N
3	letters	Y/N	Y/N	Y/N	Y/N	Y/N
3g	generalization	Y/N	Y/N	Y/N	Y/N	Y/N
4	numbers	Y/N	Y/N	Y/N	Y/N	Y/N
4g	generalization	Y/N	Y/N	Y/N	Y/N	Y/N
5	shapes	Y/N	Y/N	Y/N	Y/N	Y/N
5g	generalization	Y/N	Y/N	Y/N	Y/N	Y/N
6	vehicles	Y/N	Y/N	Y/N	Y/N	Y/N
6g	generalization	Y/N	Y/N	Y/N	Y/N	Y/N
7	things found at a playground	Y/N	Y/N	Y/N	Y/N	Y/N
7g	generalization	Y/N	Y/N	Y/N	Y/N	Y/N
8	things found in the home	Y/N	Y/N	Y/N	Y/N	Y/N
8g	generalization	Y/N	Y/N	Y/N	Y/N	Y/N
9	things found outside	Y/N	Y/N	Y/N	Y/N	Y/N
9g	generalization	Y/N	Y/N	Y/N	Y/N	Y/N
10	things found in the bedroom	Y/N	Y/N	Y/N	Y/N	Y/N
10g	generalization	Y/N	Y/N	Y/N	Y/N	Y/N

Child Name: . . . .

Answers Questions About Items

Teaching Procedure: Present the child with the Sd, which are the words not in parentheses in each step.

Prompt Hierarchy: Use the least intrusive prompt required in order for the child to be successful (gesture, faded physical, physical; faded verbal and verbal to be used **only** with verbal programs).

Materials: None.

	STEPS	date:	date:	date:	date:	date:
1	you ride in a ___ (car)	Y/N	Y/N	Y/N	Y/N	Y/N
1g	generalization	Y/N	Y/N	Y/N	Y/N	Y/N
2	you write with a ___ (pencil/pen)	Y/N	Y/N	Y/N	Y/N	Y/N
2g	generalization	Y/N	Y/N	Y/N	Y/N	Y/N
3	you wear ___ (a shirt, pants, shoes, etc.)	Y/N	Y/N	Y/N	Y/N	Y/N
3g	generalization	Y/N	Y/N	Y/N	Y/N	Y/N
4	you eat in a ___ (restaurant)	Y/N	Y/N	Y/N	Y/N	Y/N
4g	generalization	Y/N	Y/N	Y/N	Y/N	Y/N
5	you eat with a ___ (fork)	Y/N	Y/N	Y/N	Y/N	Y/N
5g	generalization	Y/N	Y/N	Y/N	Y/N	Y/N
6	you sleep in a ___ (bed)	Y/N	Y/N	Y/N	Y/N	Y/N
6g	generalization	Y/N	Y/N	Y/N	Y/N	Y/N
7	you wash your hands with ___ (soap)	Y/N	Y/N	Y/N	Y/N	Y/N
7g	generalization	Y/N	Y/N	Y/N	Y/N	Y/N
8	you smell with your ___ (nose)	Y/N	Y/N	Y/N	Y/N	Y/N
8g	generalization	Y/N	Y/N	Y/N	Y/N	Y/N
9	you blow ___ (bubbles)	Y/N	Y/N	Y/N	Y/N	Y/N
9g	generalization	Y/N	Y/N	Y/N	Y/N	Y/N
10	you live in a ___ (house)	Y/N	Y/N	Y/N	Y/N	Y/N
10g	generalization	Y/N	Y/N	Y/N	Y/N	Y/N
11	you read a ___ (book)	Y/N	Y/N	Y/N	Y/N	Y/N
11g	generalization	Y/N	Y/N	Y/N	Y/N	Y/N
12	you sit on a ___ (chair)	Y/N	Y/N	Y/N	Y/N	Y/N

12g	generalization	Y/N	Y/N	Y/N	Y/N	Y/N
13	you drink from a ___ (cup)	Y/N	Y/N	Y/N	Y/N	Y/N
13g	generalization	Y/N	Y/N	Y/N	Y/N	Y/N
14	you see with your ___ (eyes)	Y/N	Y/N	Y/N	Y/N	Y/N
14g	generalization	Y/N	Y/N	Y/N	Y/N	Y/N
15	you hear with your ___ (ears)	Y/N	Y/N	Y/N	Y/N	Y/N
15g	generalization	Y/N	Y/N	Y/N	Y/N	Y/N
16	you cut with ___ (scissors)	Y/N	Y/N	Y/N	Y/N	Y/N
16g	generalization	Y/N	Y/N	Y/N	Y/N	Y/N
17	you watch ___ (TV)	Y/N	Y/N	Y/N	Y/N	Y/N
17g	generalization	Y/N	Y/N	Y/N	Y/N	Y/N
18	you throw a ___ (ball)	Y/N	Y/N	Y/N	Y/N	Y/N
18g	generalization	Y/N	Y/N	Y/N	Y/N	Y/N
19	you listen to ___ (music)	Y/N	Y/N	Y/N	Y/N	Y/N
19g	generalization	Y/N	Y/N	Y/N	Y/N	Y/N
20	you play with ___ (toys)	Y/N	Y/N	Y/N	Y/N	Y/N
20g	generalization	Y/N	Y/N	Y/N	Y/N	Y/N

Child Name: ....

Answers "What" Questions

Teaching Procedure: Present the child with the "what" question in each step.

Prompt Hierarchy: Use the least intrusive prompt required in order for the child to be successful (gesture, faded physical, physical; faded verbal and verbal to be used **only** with verbal programs).

Materials: None.

	STEPS	date:	date:	date:	date:	date:
1	What do you see in the park?	Y/N	Y/N	Y/N	Y/N	Y/N
1g	generalization	Y/N	Y/N	Y/N	Y/N	Y/N
2	What do you see at the library?	Y/N	Y/N	Y/N	Y/N	Y/N
2g	generalization	Y/N	Y/N	Y/N	Y/N	Y/N
3	What do you see at the restaurant?	Y/N	Y/N	Y/N	Y/N	Y/N
3g	generalization	Y/N	Y/N	Y/N	Y/N	Y/N
4	What do you see at the bank?	Y/N	Y/N	Y/N	Y/N	Y/N
4g	generalization	Y/N	Y/N	Y/N	Y/N	Y/N
5	What do you see at the fire station?	Y/N	Y/N	Y/N	Y/N	Y/N
5g	generalization	Y/N	Y/N	Y/N	Y/N	Y/N
6	What do you do at the farm?	Y/N	Y/N	Y/N	Y/N	Y/N
6g	generalization	Y/N	Y/N	Y/N	Y/N	Y/N
7	What do you see at a the ice-cream store?	Y/N	Y/N	Y/N	Y/N	Y/N
7g	generalization	Y/N	Y/N	Y/N	Y/N	Y/N
8	What do you get at a restaurant?	Y/N	Y/N	Y/N	Y/N	Y/N
8g	generalization	Y/N	Y/N	Y/N	Y/N	Y/N
9	What do you see in a supermarket?	Y/N	Y/N	Y/N	Y/N	Y/N
9g	generalization	Y/N	Y/N	Y/N	Y/N	Y/N
10	What do you see at the gym?	Y/N	Y/N	Y/N	Y/N	Y/N
10g	generalization	Y/N	Y/N	Y/N	Y/N	Y/N
11	What do you see at the zoo?	Y/N	Y/N	Y/N	Y/N	Y/N
11g	generalization	Y/N	Y/N	Y/N	Y/N	Y/N
12	What do you see at the mall?	Y/N	Y/N	Y/N	Y/N	Y/N

12g	generalization	Y/N	Y/N	Y/N	Y/N	Y/N
13	What do you see in the cafeteria?	Y/N	Y/N	Y/N	Y/N	Y/N
13g	generalization	Y/N	Y/N	Y/N	Y/N	Y/N
14	What do you see at the bowling ally?	Y/N	Y/N	Y/N	Y/N	Y/N
14g	generalization	Y/N	Y/N	Y/N	Y/N	Y/N
15	What do you see at the movie theater?	Y/N	Y/N	Y/N	Y/N	Y/N
15g	generalization	Y/N	Y/N	Y/N	Y/N	Y/N
16	What do you see at the post office?	Y/N	Y/N	Y/N	Y/N	Y/N
16g	generalization	Y/N	Y/N	Y/N	Y/N	Y/N
17	What do you see at the police station?	Y/N	Y/N	Y/N	Y/N	Y/N
17g	generalization	Y/N	Y/N	Y/N	Y/N	Y/N
18	What do you see at the hair salon?	Y/N	Y/N	Y/N	Y/N	Y/N
18g	generalization	Y/N	Y/N	Y/N	Y/N	Y/N
19	What do you see at an airport?	Y/N	Y/N	Y/N	Y/N	Y/N
19g	generalization	Y/N	Y/N	Y/N	Y/N	Y/N
20	What do you see at a train station?	Y/N	Y/N	Y/N	Y/N	Y/N
20g	generalization	Y/N	Y/N	Y/N	Y/N	Y/N

Child Name: . . . .

Answers "When" Questions

Teaching Procedure: Present the child with the "when" question in each step.

Prompt Hierarchy: Use the least intrusive prompt required in order for the child to be successful (gesture, faded physical, physical; faded verbal and verbal to be used **only** with verbal programs).

Materials: None.

	STEPS	date:	date:	date:	date:	date:
1	When do you sleep?	Y/N	Y/N	Y/N	Y/N	Y/N
1g	generalization	Y/N	Y/N	Y/N	Y/N	Y/N
2	When do you eat breakfast?	Y/N	Y/N	Y/N	Y/N	Y/N
2g	generalization	Y/N	Y/N	Y/N	Y/N	Y/N
3	When do you eat dinner?	Y/N	Y/N	Y/N	Y/N	Y/N
3g	generalization	Y/N	Y/N	Y/N	Y/N	Y/N
4	When do you watch TV?	Y/N	Y/N	Y/N	Y/N	Y/N
4g	generalization	Y/N	Y/N	Y/N	Y/N	Y/N
5	When do you play?	Y/N	Y/N	Y/N	Y/N	Y/N
5g	generalization	Y/N	Y/N	Y/N	Y/N	Y/N
6	When do you take a bath?	Y/N	Y/N	Y/N	Y/N	Y/N
6g	generalization	Y/N	Y/N	Y/N	Y/N	Y/N
7	When do you go to school?	Y/N	Y/N	Y/N	Y/N	Y/N
7g	generalization	Y/N	Y/N	Y/N	Y/N	Y/N
8	When do you swim in the ocean?	Y/N	Y/N	Y/N	Y/N	Y/N
8g	generalization	Y/N	Y/N	Y/N	Y/N	Y/N
9	When does it snow?	Y/N	Y/N	Y/N	Y/N	Y/N
9g	generalization	Y/N	Y/N	Y/N	Y/N	Y/N
10	When do you put sunglasses on?	Y/N	Y/N	Y/N	Y/N	Y/N
10g	generalization	Y/N	Y/N	Y/N	Y/N	Y/N
11	When do you wear gloves?	Y/N	Y/N	Y/N	Y/N	Y/N
11g	generalization	Y/N	Y/N	Y/N	Y/N	Y/N
12	When do you build a snowman?	Y/N	Y/N	Y/N	Y/N	Y/N
12g	generalization	Y/N	Y/N	Y/N	Y/N	Y/N

13	When do you eat a snack?	Y/N	Y/N	Y/N	Y/N	Y/N
13g	generalization	Y/N	Y/N	Y/N	Y/N	Y/N
14	When do you eat lunch?	Y/N	Y/N	Y/N	Y/N	Y/N
14g	generalization	Y/N	Y/N	Y/N	Y/N	Y/N
15	When do you see your friends?	Y/N	Y/N	Y/N	Y/N	Y/N
15g	generalization	Y/N	Y/N	Y/N	Y/N	Y/N
16	When do you drink?	Y/N	Y/N	Y/N	Y/N	Y/N
16g	generalization	Y/N	Y/N	Y/N	Y/N	Y/N
17	When do you wear shorts?	Y/N	Y/N	Y/N	Y/N	Y/N
17g	generalization	Y/N	Y/N	Y/N	Y/N	Y/N
18	When do you use a vacuum cleaner?	Y/N	Y/N	Y/N	Y/N	Y/N
18g	generalization	Y/N	Y/N	Y/N	Y/N	Y/N
19	When do you see a doctor?	Y/N	Y/N	Y/N	Y/N	Y/N
19g	generalization	Y/N	Y/N	Y/N	Y/N	Y/N
20	When do you go to the mall?	Y/N	Y/N	Y/N	Y/N	Y/N
20g	generalization	Y/N	Y/N	Y/N	Y/N	Y/N

Child Name: . . . .

Answers "Where" Questions

Teaching Procedure: Present the child with the words in each step.

Prompt Hierarchy: Use the least intrusive prompt required in order for the child to be successful (gesture, faded physical, physical; faded verbal and verbal to be used **only** with verbal programs).

Materials: None.

	STEPS	date:	date:	date:	date:	date:
1	Where do you find milk?	Y/N	Y/N	Y/N	Y/N	Y/N
1g	generalization	Y/N	Y/N	Y/N	Y/N	Y/N
2	Where do you hang your coat?	Y/N	Y/N	Y/N	Y/N	Y/N
2g	generalization	Y/N	Y/N	Y/N	Y/N	Y/N
3	Where do you get a spoon?	Y/N	Y/N	Y/N	Y/N	Y/N
3g	generalization	Y/N	Y/N	Y/N	Y/N	Y/N
4	Where do you sleep?	Y/N	Y/N	Y/N	Y/N	Y/N
4g	generalization	Y/N	Y/N	Y/N	Y/N	Y/N
5	Where do you wash your face?	Y/N	Y/N	Y/N	Y/N	Y/N
5g	generalization	Y/N	Y/N	Y/N	Y/N	Y/N
6	Where do you go to the bathroom?	Y/N	Y/N	Y/N	Y/N	Y/N
6g	generalization	Y/N	Y/N	Y/N	Y/N	Y/N
7	Where do you eat dinner?	Y/N	Y/N	Y/N	Y/N	Y/N
7g	generalization	Y/N	Y/N	Y/N	Y/N	Y/N
8	Where do you watch TV?	Y/N	Y/N	Y/N	Y/N	Y/N
8g	generalization	Y/N	Y/N	Y/N	Y/N	Y/N
9	Where is your bed?	Y/N	Y/N	Y/N	Y/N	Y/N
9g	generalization	Y/N	Y/N	Y/N	Y/N	Y/N
10	Where is the couch?	Y/N	Y/N	Y/N	Y/N	Y/N
10g	generalization	Y/N	Y/N	Y/N	Y/N	Y/N
11	Where are your clothes?	Y/N	Y/N	Y/N	Y/N	Y/N
11g	generalization	Y/N	Y/N	Y/N	Y/N	Y/N
12	Where do you get ice?	Y/N	Y/N	Y/N	Y/N	Y/N

12g	generalization	Y/N	Y/N	Y/N	Y/N	Y/N
13	Where do you play?	Y/N	Y/N	Y/N	Y/N	Y/N
13g	generalization	Y/N	Y/N	Y/N	Y/N	Y/N
14	Where do you find the toilet?	Y/N	Y/N	Y/N	Y/N	Y/N
14g	generalization	Y/N	Y/N	Y/N	Y/N	Y/N
15	Where do you put sheets?	Y/N	Y/N	Y/N	Y/N	Y/N
15g	generalization	Y/N	Y/N	Y/N	Y/N	Y/N
16	Where do you heat food up?	Y/N	Y/N	Y/N	Y/N	Y/N
16g	generalization	Y/N	Y/N	Y/N	Y/N	Y/N
17	Where do you put eggs?	Y/N	Y/N	Y/N	Y/N	Y/N
17g	generalization	Y/N	Y/N	Y/N	Y/N	Y/N
18	Where do you wash clothes?	Y/N	Y/N	Y/N	Y/N	Y/N
18g	generalization	Y/N	Y/N	Y/N	Y/N	Y/N
19	Where do you find your socks?	Y/N	Y/N	Y/N	Y/N	Y/N
19g	generalization	Y/N	Y/N	Y/N	Y/N	Y/N
20	Where do you find the computer at school?	Y/N	Y/N	Y/N	Y/N	Y/N
20g	generalization	Y/N	Y/N	Y/N	Y/N	Y/N

Child Name:..

Answers "Which" Questions

Teaching Procedure: Present the child with the "which" question in each step.

Prompt Hierarchy: Use the least intrusive prompt required in order for the child to be successful (gesture, faded physical, physical; faded verbal and verbal to be used **only** with verbal programs).

Materials: None.

	STEPS	date:	date:	date:	date:	date:
1	Which is an animal, cat or apple?	Y/N	Y/N	Y/N	Y/N	Y/N
1g	generalization	Y/N	Y/N	Y/N	Y/N	Y/N
2	Which is a food, dog or pizza?	Y/N	Y/N	Y/N	Y/N	Y/N
2g	generalization	Y/N	Y/N	Y/N	Y/N	Y/N
3	Which is a color, square or red?	Y/N	Y/N	Y/N	Y/N	Y/N
3g	generalization	Y/N	Y/N	Y/N	Y/N	Y/N
4	Which is a shape, circle or desk?	Y/N	Y/N	Y/N	Y/N	Y/N
4g	generalization	Y/N	Y/N	Y/N	Y/N	Y/N
5	Which is a body part, arm or phone?	Y/N	Y/N	Y/N	Y/N	Y/N
5g	generalization	Y/N	Y/N	Y/N	Y/N	Y/N
6	Which is a month, Tuesday or January?	Y/N	Y/N	Y/N	Y/N	Y/N
6g	generalization	Y/N	Y/N	Y/N	Y/N	Y/N
7	Which is clothing, watch or pants?	Y/N	Y/N	Y/N	Y/N	Y/N
7g	generalization	Y/N	Y/N	Y/N	Y/N	Y/N
8	Which is jewelry, hair or ring?	Y/N	Y/N	Y/N	Y/N	Y/N
8g	generalization	Y/N	Y/N	Y/N	Y/N	Y/N
9	Which happens in winter, snow or swimming?	Y/N	Y/N	Y/N	Y/N	Y/N
9g	generalization	Y/N	Y/N	Y/N	Y/N	Y/N
10	Which is a drink, milk or cereal?	Y/N	Y/N	Y/N	Y/N	Y/N
10g	generalization	Y/N	Y/N	Y/N	Y/N	Y/N
11	Which has a tail, dog or flower?	Y/N	Y/N	Y/N	Y/N	Y/N
11g	generalization	Y/N	Y/N	Y/N	Y/N	Y/N
12	Which has ears, plant or bunny?	Y/N	Y/N	Y/N	Y/N	Y/N

12g	generalization	Y/N	Y/N	Y/N	Y/N	Y/N
13	Which do you sleep in, bed or car?	Y/N	Y/N	Y/N	Y/N	Y/N
13g	generalization	Y/N	Y/N	Y/N	Y/N	Y/N
14	Which goes in the sky, boat or plane?	Y/N	Y/N	Y/N	Y/N	Y/N
14g	generalization	Y/N	Y/N	Y/N	Y/N	Y/N
15	Which goes in the water, shoes or boat?	Y/N	Y/N	Y/N	Y/N	Y/N
15g	generalization	Y/N	Y/N	Y/N	Y/N	Y/N
16	Which do you read, book or pencil?	Y/N	Y/N	Y/N	Y/N	Y/N
16g	generalization	Y/N	Y/N	Y/N	Y/N	Y/N
17	Which do you write with, paper or pencil?	Y/N	Y/N	Y/N	Y/N	Y/N
17g	generalization	Y/N	Y/N	Y/N	Y/N	Y/N
18	Which do you write on, paper or door?	Y/N	Y/N	Y/N	Y/N	Y/N
18g	generalization	Y/N	Y/N	Y/N	Y/N	Y/N
19	Which do you eat with, fork or pen?	Y/N	Y/N	Y/N	Y/N	Y/N
19g	generalization	Y/N	Y/N	Y/N	Y/N	Y/N
20	Which do you cut with, napkin or scissors?	Y/N	Y/N	Y/N	Y/N	Y/N
20g	generalization	Y/N	Y/N	Y/N	Y/N	Y/N

Child Name: . . . .

Answers "Who" Questions

Teaching Procedure: Present the child with the "who" question in each step.

Prompt Hierarchy: Use the least intrusive prompt required in order for the child to be successful (gesture, faded physical, physical; faded verbal and verbal to be used **only** with verbal programs).

Materials: None.

	STEPS	date:	date:	date:	date:	date:
1	Who do you see when you are sick?	Y/N	Y/N	Y/N	Y/N	Y/N
1g	generalization	Y/N	Y/N	Y/N	Y/N	Y/N
2	Who puts out fires?	Y/N	Y/N	Y/N	Y/N	Y/N
2g	generalization	Y/N	Y/N	Y/N	Y/N	Y/N
3	Who do you go to if you are lost?	Y/N	Y/N	Y/N	Y/N	Y/N
3g	generalization	Y/N	Y/N	Y/N	Y/N	Y/N
4	Who puts you to bed at night?	Y/N	Y/N	Y/N	Y/N	Y/N
4g	generalization	Y/N	Y/N	Y/N	Y/N	Y/N
5	Whose turn is it?	Y/N	Y/N	Y/N	Y/N	Y/N
5g	generalization	Y/N	Y/N	Y/N	Y/N	Y/N
6	Whose shoe is this?	Y/N	Y/N	Y/N	Y/N	Y/N
6g	generalization	Y/N	Y/N	Y/N	Y/N	Y/N
7	Who wants a snack?	Y/N	Y/N	Y/N	Y/N	Y/N
7g	generalization	Y/N	Y/N	Y/N	Y/N	Y/N
8	Who is standing up?	Y/N	Y/N	Y/N	Y/N	Y/N
8g	generalization	Y/N	Y/N	Y/N	Y/N	Y/N
9	Who is sitting down?	Y/N	Y/N	Y/N	Y/N	Y/N
9g	generalization	Y/N	Y/N	Y/N	Y/N	Y/N
10	Who wants to go outside?	Y/N	Y/N	Y/N	Y/N	Y/N
10g	generalization	Y/N	Y/N	Y/N	Y/N	Y/N
11	Whose lunch box is this?	Y/N	Y/N	Y/N	Y/N	Y/N
11g	generalization	Y/N	Y/N	Y/N	Y/N	Y/N
12	Who is the line leader?	Y/N	Y/N	Y/N	Y/N	Y/N
12g	generalization	Y/N	Y/N	Y/N	Y/N	Y/N

13	Who wants to be my helper?	Y/N	Y/N	Y/N	Y/N	Y/N
13g	generalization	Y/N	Y/N	Y/N	Y/N	Y/N
14	Who can tell me the weather?	Y/N	Y/N	Y/N	Y/N	Y/N
14g	generalization	Y/N	Y/N	Y/N	Y/N	Y/N
15	Who delivers the mail?	Y/N	Y/N	Y/N	Y/N	Y/N
15g	generalization	Y/N	Y/N	Y/N	Y/N	Y/N
16	Who knows what color a zebra is?	Y/N	Y/N	Y/N	Y/N	Y/N
16g	generalization	Y/N	Y/N	Y/N	Y/N	Y/N
17	Who wants a drink?	Y/N	Y/N	Y/N	Y/N	Y/N
17g	generalization	Y/N	Y/N	Y/N	Y/N	Y/N
18	Who likes soccer?	Y/N	Y/N	Y/N	Y/N	Y/N
18g	generalization	Y/N	Y/N	Y/N	Y/N	Y/N
19	Who wants to sing a song?	Y/N	Y/N	Y/N	Y/N	Y/N
19g	generalization	Y/N	Y/N	Y/N	Y/N	Y/N
20	Who likes ice-cream?	Y/N	Y/N	Y/N	Y/N	Y/N
20g	generalization	Y/N	Y/N	Y/N	Y/N	Y/N

Child Name: ....

Answers "How" Questions

Teaching Procedure: Present the child with the "how" question in each step.

Prompt Hierarchy: Use the least intrusive prompt required in order for the child to be successful (gesture, faded physical, physical; faded verbal and verbal to be used **only** with verbal programs).

Materials: None.

	STEPS	date:	date:	date:	date:	date:
1	How do you get to school?	Y/N	Y/N	Y/N	Y/N	Y/N
1g	generalization	Y/N	Y/N	Y/N	Y/N	Y/N
2	How do you get dressed?	Y/N	Y/N	Y/N	Y/N	Y/N
2g	generalization	Y/N	Y/N	Y/N	Y/N	Y/N
3	How do you ride a bike?	Y/N	Y/N	Y/N	Y/N	Y/N
3g	generalization	Y/N	Y/N	Y/N	Y/N	Y/N
4	How do you answer a phone?	Y/N	Y/N	Y/N	Y/N	Y/N
4g	generalization	Y/N	Y/N	Y/N	Y/N	Y/N
5	How do you drink?	Y/N	Y/N	Y/N	Y/N	Y/N
5g	generalization	Y/N	Y/N	Y/N	Y/N	Y/N
6	How do you eat pasta?	Y/N	Y/N	Y/N	Y/N	Y/N
6g	generalization	Y/N	Y/N	Y/N	Y/N	Y/N
7	How do you color?	Y/N	Y/N	Y/N	Y/N	Y/N
7g	generalization	Y/N	Y/N	Y/N	Y/N	Y/N
8	How do you wash your hands?	Y/N	Y/N	Y/N	Y/N	Y/N
8g	generalization	Y/N	Y/N	Y/N	Y/N	Y/N
9	How do you sit in a movie?	Y/N	Y/N	Y/N	Y/N	Y/N
9g	generalization	Y/N	Y/N	Y/N	Y/N	Y/N
10	How do you make a sandwich?	Y/N	Y/N	Y/N	Y/N	Y/N
10g	generalization	Y/N	Y/N	Y/N	Y/N	Y/N
11	How do you cut paper?	Y/N	Y/N	Y/N	Y/N	Y/N
11g	generalization	Y/N	Y/N	Y/N	Y/N	Y/N
12	How do you throw a ball?	Y/N	Y/N	Y/N	Y/N	Y/N
12g	generalization	Y/N	Y/N	Y/N	Y/N	Y/N

13	How are you?	Y/N	Y/N	Y/N	Y/N	Y/N
13g	generalization	Y/N	Y/N	Y/N	Y/N	Y/N
14	How do you take a bath?	Y/N	Y/N	Y/N	Y/N	Y/N
14g	generalization	Y/N	Y/N	Y/N	Y/N	Y/N
15	How do you heat up soup?	Y/N	Y/N	Y/N	Y/N	Y/N
15g	generalization	Y/N	Y/N	Y/N	Y/N	Y/N
16	How do you make cookies?	Y/N	Y/N	Y/N	Y/N	Y/N
16g	generalization	Y/N	Y/N	Y/N	Y/N	Y/N
17	How do you plant flowers?	Y/N	Y/N	Y/N	Y/N	Y/N
17g	generalization	Y/N	Y/N	Y/N	Y/N	Y/N
18	How do you set the table?	Y/N	Y/N	Y/N	Y/N	Y/N
18g	generalization	Y/N	Y/N	Y/N	Y/N	Y/N
19	How do you mail a letter?	Y/N	Y/N	Y/N	Y/N	Y/N
19g	generalization	Y/N	Y/N	Y/N	Y/N	Y/N
20	How do you buy food?	Y/N	Y/N	Y/N	Y/N	Y/N
20g	generalization	Y/N	Y/N	Y/N	Y/N	Y/N

Child Name: . . . .

Answers "Why" Questions

Teaching Procedure: Present the child with the "why" question in each step.

Prompt Hierarchy: Use the least intrusive prompt required in order for the child to be successful (gesture, faded physical, physical; faded verbal and verbal to be used **only** with verbal programs).

Materials: None.

	STEPS	date:	date:	date:	date:	date:
1	Why do you sleep?	Y/N	Y/N	Y/N	Y/N	Y/N
1g	generalization	Y/N	Y/N	Y/N	Y/N	Y/N
2	Why do you wash your hands?	Y/N	Y/N	Y/N	Y/N	Y/N
2g	generalization	Y/N	Y/N	Y/N	Y/N	Y/N
3	Why do you eat?	Y/N	Y/N	Y/N	Y/N	Y/N
3g	generalization	Y/N	Y/N	Y/N	Y/N	Y/N
4	Why do you drink?	Y/N	Y/N	Y/N	Y/N	Y/N
4g	generalization	Y/N	Y/N	Y/N	Y/N	Y/N
5	Why do you take a bath?	Y/N	Y/N	Y/N	Y/N	Y/N
5g	generalization	Y/N	Y/N	Y/N	Y/N	Y/N
6	Why do you wear clothes?	Y/N	Y/N	Y/N	Y/N	Y/N
6g	generalization	Y/N	Y/N	Y/N	Y/N	Y/N
7	Why do you wear a hat?	Y/N	Y/N	Y/N	Y/N	Y/N
7g	generalization	Y/N	Y/N	Y/N	Y/N	Y/N
8	Why do you wear gloves?	Y/N	Y/N	Y/N	Y/N	Y/N
8g	generalization	Y/N	Y/N	Y/N	Y/N	Y/N
9	Why do you wear shoes?	Y/N	Y/N	Y/N	Y/N	Y/N
9g	generalization	Y/N	Y/N	Y/N	Y/N	Y/N
10	Why do you take a bus to school?	Y/N	Y/N	Y/N	Y/N	Y/N
10g	generalization	Y/N	Y/N	Y/N	Y/N	Y/N
11	Why do you go to school?	Y/N	Y/N	Y/N	Y/N	Y/N
11g	generalization	Y/N	Y/N	Y/N	Y/N	Y/N
12	Why do you use covers?	Y/N	Y/N	Y/N	Y/N	Y/N
12g	generalization	Y/N	Y/N	Y/N	Y/N	Y/N

13	Why do you talk on a phone?	Y/N	Y/N	Y/N	Y/N	Y/N
13g	generalization	Y/N	Y/N	Y/N	Y/N	Y/N
14	Why do you take a car?	Y/N	Y/N	Y/N	Y/N	Y/N
14g	generalization	Y/N	Y/N	Y/N	Y/N	Y/N
15	Why do you wear a bathing suit?	Y/N	Y/N	Y/N	Y/N	Y/N
15g	generalization	Y/N	Y/N	Y/N	Y/N	Y/N
16	Why do you read a book?	Y/N	Y/N	Y/N	Y/N	Y/N
16g	generalization	Y/N	Y/N	Y/N	Y/N	Y/N
17	Why do you say "hi" to people?	Y/N	Y/N	Y/N	Y/N	Y/N
17g	generalization	Y/N	Y/N	Y/N	Y/N	Y/N
18	Why do you watch TV?	Y/N	Y/N	Y/N	Y/N	Y/N
18g	generalization	Y/N	Y/N	Y/N	Y/N	Y/N
19	Why do you heat up soup?	Y/N	Y/N	Y/N	Y/N	Y/N
19g	generalization	Y/N	Y/N	Y/N	Y/N	Y/N
20	Why do you use an ice cube?	Y/N	Y/N	Y/N	Y/N	Y/N
20g	generalization	Y/N	Y/N	Y/N	Y/N	Y/N

Child Name: . . . .

What Can You Do in the Community?

Teaching Procedure: Present the child with the question in each step.

Prompt Hierarchy: Use the least intrusive prompt required in order for the child to be successful (gesture, faded physical, physical; faded verbal and verbal to be used **only** with verbal programs).

Materials: None.

	STEPS	date:	date:	date:	date:	date:
1	What can you do at a restaurant?	Y/N	Y/N	Y/N	Y/N	Y/N
1g	generalization	Y/N	Y/N	Y/N	Y/N	Y/N
2	What can you do at the park?	Y/N	Y/N	Y/N	Y/N	Y/N
2g	generalization	Y/N	Y/N	Y/N	Y/N	Y/N
3	What can you do at the library?	Y/N	Y/N	Y/N	Y/N	Y/N
3g	generalization	Y/N	Y/N	Y/N	Y/N	Y/N
4	What can you do at the bank?	Y/N	Y/N	Y/N	Y/N	Y/N
4g	generalization	Y/N	Y/N	Y/N	Y/N	Y/N
5	What can you do at the supermarket?	Y/N	Y/N	Y/N	Y/N	Y/N
5g	generalization	Y/N	Y/N	Y/N	Y/N	Y/N
6	What can you do at the zoo?	Y/N	Y/N	Y/N	Y/N	Y/N
6g	generalization	Y/N	Y/N	Y/N	Y/N	Y/N
7	What can you do at the police station?	Y/N	Y/N	Y/N	Y/N	Y/N
7g	generalization	Y/N	Y/N	Y/N	Y/N	Y/N
8	What can you do at the fire station?	Y/N	Y/N	Y/N	Y/N	Y/N
8g	generalization	Y/N	Y/N	Y/N	Y/N	Y/N
9	What can you do at the hair salon?	Y/N	Y/N	Y/N	Y/N	Y/N
9g	generalization	Y/N	Y/N	Y/N	Y/N	Y/N
10	What can you do at the post office?	Y/N	Y/N	Y/N	Y/N	Y/N
10g	generalization	Y/N	Y/N	Y/N	Y/N	Y/N
11	What can you do at the airport?	Y/N	Y/N	Y/N	Y/N	Y/N
11g	generalization	Y/N	Y/N	Y/N	Y/N	Y/N
12	What can you do at the bowling alley?	Y/N	Y/N	Y/N	Y/N	Y/N
12g	generalization	Y/N	Y/N	Y/N	Y/N	Y/N

13	What can you do at the movie theater?	Y/N	Y/N	Y/N	Y/N	Y/N
13g	generalization	Y/N	Y/N	Y/N	Y/N	Y/N
14	What can you do at the gym?	Y/N	Y/N	Y/N	Y/N	Y/N
14g	generalization	Y/N	Y/N	Y/N	Y/N	Y/N
15	What can you do at the train station?	Y/N	Y/N	Y/N	Y/N	Y/N
15g	generalization	Y/N	Y/N	Y/N	Y/N	Y/N
16	What can you do at the cafeteria?	Y/N	Y/N	Y/N	Y/N	Y/N
16g	generalization	Y/N	Y/N	Y/N	Y/N	Y/N
17	What do you do at the farm?	Y/N	Y/N	Y/N	Y/N	Y/N
17g	generalization	Y/N	Y/N	Y/N	Y/N	Y/N
18	What do you do at the ice-cream store?	Y/N	Y/N	Y/N	Y/N	Y/N
18g	generalization	Y/N	Y/N	Y/N	Y/N	Y/N
19	What do you do at the mall?	Y/N	Y/N	Y/N	Y/N	Y/N
19g	generalization	Y/N	Y/N	Y/N	Y/N	Y/N
20	What do you do at school?	Y/N	Y/N	Y/N	Y/N	Y/N
20g	generalization	Y/N	Y/N	Y/N	Y/N	Y/N

Child Name: . . . .

"Tell Me About..."

Teaching Procedure: Present the child with the Sd "tell me about..." (name the item in each step). The child will need to give at least two details per item in order for it to be considered mastered.

Prompt Hierarchy: Use the least intrusive prompt required in order for the child to be successful (gesture, faded physical, physical; faded verbal and verbal to be used **only** with verbal programs).

Materials: None.

	STEPS	date:	date:	date:	date:	date:
1	cat	Y/N	Y/N	Y/N	Y/N	Y/N
1g	generalization	Y/N	Y/N	Y/N	Y/N	Y/N
2	dog	Y/N	Y/N	Y/N	Y/N	Y/N
2g	generalization	Y/N	Y/N	Y/N	Y/N	Y/N
3	pizza	Y/N	Y/N	Y/N	Y/N	Y/N
3g	generalization	Y/N	Y/N	Y/N	Y/N	Y/N
4	cereal	Y/N	Y/N	Y/N	Y/N	Y/N
4g	generalization	Y/N	Y/N	Y/N	Y/N	Y/N
5	school bus	Y/N	Y/N	Y/N	Y/N	Y/N
5g	generalization	Y/N	Y/N	Y/N	Y/N	Y/N
6	classroom	Y/N	Y/N	Y/N	Y/N	Y/N
6g	generalization	Y/N	Y/N	Y/N	Y/N	Y/N
7	house	Y/N	Y/N	Y/N	Y/N	Y/N
7g	generalization	Y/N	Y/N	Y/N	Y/N	Y/N
8	car	Y/N	Y/N	Y/N	Y/N	Y/N
8g	generalization	Y/N	Y/N	Y/N	Y/N	Y/N
9	park	Y/N	Y/N	Y/N	Y/N	Y/N
9g	generalization	Y/N	Y/N	Y/N	Y/N	Y/N
10	beach	Y/N	Y/N	Y/N	Y/N	Y/N
10g	generalization	Y/N	Y/N	Y/N	Y/N	Y/N
11	computer	Y/N	Y/N	Y/N	Y/N	Y/N
11g	generalization	Y/N	Y/N	Y/N	Y/N	Y/N
12	crayons	Y/N	Y/N	Y/N	Y/N	Y/N

12g	generalization	Y/N	Y/N	Y/N	Y/N	Y/N
13	desk	Y/N	Y/N	Y/N	Y/N	Y/N
13g	generalization	Y/N	Y/N	Y/N	Y/N	Y/N
14	refrigerator	Y/N	Y/N	Y/N	Y/N	Y/N
14g	generalization	Y/N	Y/N	Y/N	Y/N	Y/N
15	book	Y/N	Y/N	Y/N	Y/N	Y/N
15g	generalization	Y/N	Y/N	Y/N	Y/N	Y/N
16	shoes	Y/N	Y/N	Y/N	Y/N	Y/N
16g	generalization	Y/N	Y/N	Y/N	Y/N	Y/N
17	horse	Y/N	Y/N	Y/N	Y/N	Y/N
17g	generalization	Y/N	Y/N	Y/N	Y/N	Y/N
18	cow	Y/N	Y/N	Y/N	Y/N	Y/N
18g	generalization	Y/N	Y/N	Y/N	Y/N	Y/N
19	apple juice	Y/N	Y/N	Y/N	Y/N	Y/N
19g	generalization	Y/N	Y/N	Y/N	Y/N	Y/N
20	telephone	Y/N	Y/N	Y/N	Y/N	Y/N
20g	generalization	Y/N	Y/N	Y/N	Y/N	Y/N

Child Name: . . . .

Recall

Teaching Procedure: Present the child with the question in each step.

Prompt Hierarchy: Use the least intrusive prompt required in order for the child to be successful (gesture, faded physical, physical; faded verbal and verbal to be used **only** with verbal programs).

Materials: None.

	STEPS	date:	date:	date:	date:	date:
1	What did you have for breakfast today?	Y/N	Y/N	Y/N	Y/N	Y/N
1g	generalization	Y/N	Y/N	Y/N	Y/N	Y/N
2	What did you have for dinner last night?	Y/N	Y/N	Y/N	Y/N	Y/N
2g	generalization	Y/N	Y/N	Y/N	Y/N	Y/N
3	What did you do over the weekend?	Y/N	Y/N	Y/N	Y/N	Y/N
3g	generalization	Y/N	Y/N	Y/N	Y/N	Y/N
4	What did you play with during recess today?	Y/N	Y/N	Y/N	Y/N	Y/N
4g	generalization	Y/N	Y/N	Y/N	Y/N	Y/N
5	What did you do after school yesterday?	Y/N	Y/N	Y/N	Y/N	Y/N
5g	generalization	Y/N	Y/N	Y/N	Y/N	Y/N

Child Name: . . . .

Conversation Starters

Teaching Procedure: Ask the child the question in each step. The child will need to engage another person/peer in a conversation using the topics presented in each step.

Prompt Hierarchy: Use the least intrusive prompt required in order for the child to be successful (gesture, faded physical, physical; faded verbal and verbal to be used **only** with verbal programs).

Materials: None.

	STEPS	date:	date:	date:	date:	date:
1	favorite movie	Y/N	Y/N	Y/N	Y/N	Y/N
1g	generalization	Y/N	Y/N	Y/N	Y/N	Y/N
2	favorite thing to do on the weekend	Y/N	Y/N	Y/N	Y/N	Y/N
2g	generalization	Y/N	Y/N	Y/N	Y/N	Y/N
3	favorite thing to do outside	Y/N	Y/N	Y/N	Y/N	Y/N
3g	generalization	Y/N	Y/N	Y/N	Y/N	Y/N
4	tell me about your family	Y/N	Y/N	Y/N	Y/N	Y/N
4g	generalization	Y/N	Y/N	Y/N	Y/N	Y/N
5	favorite toy	Y/N	Y/N	Y/N	Y/N	Y/N
5g	generalization	Y/N	Y/N	Y/N	Y/N	Y/N

Self Help and Daily Living Skills

Child Name: . . . .

Brushes Teeth

Teaching Procedure: Present the student with the direction "brush teeth."

Prompt Hierarchy: Use the least intrusive prompt required in order for the child to be successful (gesture, faded physical, physical; faded verbal and verbal to be used **only** with verbal programs).

Materials: Toothbrush and toothpaste.

	STEPS	date:	date:	date:	date:	date:
1	gets toothbrush	Y/N	Y/N	Y/N	Y/N	Y/N
1g	generalization	Y/N	Y/N	Y/N	Y/N	Y/N
2	turns on cold water	Y/N	Y/N	Y/N	Y/N	Y/N
2g	generalization	Y/N	Y/N	Y/N	Y/N	Y/N
3	wets the toothbrush	Y/N	Y/N	Y/N	Y/N	Y/N
3g	generalization	Y/N	Y/N	Y/N	Y/N	Y/N
4	gets toothpaste	Y/N	Y/N	Y/N	Y/N	Y/N
4g	generalization	Y/N	Y/N	Y/N	Y/N	Y/N
5	puts toothpaste on the toothbrush	Y/N	Y/N	Y/N	Y/N	Y/N
5g	generalization	Y/N	Y/N	Y/N	Y/N	Y/N
6	wets the toothbrush	Y/N	Y/N	Y/N	Y/N	Y/N
6g	generalization	Y/N	Y/N	Y/N	Y/N	Y/N
7	brushes top teeth	Y/N	Y/N	Y/N	Y/N	Y/N
7g	generalization	Y/N	Y/N	Y/N	Y/N	Y/N
8	brushes bottom teeth	Y/N	Y/N	Y/N	Y/N	Y/N
8g	generalization	Y/N	Y/N	Y/N	Y/N	Y/N
9	brushes tongue	Y/N	Y/N	Y/N	Y/N	Y/N
9g	generalization	Y/N	Y/N	Y/N	Y/N	Y/N
10	spits out toothpaste	Y/N	Y/N	Y/N	Y/N	Y/N
10g	generalization	Y/N	Y/N	Y/N	Y/N	Y/N
11	rinses toothbrush under cold water	Y/N	Y/N	Y/N	Y/N	Y/N
11g	generalization	Y/N	Y/N	Y/N	Y/N	Y/N
12	puts toothbrush away	Y/N	Y/N	Y/N	Y/N	Y/N
12g	generalization	Y/N	Y/N	Y/N	Y/N	Y/N

13	turns off cold water	Y/N	Y/N	Y/N	Y/N	Y/N
13g	generalization	Y/N	Y/N	Y/N	Y/N	Y/N
14	wipes mouth	Y/N	Y/N	Y/N	Y/N	Y/N
14g	generalization	Y/N	Y/N	Y/N	Y/N	Y/N

Child Name: . . . .

Washes Face

Teaching Procedure: Present the student with the direction "wash face."

Prompt Hierarchy: Use the least intrusive prompt required in order for the child to be successful (gesture, faded physical, physical; faded verbal and verbal to be used **only** with verbal programs).

Materials: Sink, water, face soap, towel.

	STEPS	date:	date:	date:	date:	date:
1	turns on cold water	Y/N	Y/N	Y/N	Y/N	Y/N
1g	generalization	Y/N	Y/N	Y/N	Y/N	Y/N
2	wets face with water	Y/N	Y/N	Y/N	Y/N	Y/N
2g	generalization	Y/N	Y/N	Y/N	Y/N	Y/N
3	gets face soap	Y/N	Y/N	Y/N	Y/N	Y/N
3g	generalization	Y/N	Y/N	Y/N	Y/N	Y/N
4	puts soap into hands	Y/N	Y/N	Y/N	Y/N	Y/N
4g	generalization	Y/N	Y/N	Y/N	Y/N	Y/N
5	rubs hands together	Y/N	Y/N	Y/N	Y/N	Y/N
5g	generalization	Y/N	Y/N	Y/N	Y/N	Y/N
6	washes right side of face	Y/N	Y/N	Y/N	Y/N	Y/N
6g	generalization	Y/N	Y/N	Y/N	Y/N	Y/N
7	washes left side of face	Y/N	Y/N	Y/N	Y/N	Y/N
7g	generalization	Y/N	Y/N	Y/N	Y/N	Y/N
8	washes forehead	Y/N	Y/N	Y/N	Y/N	Y/N
8g	generalization	Y/N	Y/N	Y/N	Y/N	Y/N
9	rinses soap off of hands	Y/N	Y/N	Y/N	Y/N	Y/N
9g	generalization	Y/N	Y/N	Y/N	Y/N	Y/N
10	puts water into hands	Y/N	Y/N	Y/N	Y/N	Y/N
10g	generalization	Y/N	Y/N	Y/N	Y/N	Y/N
11	splashes water on face until soap is off	Y/N	Y/N	Y/N	Y/N	Y/N
11g	generalization	Y/N	Y/N	Y/N	Y/N	Y/N
12	gets a towel	Y/N	Y/N	Y/N	Y/N	Y/N
12g	generalization	Y/N	Y/N	Y/N	Y/N	Y/N

| 13 | dries face | Y/N | Y/N | Y/N | Y/N | Y/N |
| 13g | generalization | Y/N | Y/N | Y/N | Y/N | Y/N |

Child Name: . . . .

Puts Shirt On

Teaching Procedure: Provide the student with the direction "put shirt on."

Prompt Hierarchy: Use the least intrusive prompt required in order for the child to be successful (gesture, faded physical, physical; faded verbal and verbal to be used **only** with verbal programs).

Materials: Shirt that is on the bigger side.

	STEPS	date:	date:	date:	date:	date:
1	lays shirt on a table face down	Y/N	Y/N	Y/N	Y/N	Y/N
1g	generalization	Y/N	Y/N	Y/N	Y/N	Y/N
2	picks up the bottom backside of the shirt	Y/N	Y/N	Y/N	Y/N	Y/N
2g	generalization	Y/N	Y/N	Y/N	Y/N	Y/N
3	puts the shirt over the head	Y/N	Y/N	Y/N	Y/N	Y/N
3g	generalization	Y/N	Y/N	Y/N	Y/N	Y/N
4	takes right hand and holds bottom of the shirt while the left hand goes into the sleeve	Y/N	Y/N	Y/N	Y/N	Y/N
4g	generalization	Y/N	Y/N	Y/N	Y/N	Y/N
5	takes left hand and holds bottom of the shirt while the right hand goes into the sleeve	Y/N	Y/N	Y/N	Y/N	Y/N
5g	generalization	Y/N	Y/N	Y/N	Y/N	Y/N
6	pulls shirt down	Y/N	Y/N	Y/N	Y/N	Y/N
6g	generalization	Y/N	Y/N	Y/N	Y/N	Y/N

Child Name: . . . .

Ties Shoes

Teaching Procedure: Present the student with the direction "tie shoes."

Prompt Hierarchy: Use the least intrusive prompt required in order for the child to be successful (gesture, faded physical, physical; faded verbal and verbal to be used **only** with verbal programs).

Materials: Shoes with laces.

	STEPS	date:	date:	date:	date:	date:
1	picks up laces	Y/N	Y/N	Y/N	Y/N	Y/N
1g	generalization	Y/N	Y/N	Y/N	Y/N	Y/N
2	crosses laces (makes an X)	Y/N	Y/N	Y/N	Y/N	Y/N
2g	generalization	Y/N	Y/N	Y/N	Y/N	Y/N
3	puts a lace in each hand	Y/N	Y/N	Y/N	Y/N	Y/N
3g	generalization	Y/N	Y/N	Y/N	Y/N	Y/N
4	puts one lace under the other lace and pulls tight	Y/N	Y/N	Y/N	Y/N	Y/N
4g	generalization	Y/N	Y/N	Y/N	Y/N	Y/N
5	makes a loop with one lace	Y/N	Y/N	Y/N	Y/N	Y/N
5g	generalization	Y/N	Y/N	Y/N	Y/N	Y/N
6	wraps the other lace around the loop	Y/N	Y/N	Y/N	Y/N	Y/N
6g	generalization	Y/N	Y/N	Y/N	Y/N	Y/N
7	pushes the lace that was wrapped around the loop through the opening (where the thumb is)	Y/N	Y/N	Y/N	Y/N	Y/N
7g	generalization	Y/N	Y/N	Y/N	Y/N	Y/N
8	pulls it through while pulling the other loop in the opposite direction at the same time	Y/N	Y/N	Y/N	Y/N	Y/N
8g	generalization	Y/N	Y/N	Y/N	Y/N	Y/N

Child Name: . . . .

Toileting

Teaching Procedure: The purpose of this program is for the student to be able to use the bathroom independently. Therefore, this program should be taught by getting the child to mand (request without being asked) for the bathroom. Once you start this program, students should be placed into underwear and no longer be in a diaper or pull-up. This will help them feel when they are wet or dry.

Prompt Hierarchy: Use the least intrusive prompt required in order for the child to be successful (gesture, faded physical, physical; faded verbal and verbal to be used **only** with verbal programs).

Materials: Toilet, toilet paper.

	STEPS	date:	date:	date:	date:	date:
1	Set a timer according to the baseline data. When the timer beeps, do not ask the child if he needs to use the bathroom; instead prompt the child to request "bathroom." This can be done through sign language, visual picture, or through verbal language. Bring the student into the bathroom and get him to take down his pants and underwear. Have him check to see if he is wet or dry. If he is dry give lots of praise. If wet, neutrally say, "you are wet, we need to go in the potty/toilet." Then get the student to sit on/stand at the toilet. You can run water if you think that may help him void in the toilet. Have the student stay there for two to three minutes. If he voids, give lots of praise and reinforcement, otherwise just say "good job trying." Then reset the timer.	Y/N	Y/N	Y/N	Y/N	Y/N
1g	generalization	Y/N	Y/N	Y/N	Y/N	Y/N

2	The remainder of the steps should occur in the exact same way; the only difference is you will increase the interval by 15 minutes to try and get the student to be able to last longer in between going to the bathroom. So step 2 would be every hour if you started on step 1 at every 45 minutes.	Y/N	Y/N	Y/N	Y/N	Y/N
2g	generalization	Y/N	Y/N	Y/N	Y/N	Y/N
3	The last step is for the student to independently request going to the bathroom without being prompted by a timer.	Y/N	Y/N	Y/N	Y/N	Y/N
3g	generalization	Y/N	Y/N	Y/N	Y/N	Y/N

Data Sheets

Trial-by-trial data sheet

PROGRAM NAME	STEP/ SET	1	2	3	4	5	6	7	8	9	10	TOTAL %

Probe data sheet per program

Directions: This data sheet is intended to be used as a probe data sheet per program. The first time you probe a step each day/session, circle a Y if the student responded correctly or an N if the student needed a prompt.

PROGRAM . . . . CRITERIA . . . .

Date:											
Steps:											
	Y/N	Y/N	Y/N	Y/N	Y/N	Y/N	Y/N	Y/N	Y/N	Y/N	Y/N
Date:											
	Y/N	Y/N	Y/N	Y/N	Y/N	Y/N	Y/N	Y/N	Y/N	Y/N	Y/N
Date:											
	Y/N	Y/N	Y/N	Y/N	Y/N	Y/N	Y/N	Y/N	Y/N	Y/N	Y/N
Date:											
	Y/N	Y/N	Y/N	Y/N	Y/N	Y/N	Y/N	Y/N	Y/N	Y/N	Y/N
Date:											
	Y/N	Y/N	Y/N	Y/N	Y/N	Y/N	Y/N	Y/N	Y/N	Y/N	Y/N
Date:											
	Y/N	Y/N	Y/N	Y/N	Y/N	Y/N	Y/N	Y/N	Y/N	Y/N	Y/N
Date:											
	Y/N	Y/N	Y/N	Y/N	Y/N	Y/N	Y/N	Y/N	Y/N	Y/N	Y/N
Date:											
	Y/N	Y/N	Y/N	Y/N	Y/N	Y/N	Y/N	Y/N	Y/N	Y/N	Y/N

Probe data sheet per program (you fill in the prompt)

Directions: This data sheet is intended to be used as a first trial probe data sheet with prompt levels. This means the first time a step you probe each day/session, write the prompt that was necessary in order for the child to be successful, or write a +, Y, or I for independent. The data should then be transferred to the first trial probe graph.

KEY: Y = independent, S/G = shadow/gesture, FP/FV = faded physical/faded verbal, P/VP = physical prompt/verbal prompt.

PROGRAM . . . .   CRITERIA . . . .

Date:														
Steps:														
Date:														
Date:														
Date:														
Date:														
Date:														
Date:														

First trial probe with prompts graph

Directions: Take the prompt that was needed in order for the student to be successful and graph that data point. For example, if the student needed a physical prompt, you would mark the data point on the bottom line (P/VP).

KEY: Y = independent, S/G = shadow/gesture, FP/FV = faded physical/faded verbal, P/VP = physical prompt/verbal prompt.

PROGRAM . . . . CRITERIA . . . .
(three consecutive Ys in a row are considered mastery)

Y												
S/G												

Y												
S/G												

STEPS:

% correct graph

PROGRAM . . . .   CRITERIA . . . .

Steps:

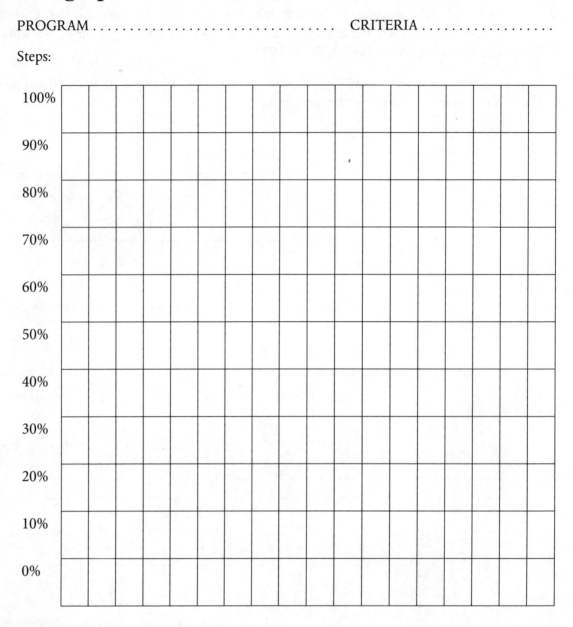

DATES: